T0204734

The
Dialogical
Self

The Dialogical Self

Meaning as Movement

Hubert J. M. Hermans

Harry J. G. Kempen

Psychological Laboratory
University of Nijmegen
Nijmegen, The Netherlands

Academic Press, Inc.

A Division of Harcourt Brace & Company

San Diego   New York   Boston   London   Sydney   Tokyo   Toronto

This book is printed on acid-free paper. ∞

Academic Press, Inc.
1250 Sixth Avenue, San Diego, California 92101-4311

United Kingdom Edition published by
Academic Press Limited
24–28 Oval Road, London NW1 7DX

Library of Congress Cataloging-in-Publication Data

Hermans, H. J. M.
    The dialogical self : meaning as movement / Hubert J.M. Hermans,
Harry J.G. Kempen.
        p.   cm.
    Includes bibliographical references and index.
    ISBN: 0-12-342320-1
    1. Self.   2. Mind and body.   3. Social perception.   I. Kempen,
Harry J. G.   II. Title
    BF697.H437   1993   93-16702
    155.2--dc20   CIP

The human transcends the human unceasingly

Pascal (1667/1963, p. 531)

CONTENTS

Chapter 3   The Decentralization of the Self

Chapter 4   Developments in Modern Novelistic Literature

Chapter 9   The Construction and Co-Construction of Meaning: Explorations into a Psychology of Valuation

FOREWORD

The reader will recognize this work as an example of the figural shift in the human sciences that has occurred in the post-modern era. C. Geertz [*American Scholar*, **80**, 165–179 (1980)] and others have noted that the human sciences have been retreating from relying on metaphors drawn from the more established physical sciences to adopting metaphors drawn from history, biography, literature, drama, and rhetoric. For too long, psychology, under the impetus of the mechanistic world view, has sought to explain human action as the result of *naturwissenschaftliche* constructions such as forces, energies, elements, drives, and valences. By drawing on metaphors, the source of which is to be found in the *geisteswissenschaftliche* tradition, Doctors Hermans and Kempen offer a challenging treatise on the psychology of human action.

I am complimented that the authors have found my formulations on narrative psychology useful. The dialogical self makes sense in the context of story making and story telling. The conception of the dialogical self helps to clarify and to give body to a central feature of narrative psychology: to wit, the collaborative nature of self-narratives. Contrary to the implications of a monological view of self, the dialogical self is formed out of the construction and reconstruction of encounters with others and the reciprocal influences of multiple others. Reading this manuscript, I was reminded of my early explorations of self [T. R. Sarbin, *Psychological Review*, **50**, 11–22 (1952)]. At that time, I tried to spell out a set of conceptions that leaned on but went beyond the social behaviorist ideas advanced by George Herbert Mead. In so doing, I ventured close to the constructions advanced by Doctors Hermans and Kempen.

Initially influenced by William James and George Herbert Mead, I found the grammatical analyses of the pronouns *I* and *me* especially useful as clues to understanding the subjective and objective features of self-reference. I questioned the conventional wisdom of regarding the self as the central core of personality (hardly distinguishable from the theological notion of soul) by pointing, for example, to the variable referents for *I*. Such sentences as "I am hungry," "I am in love," "I am a woman," and "I am a teacher" illustrate the variability. In short, the linguistic context determines the meaning of *I*, the linguistic expressions presumably connecting with a person's constructions of occurrences in the distal and proximal worlds. The multiplicity of referents for *I* is nowhere better illustrated than in the notion of the social self, composed of roles. The enactment of a role is reflexively a *me*, and every human actor enacts multiple roles ("I am a father," "I am a son," "I am a doctor," "I am a citizen"), reciprocating or complementing the role enactments of others. In any dialogue, action entails reciprocal action. Whenever we have an *I*, a *you* (thou) is necessarily a part of the social context and ultimately enters into the construction of self. In past theoretical formulations of self, most writers have constructed a Berlin wall between the *I* and the *you*. *I* and *you* have been construed as discrete hermetic entities, following the implications of entrenched Cartesian arguments and the residues of theological doctrine.

Had I been privy to the contemporary thinking of Doctors Hermans and Kempen, and their creative adaptation of Bakhtin's idea of multiple voices, I would have discovered that the dialogical self is the most felicitous way of denoting the social context-dependent nature of reflexive constructions denoted by first person pronouns. I am wholeheartedly in agreement with Doctors Hermans and Kempen that the older theologically derived monological view of self is inadequate as a formulation for the multiplex and changing nature of self. The meaning of self must be flexible and context-dependent.

The insights contained in *The Dialogical Self* stimulate the reader to consider the origin of the systematic study of psychology, especially Anglo-American psychology. In constructing its subject matter, the encapsulated and self-contained individual, psychology reflected the existing social order. One of the corollaries of the focus on the self-contained individual is the arbitrary separation of self and society. This separation has enabled psychologists, in the main, to ignore the social and moral orders as contexts for action and for self-appraisal. The construction of the dialogical self is a corrective to the belief that self and society are discrete conceptions.

Doctors Hermans and Kempen take us on a wonder-filled journey. We are invited to view the contrasting landscapes of the rationalist philosophy of Descartes and the *Scienza Nuova* of Giambattista Vico. The latter is not only a progenitor of conceptions that support the idea of the dialogical self, but also a progenitor of contextualism as a world view and constructionism as an epistemology. On this journey, we are also invited to view the contributions of the literary theorist Mikhael Bakhtin, whose discourse on polyphony provides the key metaphor for the dialogical self. The validity of the notion of multivoiced selves is immediately apparent when we reflect on the complexities of decision-making, especially in the context of moral conflict. We are taken into the intricacies of developmental research—how the infant develops a self in interaction. One of the features in the development of the dialogical self is the skill in imagining. Stories about one's self and about others are told in the context of social action and imagined interaction. We are greeted with a pleasant surprise in a discussion of imaginal dialogues in adult life. Actions that are labeled *real* and actions that are denoted as *imagined* both contribute to the multivoiced self. Both *real* and *imagined* actors populate the narratives that provide guidance for our self-constructions. Our self-narratives are necessarily an amalgam of our involvements in a consensually experienced social community, an imagined social community, and even an imagined autistic community.

Doctors Hermans and Kempen introduce an innovative metaphor to identify organized actions that are often called *traits*. The term *trait* is derived from the Latin *trahere*, to draw, and was employed to connote features that could be drawn, such as high cheekbones or a prominent nose. Traits, then, refer to thing-like features. The metaphor was extended to purported thing-like inner features, an extension that was congruent with the notion of a monological self. The authors of *The Dialogical Self* make use of a radically different metaphor, *characters*, to denote organized acts. The metaphor of *characters* is consistent with the notion of the dialogical self with its many voices, multiple dramas, and overlapping narratives. In regarding organized acts as characters, rather than traits, our constructions of self are necessarily dialogical, dramatic, and narrative rather than a catalogue of thing-like features, the latter illustrated by the now discredited hypothesis of traits residing in phrenological bumps.

In this connection, it is instructive to compare the utility of *characters* as a metaphor for organized acts with conceptions offered by other theorists. Freud, for example, employed *das Ich* as an allegorical figure engaged in warfare and diplomacy with other allegorical figures, the action taking place on a private stage, accessible only to specially trained analysts. Mead's discussion of the interchanges between the *I* and the *me* provided the basis for looking upon organized acts as parts of a monodrama being performed on an internal stage. Goffman supplemented Mead's monodrama by placing the actors on a public stage. He perceived organized acts as roles performed in the interest of solving identity problems. The formulation of organized acts as *characters* takes advantage of both Mead's monodrama and Goffman's roles. The roles enacted in public life vis à vis other actors become incorporated into the dialogical self, the referents for which are the constantly emerging relationships between the *I* and the *me*. Bakhtin's key metaphor, polyphony, is consistent with this formulation.

The concept of self appears to be indispensable for a complete psychology. The traditional monological view of self, however, has not been very helpful in understanding the complexities of human action. The dialogical self has an instant appeal to psychologists and other scientists who recognize the multi-faceted and contextual nature of social behavior. Doctors Hermans and Kempen are to be commended for their bold undertaking: to honor the complexities of human conduct.

Theodore R. Sarbin

ACKNOWLEDGMENTS

The foundation of this book is laid by our teachers, who stimulated us to transcend the limits of specializations: Frederik J. J. Buytendijk, Petrus J. A. Calon, Han M. M. Fortmann, Karel J. M. van de Loo, Joseph J. G. Prick, F. J. Theodorus Rutten, and Stephan S. Strasser.

We thank our colleagues who have given their support during the preparation and writing of this work: Kenneth and Mary Gergen, Els Hermans-Jansen, James Lamiell, Mikael Leiman, Michael Mahoney, Dan McAdams, Piotr Oleś, Theodore Sarbin, M. Brewster Smith, Arne Stiksrud, and Lenie Verhofstadt-Denève.

Brigit van Widenfelt has considerably improved the manuscript with her detailed editorial comments. Wies Cloosterman has with great care worked on the layout of the text.

Finally, we are indebted also to our colleagues all over the world, who have sent us their reactions to our first publication on the dialogical self in the January issue of the *American Psychologist* (1992).

INTRODUCTION

This book is the result of 25 years of conversation of the two authors, with each other, with themselves, and with collective voices of contemporary psychology. As young students of psychology in Nijmegen in the 1960s, we, Hubert Hermans and Harry Kempen, found ourselves placed between two streams of thought, one European and philosophical, the other American and empirical. Most of our teachers at that time were deeply involved in existential and phenomenological thought, originating from Germany (e.g., Heidegger, Binswanger, Straus) and France (e.g., Merleau-Ponty, Sartre, Camus). Though some of these teachers were rather skeptical of the developments in American psychology, particularly of behaviorism and experimentation, they found it necessary to send their younger staff members to the United States in the 1950s and 1960s, for training. In this way American psychology was imported to our psychology lab, and the names of such divergent authors as Coombs, Cronbach, Goldberg, Hilgard, Krech, Sarbin, and many others became familiar in the psychology circles of the Nijmegen University. The fact that some of these persons also visited Nijmegen to give lectures further stimulated interest in new developments in American psychology, so that its influence increased strongly over the years.

When we look back to the decades behind us, we see that empirical psychology, with its first instigation in the 1950s, has become the dominant paradigm of our psychology lab over the years. This development was associated with the growing numbers of staff members (particularly in the rich 1960s), the proliferation of specializations (and departments), and the emphasis on publications, fund raising, and international cooperation.

Over the years we became aware of experiencing ourselves in and between two contrasting cultures. One was the culture of our teachers, who were interested in psychology as a whole and were concerned with philosophical reflections about the person as a whole. We admired their strongly integrative minds, always looking for relationships. The term *meaning* was frequently heard in their lectures, often in association with concepts as "encounter," "history," and *Dasein* (literally "being there" or even better "being the there," but usually translated as "existence").

The other culture we were confronted with reflected the American approach of the empirical investigation of specific aspects of individual behavior, which greatly impressed us with its inventive ways of performing research and rigorous methodology. The most decisive influence, however, came from the more recent upsurge of the narrative approach which, in its different manifestations, was proposed by such thinkers as Bruner, the Gergens, Gregg, Harré, McAdams, and Sarbin. Reading their works and discussing them, we became aware that we did not want to go back to a purely interpretive approach, as exemplified in the works of Dilthey and other European thinkers. We realized the two-sided promise that the narrative approach had to offer. First, it functions as a road to philosophical thinking in general and to a deepening of the concepts of meaning and self in particular. Second, it has the potential of translating theoretical notions into empirical research, both qualitative and quantitative. It is precisely on this interface of philosophical–theoretical thinking and empirical explorations that we want to make a contribution with this book. It is not our intention to present an extensive description of a research project. Rather, we want to present (in Chapters 6 and 9) some empirical explorations that serve as illustrations of our more extensive theoretical and conceptual discussions.

The main purpose of this work is to bring together two familiar concepts, dialogue and self, and combine them in such a way that a more extended view on the possibilities of the mind becomes visible. One of the reasons to explore the "composite concept" of dialogical self is rooted in recent discussions on "individualism" and "rationalism" of Western culture (e.g., Hermans, Kempen, & Van Loon, 1992). As many scholars have argued, this cultural bias has had a strong influence on psychological conceptions of the self that have been proposed over the course of this century. Such developments challenge psychologists, in the words of Spence (1985), "to attempt to rise above their own culture" (p. 1286).

It is the narrative approach (Chapter 2) that provides direct access to the self as a dialogical phenomenon and, along these lines, offers a possibility to transcend the cultural boundaries described above. The notion of "story" or "narrative" assumes the existence of a person who tells and an actual or imaginal person who listens. The fact that a listener, another person, is always present or implied, makes the self a dialogical phenomenon *par excellence*. The view of the self as a narrative does not only apply to Western culture, but also to other cultures, as people of all times and places have told each other stories about the world and themselves.

This view of "the self as relationship" is certainly not an isolated phenomenon in psychology. Recently, Hilton (1990) presented arguments, in the area of attribution theory, for substituting the concept of "causal attribution" for "causal explanation." Whereas the former term is rooted in the metaphor of "the person as scientist," the latter is based on the "person in conversation." Recent views on moral development are going in similar directions. There is a growing tendency to study morality from the perspective of narrative (e.g., anecdotes, case descriptions, parables). Narratives or stories always refer to morality in terms of the particulars in time and space, instead of considering it as an abstract reasoning process (see Vitz, 1990, for a review). An important implication of the dialogical or conversational view is that the self is not an intrapsychic but a relational phenomenon, that typically transcends the boundaries between the "inside" and the "outside." This view of the self opens a possibility to study "meaning," and "meaning making" in particular, as a "movement" between dialogical positions. With the concept of meaning, we are, as Bruner (1991) and Harré (1992) have argued, at the heart of the "second revolution in cognitive psychology."

Another important development in psychology goes back to the beginning of this century, when the Russian literary scholar Michael Bakhtin devised an intriguing concept, the polyphonic novel, which he based on the works of Dostoevsky (Chapter 3). Closely associated with the musical idea of "polyphony" and with the oppositional relationships between the main figures of Dostoevsky's novels, Bakhtin held that there is a fundamental difference between logical and dialogical relationships (Chapter 3). Inspired by Bakhtin's ideas, we show that the notion of dialogue is not only profoundly different from the rationalistic *Cogito* (I think) of Descartes, but also leads to the "spatialization" of temporal differences. That is, developments over time can be juxtaposed in spatial structures, leading to new relationships between dialogical positions. This spatialization of temporal differences is elaborated on by analyzing recent developments in novelistic literature (e.g., the works of Gustave Flaubert, James Joyce, Virginia Woolf, Gertrude Stein, and other modernist novelists) (Chapter 4). A relevant implication of the notion of spatialization is that it allows us to move beyond the prevailing definition of narrative as intrinsically temporal, that is, as having a beginning, development, and ending. Instead, time and space are assumed equally important, resulting in a view of narrative that, as a spatio–temporal structure, is intrinsically open ended.

Bakhtin's polyphonic novel and the spatialization of narrative implies a "retreat of the omniscient narrator" (Chapter 4). The idea that the author has a perfect overview of characters and events of the story is vanishing in the modernist novel. Instead, the author enters the novel and, disguised as a character, speaks via the voice of this character or even via the voices of more characters, who often express opposing views of the world. Along similar lines, we define, building on James' classic distinction between *I* and *Me*, and on Sarbin's narrative translation of the same terms, the self as a "multiplicity of *I* positions" (Chapter 5). That is, the self is decentralized, in so far as there is no omniscient centralized *I*. Instead, the self is a "decentralized manyness" of *I* positions that each have a voice and can tell their own stories about their respective *Me*s. The *I* moves, in an imaginal landscape, from one position to another in such a way that dialogical relationships in a multivoiced self become possible.

The decentralization of the self, which appeared in the works of the American pragmatists (e.g., Dewey and James) and was more recently propagated by the French structuralists (e.g., Lévi-Strauss and Lacan), poses the problem of synthesis. The opposition between the fragmentation of the self and its synthesis is examined by assuming two forces at work: centripetal and centrifugal. An exclusive emphasis on the latter type of forces tears the self into pieces, as we see, for example, in the dysfunction called "multiple personality." A dominance of the former type, however, makes the self rigid and closed to innovative impulses. It is argued that a "new synthesis" can be conceptualized by taking both forces, in their dialectic relationship, into account (Chapter 6).

The analysis of the self in terms of centripetal and centrifugal forces applies also to psychology as a discipline (Chapter 8). From a historical analysis, we can learn that periods in which centripetal forces prevail alternate with periods in which centrifugal forces are predominant. An example of the former is the first half of this century in which the "grand theories" were dominating the psychology scene. An example of the latter are the past decades that are characterized by the proliferation of specializations and schisms in psychology as a field. More specifically, we discuss in Chapter 8 three separations: (1) between psychologist and subject,(2) between scientist and practioner, and (3) between different psychological subdisciplines. Further, in Chapter 8, strategies and models for research and practice are discussed that function as vehicles for substituting these separations by procedures of a more dialogical nature.

As Mead (1934) has extensively argued, the self is a social phenomenon and must, therefore, be studied in close relationship with society. Moreover, the way the self functions socially largely depends on the institutions that play a central role in society. The main concept for Mead was the "generalized other," an elaboration of James' "social *Me.*" In view of the pervasive influence of society and its institutions on the development of the mature self, we discuss in Chapter 7 Mead's "generalized other" in detail. Mead's view on the self is criticized from the perspective of the two main features of dialogue (discussed in Chapter 5), that is, intersubjective exchange and dominance. Finally, we redefine the "generalized other" as a "collective voice" and demonstrate how collective voices speak through the voice of the individual person. The theoretical possibilities, resulting from studying the self as a multiplicity of personal voices in direct alliance with the generalized other as a multiplicity of collective voices, are explored. Discussion of these possibilities is continued in Chapter 8, in which psychology is analyzed as an institution characterized by divergent and even conflicting collective voices. On historical grounds this has resulted in a situation in which some voices are more dominant (e.g., more "scientific" or more "basic") than others.

Finally, Chapter 9 deals with the concept of meaning in more detail. The main features of a dialogical meaning are discussed. Meaning assumes (1) the existence of an imaginal space side by side and interwoven with physical space; (2) a multiplicity of *I* positions located in this imaginal space; (3) dialogical movements, hence and forth, between positions; and (4) the existence of suppressed meanings, that is, the dominance of one meaning always implies the temporary suppression of another. In close relation with the last feature, the phenomenon of "suppressed voices" is examined. It is argued that the notion of suppressed voices opens perspectives for the investigation of experiences on lower levels of consciousness, without the necessity of taking traditional psychoanalytic assumptions as a starting point. In order to study the structure and process of meaning, a theory of valuation is explained that permits, in the form of a concrete procedure of self-investigation, a way of studying meaning as a dialogical movement.

Guidelines to the Reader

For those who do not plan to read all the chapters of the book, some reader advice follows here. *Social psychologists* can find the basic features of narrative in close relation with the root metaphor of contextualism discussed in Chapter 2 and the central features of dialogue, intersubjective exchange, and dominance (social power) analyzed in Chapter 5. Moreover, it may be useful for social psychologists and *sociologists* to follow in Chapter 7 the argumentation that Mead did, in fact, not develop one unified theory but two conflicting theories, one emphasizing unity of society and the other stressing conflict and dominance in society. *Developmental psychologists* can find a review of literature about the genesis of the dialogical self in Chapter 5 (e.g., pseudodialogues between mother and child, imaginal dialogues, self-recognition, personal space, role playing, and the use of the pronoun *I*). *Clinical psychologists* and *psychotherapists* can find much about the process of synthesis in Chapter 6 and a concrete procedure to study synthesis as a process in Chapter 9. Moreover, they might be interested in a discussion of the scientist–practitioner split and suggestions for a more collaborative relationship between the two groups in Chapter 8. *Personality psychologists* can find a review of studies referring to the growing emphasis on the person as a self-expert and knowledgeable co-worker of the psychologists in Chapter 8 and a procedure for studying personality traits as characters in a self-narrative in Chapters 6 and 9.

Psychologists interested in novelistic literature and its fertile contribution to the understanding of narrative should concentrate on Chapters 3 and 4. For psychologists interested in culture and in the cultural biases inherent in the Western self, the insights of Vico, who can be considered the founder of constructionism, are particularly relevant (Chapter 1). His concept of "corporeal imagination" that is elaborated on in later chapters functions as a powerful correction of the disembodied Descartean *Cogito*. Some cultural anthropological work, reported in Chapter 5, is of direct interest for those who want to compare Western culture with non-Western cultures.

Let us open the curtain with a confrontation between Descartes and Vico, who enter the stage as protagonist and antagonist, respectively. These two figures crop up in the book incidentally, in an explicit way, but they are permanently present as an understream of thought.

CHAPTER 1

Vico versus Descartes

"I will now shut my eyes, stop my ears, and withdraw all my senses. I will eliminate from my thoughts all images of bodily things. . . I will regard all such images as vacuous, false and worthless. I will converse with myself and scrutinize myself more deeply; and in this way I will attempt to achieve, little by little, a more intimate knowledge of myself." In this quotation from *Third Meditation* (1641/1984, p. 24) Descartes proceeded in an effort to arrive at the complete certainty of his famous *Cogito, ergo sum* ("I think, therefore I am"). However, as Levin (1988) observed, the Cartesian self came out as "a self of reason completely purged of body and feeling, a self without shadows, a self totally transparent to itself, totally knowing of itself, totally self-possessed, totally certain of itself" (p. 15).

We certainly need not wait until the twentieth century to hear a voice arguing in vehement opposition to Descartes' influential thesis. Giambattista Vico, born in 1668 as the son of a bookseller in Naples, 18 years after Descartes' death, is generally recognized as one of the founders of the philosophy of history (cf. Hora, 1966). The main thesis of his famous work *Scienza Nuova* (New Science) was that this historical world is certainly created by human beings ". . . and its principles are therefore to be found within the modifications of our own human mind" (Vico, 1744/1968, p. 96). Much of Vico's thinking was in opposition to Descartes' *Cogito,* and therefore he rejected Descartes' method of systematic doubt since it ignored the role of historical knowledge in human awareness. Vico argued that *Cogito* as the final certainty is a serious reduction of the human condition, resulting in an ahistorical and disembodied conception of the mind. Instead, Vico elaborates on the view that mind and body are inseparable: "Buried in a body" the human mind is *in* history and *makes* history at the same time. ". . . It is because I consist both of body and mind that I think; so that body and mind united are the cause of thought" (Vico, 1710/1988, p. 96).

Let us consider the nature of two contrasting positions in some more detail in order to consider their far-reaching implications.

1.1 Thinking above the Body

Descartes has often been given the tribute of being "the father of modern philosophy." With equal right he can be considered as "the founder of *Enlightenment*," an era in which questions relating to the body were increasingly answered in terms of physical, mechanical, and biochemical explanations. In the Western world, particularly, questions about the body became dissociated from questions about the mind or soul (cf. F. Johnson, 1985). Such dissociation is most commonly described as "Cartesian," although it has also received support from other philosophical and theological traditions in the West. Descartes, in line with preceding and preparing traditions, stressed the essential difference between "natural" and "supernatural" phenomena and between "physical" and "metaphysical" categorization, reflecting the distinctive quality of material versus immaterial entities. Mind–body distinctions enjoyed a relative ascendency in the Western world as describing methodically and philosophically different forms of reality (see also Ryle, 1949).

The essential opposition in Descartes' philosophy is between mind (*res cogitans*) and extension (*res extensa*), the body being part of the latter. Such a dualism, however, encounters insuperable obstacles when one takes the specific experience of the body into account. Zaner (1981), referring to the work of Bergson (1907), argues that my body, even when regarded as a physiological entity, is not simply an object like other objects in the extended world. It is peculiarly "mine," that is, this one organism, as no other, is a center. It functions as a reference point around which other worldly things are placed, arranged, and organized. My body is a "centre d'action," an actional center.

Certainly, Descartes was not totally unaware of the intrinsic relatedness of body and mind. He insists that the body is "intimately unioned" with the mind. That is, he believes that the soul is not in the body in the way a boatman is in his boat, that is, removable, accidentally, revocably. Here the stress is not at all on the isolation of extension from mind, but rather on "intimacy." Descartes, forced by the necessity that there must be at least *some* relation between body and mind, assumed that a specific organ, the pineal gland, served as a bridge between the two entities. However, as Zaner (1981) argues, in a philosophy that is based on the conception that everything is *either* matter *or* mind, nothing can be *both* mind *and* matter. Therefore, any conception of the body as intimately unioned with the mind has a high risk of being incompatible with the thesis of the essential opposition between mind and extension. It is on this point, Zaner (1981) concludes, that Descartes' ontology collapses under the weight of its own insights (p. 10).

1.2 Thinking in Splendid Isolation

Closely related to the mind–body dualism is the separation of self and other. In an insightful and critical way, Straus (1958) argues that Descartes' *Cogito* implies not only a dualism between mind and body but also a dissociation between self and others. When we today speak with little hesitation (in fact too little as far as Straus is concerned) about an "outside world," we are using Cartesian terminology and are following his line of thought, whether we want to or not. To what does the word *outside* in the phrase "outside world" refer to, or *external* in the phrase "external world"? In Cartesian terms it means that the world is outside of consciousness and that, reciprocally, consciousness, including sensory experience, is outside of the world. The Cartesian dichotomy, therefore, separates not only mind from body, but also one person from another person, Me from *You.* The Cartesian ego does not have *direct* communication with any alter ego. In this view self-awareness precedes the awareness of the world. We are aware of ourselves without necessarily being aware of anything else. In the realm of consciousness, each one is alone with himself or herself. Although Descartes does not deny, or even seriously doubt, the existence of the so-called outside world, he insists that it is never *directly* accessible to us. Its existence is not more than probable; it must be proved. However, as Straus concludes, the fact that proof was needed emphasizes the distance. In this philosophy the alter ego, and external reality more in general, becomes a function of judgment and a result of proof, instead of immediate experience and starting point. Descartes' conception of reality can be expressed by the formula "something happens in the outside world in accordance with the laws of nature," whereas everyday life experience of reality adheres to the formula, "something happens *to me* in the world." In other words, the prelogical sphere of the immediate experience of reality has been eliminated.

Why does Descartes seem to neglect the world of everyday experience or what reasons does he have to disavow its evidence? This question can only be answered when we take into account the nature of his method, the method of doubt. He accepted only those ideas that led to judgments that were "so clearly and distinctly presented to his mind" that there was no reason for him to doubt. In *First Meditation* he asks his reader to imagine that all feeling and perception, including body awareness, is a lie caused by "some malicious demon," who has employed all his energies to deceive him (Descartes, 1641/1984, p. 15).

Although the wicked genius can obscure Descartes' senses and even his thoughts, he cannot destroy the assurance that there is someone who has been betrayed and who is capable to *think* about the possibility of betrayal. In other words, even when there is betrayal, one can think about being betrayed, and this thinking is of a universal philosophical validity. The term *therefore* in the sentence "I think, therefore I am" points to the perfect certainty of a conclusion resulting from a reasoning process. In this way the Cartesian self ends up, according to F. Johnson (1985), as a "fixed entity, essentially isolated and disembodied, an ego–logical thing, encapsulated in a machine of corruptible matter" (p. 15).

In summary, Descartes' philosophy is characterized by two separations, between the body and the mind and between self and other. The resulting conception of a rational and individualistic mind, however, is in apparent disagreement with everyday experience. In this experience I feel my body not simply as an object in the world, but as "mine." Moreover, the other person is not the result of a reasoning process, but of immediate presence "to me," even before I start to think explicitly.

The best way to summarize the criticism of Descartes' philosophy is with one of Straus' (1958) conclusions: "In sensory experience I always experience myself *and* the world at the same time, not myself directly and the *Other* by inference, not myself before the *Other*, not myself without the *Other*, nor the *Other* without myself." (p. 148).

1.3 To Know Is to Make

Whereas Descartes took his starting point in the thinking mind, Vico took it in the historical mind. We know human beings only if we know them from the beginning. His "New Science" was therefore a history of human ideas, based on the principle "the sciences must begin where their subject matters began" (Vico, 1744/1968, p. 104). His attempt was to go back to the moment when people began to think humanly and not when philosophers began to reflect on human thinking. In his intellectual enterprise, Vico arrived at a position that was at least in two respects opposite to Descartes' *Cogito:* (1) Human knowledge is embodied; and (2) knowing is relating to other people.

Vico, reflecting on the history of mankind, was aware that the first wisdom of people, impressed by the beauty and terror of nature as they were, was not abstract like that of learned people now, but felt and imagined. He called this kind of knowledge "poetic wisdom," and he used this term in a very constructive way: ". . . they were called 'poets,' which is Greek for 'creators.'" (Vico, 1744/1968, p. xl). Poetic knowledge was born from ignorance, for "ignorance, the mother of wonder, made everything wonderful to men who were ignorant of everything" (p. 116). Poetry was at first divine, because it imagined the causes of the things to be gods. For example, the ancient Germans dwelling about the Arctic Ocean spoke of hearing the sun pass at night from west to east through the sea and affirmed that they saw gods. The first people gave the things they wondered at substantial being after their own ideas, "just as children do, whom we see take inanimate things in their hands and play with them and talk to them as though they were living persons" (p. 117).

Vico supposed that the first people, in attempting to find causes for incomprehensible things, took their own body as a model to make their environment understandable. They did this "by virtue of a wholly corporeal imagination" (p. 117). When the sky fearfully rolled with thunder and flashed with lightning, they imagined gods and giants at work and ". . . pictured the sky to themselves as a great animated body . . ." (p. 118). Vico added to these observations that it

is for our "civilized minds" difficult to understand how these first people constructed their world, because we are "detached from the senses . . . by abstractions corresponding to all the abstract terms our languages abound in, and so
refined by the art of writing . . . that it is naturally beyond our power to form
the vast image of this mistress called 'Sympathetic Nature'" (p. 118). Our
intellectual baggage prevents us from entering into the vast imagination of these
first people "whose minds were not in the least abstract, refined, or spiritualized,
because they were entirely immersed in the senses, buffeted by the passions,
buried in the body" (p. 118).

In order to understand Vico's use of the term *imagination*, it must be emphasized that it is not to be equaled with "irrealistic fantasy." On the contrary,
imagination has its base in the perception of everyday life reality and is rooted in
the experience of the natural environment. Gifted with imagination people
select perceptual elements and combine them into meaningful, narrative configurations. In Vico's terms, ". . . imagination is nothing but extended or compounded memory" (p. 75).

The notion of imagination in Vico's world view was not only a way of
interpretation of incomprehensible phenomena, but also a force in shaping the
environment. In the awareness that the human mind cannot become a productive force in history independent of the body, Vico realized that progress with
regard to the environment has, since ancient times, been the result of *inventions*.
He therefore assumed the existence of a creative force in human nature, which
he called *ingenium*. With this force humans can alter the physical world and
make history. Endowed with ingenium, people are able to move things into "new
relationships" (Hora, 1966, p. 241). Along these lines Vico arrived at the
conclusion *verare et facere idem esse* ("knowing and doing are the same") (Hora,
1966, p. 237).[1]

The real basis for Vico's counter to Cartesian rationalism is not the arguments
with which Descartes formulates his position, but that Descartes leaves out that
part of the mind that Vico called ingenium. In his book, *On the Study Methods of
Our Time* (1709/1990), Vico holds that the great achievements such as the
machines of Archimedes and the dome of the Church of Santa Maria del Fiore
designed by Filippo Brunelleschi, the great Renaissance architect and inventor
of linear perspective, are done not primarily by geometrical method but by the
faculty of ingenium. This faculty alone is responsible for the activity of ordering
and reordering things and thoughts in such a way that new and unexpected
relationships emerge. Therefore, there is much reason to consider Vico as the
father of the social constructionist orientation (cf. Mahoney, 1988).

1.4 Knowledge Resulting from Communication

Vico's social theory assumes that mankind went through three periods: "the age
of the gods," "the age of heroes," and "the age of peoples." Since people first

translated the unfamiliar into the familiar by perceiving anthropomorphic spirits at work, these spirits had to be propitiated and placated, an activity that fell to the heads of the families. This was the beginning of the "age of the gods," the period when people lived in patriarchal communities, affiliated by blood ties, and were ruled over by strong men who combined the roles of priest and king. These primal communities expanded when fugitives from dangerous areas sought protection by the patriarchs in return for their labor. Because the refugees were not linked by blood to the primal kinship, but were affiliated only by services rendered and received, a division of power and privileges was established. This was, according to Vico, the origin of aristocracy, where the ruling group claimed descent from the gods. Thus, the "age of gods" gave way to the "age of heroes" and, correspondingly, the rule of priest-kings was replaced by the rule of nobles. The security and order established by the aristocrats, however, resulted in the enrichment of the plebeians, who grew stronger and rebelled. The struggle between aristocrats and plebeians marked the transition from the age of heroes to "the age of peoples." At the same time customary codes of conduct were replaced by the written contract that defined relations between parties enjoying definable rights.

Although Vico did not distantiate himself from all Enlightenment beliefs, he rejected the idea that humanity as a whole developed in a linear sequence from lower to higher forms of self-consciousness. He held that in most cultures each stage is an improvement over the preceding one, but every third stage (the stage of the people) is always followed by a period of decline. This conviction of necessary decline within one and the same culture did not prevent him from believing that *across cultures* there is a process of development that occurs in an ultimately progressive way. In other words, human history in general does not develop in either a linear or cyclical pattern, but more like a spiral.[2]

There are several places in Vico's work where he treats the development of language in close relation to the three periods of history. He describes the first language as a divine mental language by mute religious acts or divine ceremonies: "This language belongs to religions by the eternal property that it concerns them more to be reverenced than to be reasoned. . ." (Vico, 1744/1968, p. 340). The second language came about by heroic blazonings, ". . . with which arms are made to speak" (p. 340). This language has been survived mainly in military discipline. The third language is the articulate speech, "which is used by all nations today" (p. 340).

As Vico goes back to the earliest stages of mankind in order to find the origin of our modern society, he attempts to trace the first use of words. Human words, he explains, were formed from interjections, which are sounds articulated under the impetus of violent passions. In all languages these sounds are monosyllables:

Thus it is not beyond likelihood that, when wonder had been awakened in men by the first thunderbolts, these interjections of Jove should give birth to one produced made in the image of God, possessing the divine spark of rationality that sets them off from brute animals. However, human beings have bodies, or even better, they "are" bodies. We are not only *rational* animals, we are also rational *animals*. This balancing of the emphasis requires acknowledging the role of the body in the process of knowing itself. The most direct way to clarify this point is to show that the body, and, even broader, the reality of space, is *in* the mind, not simply outside the mind. We confine ourselves here to two phenomena, "image schema" and "metaphor," as described by Johnson (1987).

An image schema functions as a frame for orienting ourselves in varying situations on the basis of the form of our body. For example, a "verticality schema" emerges from our tendency to employ an up–down orientation in picking out meaningful structures of our experience. We stand "upright" or "lie down," climb a staircase, ask how tall our child is, wonder about the level of the water, and admire a tall tree. In other words, our body, being part of the spatial world, has a verticality structure that we use as a means of orientation in that world.

The image schema is not a purely corporeal structure. We use it also as a metaphor to organize our more abstract understanding. For example, in estimating quantities, we assume that "more is up," that is, we understand quantity in terms of verticality. We say: The prices are going up; the number of books published each year keeps rising; someone's gross earnings fell; and we turn down the heat. In all these examples we use a verticality structure as a physical base for our mental understanding, although there is no intrinsic reason why "more" should be "up." What we see, in fact, is that a given image schema emerges first as a structure of bodily interactions and is then figuratively developed as a structure around which meaning is organized at more abstract levels of cognition.

If one accepts the body as a first and basic metaphor for human understanding, then metaphor is not to be viewed as an ornament or a mere figure of speech, frequently used by poets or children. On the contrary, metaphor is an indispensable structure of human understanding by which we can figuratively comprehend our world. The central significance of image schemata and metaphor is in sharp contrast to basic notions of the objectivist view. The objectivists hold that the concepts that are used to analyze meaning must map definitive, discrete, and fixed objects, properties, and relations. Such concepts are "literal." Metaphorical projections, however, are not of that sort, for they involve category crossings that do not exist objectively in the world. In its simplest definition, metaphor is an implicit comparison between two unlike entities. The quality of one entity is transferred to the other entity (the Greek *metapherein* means "to transfer"). The two qualities form a combination that does not correspond to something that already exists in the world. Rather, metaphorical combinations imply a construction of the world. It is this notion of construction that Vico had in mind when he concluded that "to know is to make," and "to make is to know."

Image schemes and their metaphorical use are central to imagination. Imagination, in Johnson's terms, is a basic image-schematic capacity for ordering our experience. It is not a wild, nonrule-governed faculty for fantasy and creativity. The concept of imagination, that will play a role in the following chapters, can only properly be understood if one realizes that the body is in the mind and that the "external world" is not simply external but shaped and constructed by the production and use of knowledge itself.

Notes

1. The expression "moving things into new relationships" points to the historical role of creativity in restructuring the world. In a recent review, Epstein (1991) concludes that creativity has been said by many to be a result of a "combinatorial process." Einstein, for example, in explaining his creative ability, spoke of "combinatory play." Stephen Jay describes his creativity as to "make connections." Henri Poincaré said: "Ideas rose in crowds, I felt them collide until pairs interlocked . . . making a stable combination." Rothenberg (1971) describes creativity as a "Janusian" process, after Janus, the god with two faces looking in opposite directions. New ideas result from "the capacity to conceive and utilize two or more opposite or contradictory ideas, concepts, or images simultaneously" (Rothenberg, 1971, p. 195).

2. Vico's conception of inevitable decline was closely related to the changes in people's attitude: "Men first feel necessity, then look for utility, next attend to comfort, still later amuse themselves with pleasure, thence grow dissolute in luxury, and finally go mad and waste their substance" (Vico, 1744/1968, p. 78). For a review of Vico's social stages see White (1968).

CHAPTER 2

The Narrative Construction of Reality

One of the most conspicuous developments in psychology of the past decade is the upsurge of the narrative approach. Scholars from psychological sub-disciplines and related fields have shown an increasing interest in the possibilities of studying the human mind from the perspective of the "narrative" or "story." A narrative approach to reality puts heavy emphasis on the role of imagination, and is, therefore, more in the Vichean than in the Cartesian tradition. In this chapter we will investigate the nature of the narrative approach and its place in psychology.

2.1 Story as a Root Metaphor

A clarifying schema for describing the specific features of the narrative approach was offered by Pepper's (1942) treatment of "root metaphors," recently discussed as relevant to psychology by Sarbin (1986). Pepper, reflecting on the history of mankind, concluded that the hypotheses people develop about their world are derived from a basic or root metaphor guiding their perceptions and thinking. A root metaphor not only offers a basic perspective for perceiving, classifying, and interpreting events, but also constrains these activities. Metaphors, like spotlights, produce a particular view of reality. At the same time, however, each light is bound to a particular angle and, therefore, offers only *one* view. Metaphors create views and at the same time restrict these views. Let us take a closer look at four metaphors that, according to Pepper (1942), are most relevant for scientific purposes: "formism," "mechanism," "organicism," and "contextualism," the last one including the notion of narrative or story.

2.1.1 Formism: The Form of Things

Formism, as a root metaphor, stresses the organization of the environment on the basis of the form of things (big, small, short, long, round, angular). The

common sense version of formism is found in the activities of an artisan fashion-
ing products in a similar style. On the basis of their perceived forms, objects can
be classified (e.g., furniture belongs to a particular style). According to Sarbin
(1986), formism has received its expression also in the realm of psychological
theory. A familiar example is personality trait theories, in which people are
classified and compared according to psychological traits like intelligence, aggression, anxiety, shyness, impulsivity, dependency, and so on. Such traits re-
veal how people's personality or character has been "formed." Also, the use of
diagnostic categories can be viewed as representing the metaphor of formism.
For example, the *Diagnostic and Statistical Manual of Mental Disorders* (DSM)
(American Psychiatric Association, 1987) comprises descriptions and criteria
for the diagnosis of a wide variety of disorders. Such criteria may be useful for
clinicians aiming at a certain degree of consensus in the classification of clients
on the basis of clinical problems.

Formism functions as a metaphor to classify and compare people on the basis
of general traits or characteristics and provides the means for the study of
individual differences. However, general traits do not lend themselves easily to the
description of a person's individuality or to the *particulars* of his or her personal
history. When we classify somebody, for example, as aggressive, we see him or
her as more aggressive than we see most other people. Considering the person in
this way, we see him or her, more or less, as a representative of a *general* class
(aggressive people). Of course, we can use a greater number of traits in describing one and the same individual and construct a profile of traits that may be
more or less specific of this particular person (e.g., high in extraversion, low in
intelligence, high in aggression, intermediate in anxiety). However, as Lamiell
(1987) and others have argued, the individuality of such a profile is highly
restricted, in so far as it can not be more than a combination of general trait
categories. As long as the description is restricted to trait categories, nothing is
known about the particular events of the person's history or about the personal
meaning of a trait in the eyes of this particular individual.

2.1.2 Mechanicism: Cause–Effect Relationships

The most typical model of the mechanistic metaphor, the dominating view in
Western science, is the machine. Mechanicism considers the human organism as
reactive from a basic state of rest and activity as a result of external stimulation.
The most simplified example is the movement of a billiard ball: Its speed and
direction are determined by another ball that functions as the "efficient cause"
(i.e., a cause that effects subsequent movement or behavior). As the history of
learning theories has demonstrated, also more complex phenomena, such as
affect and problem solving, can be considered as ultimately reducible to processes governed by efficient causes. A mechanistic model of development typically focuses on the role of events as antecedents to various response outcomes.

Although changes in the organism may appear to be qualitative, all changes are actually quantitative (Hultsch & Plemons, 1979).

A typical example of the mechanistic view of life events is Dohrenwend's (1961) model of stress responses. The model contains four main elements: a set of *antecedent* stressors, a set of mediating factors, a social–psychological adaptation syndrome, and *consequent* adaptive or maladaptive responses. Life events, including those that are typically negative (e.g., divorce) and those that are typically positive (e.g., marriage), are considered as potential stressors. Mediating factors refer to inner resources (e.g., intellectual abilities) and external resources (e.g., social support). Social–psychological adaptation involves, for example, changes in orientation (e.g., beliefs) or activity (e.g., increasing or decreasing). These processes may, finally, lead to either functional or dysfunctional outcomes. This model is quite complex mainly by its assumption that stressors do not directly result in a particular outcome, but do so via intermediate processes. Suppose, for example, there are two people, A and B, A being more intelligent and receiving more support from significant others than B. In this case it is expected that the same stressor (e.g., a conflict in the work situation) will result in more maladaptive responses for B than for A. Dohrenwend's model can be described as mechanistic because, despite its complexity, it is formulated in antecedent–consequent relations of a quantitative nature.

The problem with mechanistic models is that the definition of antecedent–consequent relations precludes the possibility that the same event as an antecedent factor may have *qualitatively* different meanings for different people. For example, when the death of a significant other is defined as a stressor, it is assumed that this event functions as a stressor with a high degree of tension in the lives of all people who are confronted with such event. This assumption excludes the possibility that, for a particular person, the death of a significant other may have the meaning of a relief of tension, or a consolation, after a long period of suffering. Such an act of meaning construction, qualitatively different from the notion of stress as a quantitative cause, is excluded on a theoretical base.

2.1.3 Organicism: Maturation and Growth

The organismic metaphor considers the human organism as living and active. The components of the organism are seen as parts of an organized whole, and change is viewed not only quantitatively but also qualitatively (e.g., the growth and blossom of a plant). Although efficient causes are not necessarily absent, fundamental causation is teleological in nature. There is a telos, a goal, that gives unity and direction to the organized process. Development is seen as a process of structural change and is discontinuous in so far that later states are *not* reducible to previous states or antecedent factors.

A typical example of an organismic theory is, according to Hultsch and Plemons (1979), Levinson's conception of the life-span consisting of a sequence of five eras, each of roughly 20 years duration (Levinson, Darrow, Klein, Levinson, & McKee, 1974). The eras are (1) preadulthood, age 0–20; (2) early adulthood, age 20–40; (3) middle adulthood, age 40–60; (4) late adulthood, age 60–80; and (5) late late adulthood, age 80+. These eras are characterized by relatively stable periods and transitions. The stable periods (lasting 6–8 years) are marked by crucial choices and the striving for particular goals. Transition periods (lasting 4–5 years) are characterized by the termination of existing life structures and the initiation of new ones. In these transition periods the person explores new possibilities for change which provide a basis for a new stable period. Around the age of 20, for example, the person makes a transition between the previous period and the challenges of young adulthood. This task requires a change of the relationship with one's family and peers. At the same time the possibilities of the adult world are explored: starting a new education, applying for a job, sharing one's life with a partner. After these transitions, the person enters a more stable period where the new goals in work, school, or family are giving structure and direction to one's life.

Levinson's theory represents an organismic metaphor in that it is governed by final causation, in contrast to the efficient causation of the mechanistic metaphor. Moreover, the theory describes qualitative changes, that is, new phenomena emerging in the course of successive periods. This is in contrast to the mechanistic metaphor that is restricted to quantitative changes that are reducible to the workings of antecedent variables.

A recurring problem with organismic theories is that they typically assume the existence of a fixed sequence of developmental stages or tasks. It is assumed that one era or stage leads invariably to a next era or stage and that the processes involved are the same for all people. The problem with this assumption is that such a sequence is more relevant for some people than for others. For example, Levinson assumes the existence of a *midlife crisis*, in the period of transition between young and middle adulthood. However, research on this question has produced mixed results. McCrae and Costa (1982), for example, found midlife crises to crop up in only a few men and to be dispersed over a longer period of time, anywhere between the ages of 30 and 60. On the basis of a review of relevant studies, Clarke-Stewart, Perlmutter, and Friedman (1988) conclude that midlife crisis does *not* seem to be a general phenomenon. In more theoretical terms, organismic theories, in assuming a fixed sequence of developmental stages for all people irrespective of their sex, race, socioeconomic status, and family background, are quite insensitive to the apparent differences among people and, in particular, do not take into account their individual histories.

2.1.4 Contextualism: The Historical Nature of Events

Contextualism is the root metaphor that will guide the explorations in this study. The central element is the historical event that can only be understood when it is located in the context of *time* and *space*. As Sarbin (1986) has argued, contextualism presupposes an ongoing texture of elaborated events, each being influenced by collateral episodes and by multiple agents who engage in actions. There is a constant change in the structure of situations and in *positions* occupied by the actors. Sarbin (1986) argues that there is a basic similarity between the historian and the novelist, because the historical act and the narrative have approximately the same semantic structure. History is more than a simple collection of records of past or present events. Annals and chronicles are not more than the raw materials for the historian's construction of narratives, an activity involving the organization and interpretation of events. Although their emphases are different, both the historian and the novelist are narrativists. The historian writes about presumably actual events, influenced by reconstructed people who have their intentions and purposes. This reconstruction is not possible without imagination, since history can only be written on the basis of incomplete data. The novelist, on the other hand, writes about fictive characters in a context of real-world settings. Fiction always makes use of elements derived from the observed reality and is, therefore, not more than a new or unusual combination of realistic elements. Both kinds of narrative, historical and novelistic, make use of so-called "fact" *and* "fictions." Not surprisingly, "story" and "history" are etymologically related.

Not only historians and novelists are involved in the construction of stories; ordinary people also are continually ordering and reordering the events that they consider relevant to their own lives. In Cohler's (1982, 1988) view, personal narratives represent internally consistent interpretations of the past as presently understood, the experienced present, and the anticipated future. Such a conception implies that a life story is never fixed. The story is retold over time because new experiences, resulting from changes in the situation, must be integrated. The retelling of one's story follows from two characteristics of personal narratives. First, storytelling is only possible if events cohere as *interconnected* parts of an organized whole; and thanks to their interconnection they are intelligible and meaningful. Second, *new events*, particularly those that have direct implications to an existing story, may result in a new ordering of the story as a whole. New experiences may influence not only the account of one's present situation, but also of one's past and future. For example, as long as people receive the respect from significant others in their direct environment, they may remember similar experiences in their past. However, when important failures disrupt the sense of continuity, the same person may remember negative experiences in the past that were similarly threatening to his or her self-esteem. In other words, changes in the situation may have direct repercussions to the story involved, and therefore both telling and retelling are essential to personal narratives (Hermans, 1992).

2.1.5 Comparison of Root Metaphors: The Specific Angle of Contextualism

In order to further clarify the nature of contextualism, we compare this metaphor with the other ones by way of summary.

Formism classifies things (objects, persons) in such a way that general traits, types, or characteristics of an ahistorical kind are produced. Contextualism, on the contrary, is sensitive to the particulars of time and space and, therefore, will highlight a particular event in the context of other events.

Mechanism places events in antecedent–consequent relationships, where the antecedent event functions as an efficient cause. From the perspective of contextualism, it would be an oversimplification to select two events and place them in a cause–effect relationship. This objection holds even when such a model is made more complex by the inclusion of intermediate factors that may modify the cause–effect relationship. Contextualism, rather, presupposes a *multiplicity* of events, referring to past, present, and future, that form together a coherent and interconnected totality. Moreover, contextualism does not suppose efficient causation, but *final causation:* The person as a storyteller does not "react to stimuli" but is continuously involved in a process of meaning construction and is oriented to the active realization of purposes and goals.

Organicism is traditionally the most influential metaphor for developmental psychology. Besides Levinson's work, Erikson's (1950, 1963) theory of developmental stages and Havighhurst's (1972) view of developmental tasks are well known examples of this approach. The research line of Piaget and Kohlberg fits into the metaphor of organicism as well. As already discussed, a typical feature of organismic theories is the supposition of a predictable sequence of developmental stages or tasks. Contextualism, on the other hand, certainly acknowledges the importance of predictable or expected events, but differs from organicism in that it emphasizes the importance of *unexpected* events. Due to the fact that events are dependent on the changes in the situation, lives change over time in ways that are not necessarily predictable. In support of this assertion there is ample empirical evidence. Findings from longitudinal studies, together with the increased appreciation of the influence of larger historical factors on human lives (Elder, 1974, 1979), have made clear that lives are much less predictable than formerly recognized (Clausen, 1972; Gergen, 1980; Kagan, 1980; Riegel, 1975). Studies of lives over time should, therefore, be concerned with the impact of unanticipated events, particularly with the manner in which people make sense of these events (Brim & Ryff, 1980; Cohler, 1982, 1988). A broad range of events may result in unanticipated changes: economic recession, moving to another place, change of job, the sudden loss of a friend, divorce of parents, a serious accident, or a life-threatening operation. Often such events have a disrupting influence simply because the person is not "ready" for them. When changes are expected or "on schedule," there is time in advance to prepare oneself for the coming event. When, however, the event is unexpected, there is less opportunity to get accustomed to the change of situation, making adaptation more difficult. Of course, the same events may also have a challenging and renewing influence on a person's life in the long run.

2.2 The Pervasiveness of Narrative in Daily Life

It is certainly possible to describe a narrative or story as a form of "narrative thinking" if one makes sure that a clear distinction is made between thinking of a narrative nature and thinking of a rational nature. Such a distinction was made by Bruner (1986), who argued that there are basically two "modes of thought": storytelling (narrative thinking) and argumentation (propositional thinking). Each mode represents a distinct way of construing reality and has its own criteria for well formedness. Whereas arguments are intended to convince someone of their truth, stories are construed to convince someone of their lifelikeness. Argumentation appeals to formal and empirical proof procedures. Storytelling appeals to verisimilitude.[1]

The difference between the two modes can be further clarified by the distinctive function of the world *then*. This term functions differently in the logical proposition "if x, then y" than in the narrative "The king died, and then the queen." One leads to a search for universal truth conditions (x is always and necessarily followed by y), the other for particular connections between events (x is followed by y in this case). The story must, of course, conform to the canons of logical consistency to achieve truth, but violations of expected consistency also provide the basis for drama (e.g., in the story of a doublegoer the identity thesis a = a is violated, because a = b is true at the same time).

Bruner (1986) emphasizes the contrast between the imaginative quality of the narrative mode and the deductive quality of the logico–scientific mode. The former leads to "good" stories, gripping drama, and believable historical accounts; the latter refers to the ability to see possible formal connections before one is able to empirically prove them. The narrative mode deals in human intention and action and the vicissitudes that mark its course, whereas the logico–scientific mode seeks to transcend the particular by reaching for higher and higher levels of abstraction. The narrative mode aims to put the (general) human condition into the particulars of experience and attempts *to locate experience in time and space* (Bruner, 1986, p. 13).

When Bruner emphasizes the "lifelikeness" of narrative thinking, how pervasive is this kind of thinking in human life? This question can be answered by demonstrating the narrative structure of perception, emotion, and action.

2.2.1 The Narrative Structure of Perception

A most direct elucidation of the narrative organization of perception is provided by the work of the Belgian psychologist Michotte (1946/1963), who performed experiments on the human perception of causality. Michotte constructed an apparatus that allowed an observer to see two or more small rectangles in motion. The experimenter controlled the speed, direction, and distance traveled by the figures. With particular configurations, the observing subjects used causal attributions in their interpretation of the movements of the rectangles. For example, if rectangle A stopped after moving toward B, and rectangle B then started to move, the observers would say that B "got out of the way" of A. In such cases, subjects typically reported their perceptions in "as if" terms. For example, "It is as if A's approach frightened B and B ran away" or "It is as if A, in touching B, induced an electric current which set B going."

Similar observations were reported by Heider and Simmel (1944), who employed a film of a large triangle, a small triangle, and a circle. The experimenter manipulated these figures in such a way that they moved in various directions and at variable speeds within a circumscribed field. Within this field was a big rectangle, one side of which was sometimes open. One of the observers reported as follows:

> A man has planned to meet a girl and the girl comes along with another man. The first man tells the second to go; the second tells the first, and he shakes his head. Then the two men have a fight, and the girl starts to go into the room. . . She apparently does not want to be with the first man. The first man follows her into the room after having left the second in a rather weakened condition leaning on the wall outside the room. . . The girl gets out of the room in a sudden dash just as man number two gets the door open. The two chase around the outside of the room together, followed by man number one. But they finally elude him and get away. The first man goes back and tries to open his door, but he is so blinded by rage and frustration that he cannot open it. . . [Heider & Simmel, 1944, pp. 246–247]

Sarbin (1986) concludes from these studies that the meaningless movements of the geometrical figures were assigned meaning and described in the idiom of the narrative. Similarly, Bruner (1986, p. 18) concludes that it is possible to arrange the space–time relationship in such a way that intention or "animacy" are implied. We plainly *see* "search," "goal seeking," and "persistence in overcoming obstacles" as intention driven.

2.2.2 The Narrative Structure of Emotion

In one of his explorations, Sarbin (1989) asked more than 30 adults, most of them psychologists, to *define* the term *emotion*. After each respondent had formulated a definition, he asked them to give an *instance* of emotion, drawn from observation of self or others.

One of Sarbin's subjects offered the following definition of emotion: "It is something that I feel inside of me. I know when I'm having an emotion because I feel it." When asked for an illustration, he described a mistake made by his secretary that caused a great deal of distress. In this account the respondent referred to his feelings of anger and rage, but he did so in terms of an event that happened in a particular situation.

In comparing the answers from all his subjects in the first part of his study, Sarbin found that there was a great deal of variety in the definitions, except for one characteristic. Almost all the respondents referred in their definition to a locus for the emotion: *inside* the body. In the second part of the survey a variety of examples referring to different emotions was produced. Most situations depicted by the subjects focused on anger, a few on fear, and one on caring. In one respect, however, all examples were alike: They were told as narratives *without* any reference to happenings inside the body.

The apparent existence of a gap between the definition and the exemplification of emotion is perhaps not surprising, as Sarbin explains, if one realizes that psychologists are exposed to the writings of several generations of textbook authors who composed chapters on emotion often in the vocabulary of psychophysiology. The fact that the exemplifications refer to events in the immediate situation points to the relevance of the narratory principle in daily life experience. It is Sarbin's (1989) thesis that for the realm of human emotions, the narratory principle provides a more satisfying and more ecologically valid explanatory model than the traditional textbook definition. Let us follow his explanation.

In most prevailing theories, psychophysiological models encourage the detachment of phenomena identified as "emotions" from situational contexts. Many psychological writings about anger, love, shame, guilt, etc., imply that these emotions are detachable from the context of action, not unlike discourses on digestion, liver function, or vision. This isolation is traceable to the ontological status assigned to such substantives as mind, soul, psyche, and consciousness. The tendency to take emotional phenomena out of context is expressed in a particular metaphor: *The body is a container.* This metaphor suggests that an emotion is a fluidlike substance that is located in a container, separating the substance from the environment. The container metaphor suggests also a reification (objectification) of the emotion: It is not something that emanates from a living person in a particular situation (*I* as an emotional being) but something that happens in a machinelike apparatus (emotions as physiological reactions). The traditional view of emotions reflects the dominating role of the root metaphor of mechanism in psychology as a science. From the perspective of this metaphor, the body works as a machine that can be studied in its thinglike operations.

Sarbin (1989) emphasizes that the problem is not only in the answers but also in the preceding questions that invite abstract definitions of emotions per se. Questions that are in line with the root metaphor of contextualism are not "What is emotion?" or "How can it be defined?" but rather "Who are the actors?", "What is the setting?", and "When did the action take place?" When A is insulting B and B answers the insult by striking A with a blow, it is not the case that the "insult" stands alone, or that the retaliation stands alone, or that the emotion identified as anger is detachable from insult and retaliation. Rather, all these features are integral to the emplotment of an anger narrative. They are learned as parts of a patterned whole and perceived as a patterned whole (e.g., when another person hits you, you respond with a hit in return).[2]

The person who is enraged by a secretarial mistake and the one who expressed his or her anger by giving the other a blow are enacting roles demanded by a specific anger script, and they do this with high degrees of involvement. In order to explicate the narrative quality of emotions, Sarbin (1989) interprets them in terms of "rhetorical actions." This expression may be alien to psychologists schooled in the "objectivist" tradition, because these psychologists borrow their metaphors from the sciences dealing with mathematical, physical, or geological dimensions. The potential contribution of rhetoric stems from the theater, which has functioned as a source of inspiration to symbolic interaction theory and role theory. The typical vocabulary comprises dramaturgical terms as scenarios, scripts, role models, role conflict, etc.

Rhetoric is the disciplined use of gestural and oral behavior for the purpose of persuading and convincing others of the propriety of the actor's values and conduct. In classical conceptions rhetorical acts emerge when people are involved in solving their urgencies and exigencies. Rhetorical acts can be seen as problem-solving behavior in the realm of interpersonal action. In face-to-face rhetoric, the speaker and the listener invite involved actions from each other. As problem solvers the actors are performing intentional acts in the course of dealing with the strains of social living.

2.2.3 The Narrative Structure of Action

Not only emotions, but also actions are guided by narrative plots. When we tell stories or listen to them, we are involved in the actors and their vicissitudes. Actions, however, are not only *in* the story, they also follow from it. We engage in conduct to advance the plot, particularly when we imagine ourselves as the protagonist.

A concept that clearly demonstrates the narrative structure of actions is the so-called "Quixote principle" originally formulated by Levin (1970) and further developed by Sarbin (1990). This principle refers to the device of identity shaping through reading stories. The reader is at first an involved participant in the story, identifying with one of the main characters. After the role of this character is enacted in imagination, it is enacted overtly and guides the reader's behavior. The story of Don Quixote may be considered the paradigm case. It illustrates how a person forms an identity from reading fictional or historical tales and then proceeds to validate the newly acquired identity in daily life. Before he named himself Don Quixote, the lonely sixteenth century Spanish gentleman, Alonzo Quesada, became impressed by the heroic deeds and institutions of chivalry as a result of intensive reading of the adventures of knight-errants. Like many other readers who create silent fantasies in which they can participate vicariously as actor or spectator, he constructed imaginings around the deeds of his favorite knights. Quesada, however, does more than imaginatively traveling in the story; he takes the step of acting on his imaginations. He adopts an appropriately knightly name, Don Quixote, and then goes out to fight the wrongs in the world: to rescue people in distress, to foil wicked enchanters, and to slay dragons.

The influence of reading books on suicide rates also exemplifies the Quixote principle. An historical case is Goethe's novel *The Sorrows of Young Werther*, published in 1774. Sociologists have taken this book as a model for identifying the Werther effect: suicide inspired by stories of suicide. The book was written in a time when death, especially death by one's own hands, had a romantic flavor. In the literature of that time there was an aura of nobility and heroism about death and dying, especially if one composed his or her own death scenario. Werther's struggle with rejection and his ultimate suicide was taken as a guiding example by young men of fashion, particularly by those who experienced unrequited love. There was a real Werther epidemic following the publication of the book. The typical suicide was performed in full Werther costume: blue tailcoat, yellow waistcoat, and boots. The pistol was aimed just above the eye (Sarbin, 1990, p. 55).

Also assassinations or attempts in that direction may illustrate the influence of the Don Quixote principle. A well known example is that of John Hinckley, the man who attempted to assassinate former President Reagan. Hinckley constructed a self-narrative in which he and Jodi Foster, an actress in a film, were to be united as romantic partners. First he tried to validate his imaginations through letters, phone calls, and aborted visits. When he was rebuffed, he extended his self-narrative by imagining that he could reach celebrity status by the assassination of the president. International media coverage would immortalize his love by linking his name forever with the name of his imaginal lover (Caughey, 1984; Sarbin, 1990).

A final example of the Quixote principle is the phenomenon of warfare among ghetto gangs. In this case, the source of narrative guidance can be traced to tales of medieval warfare and classical literature. First of all, it must be noted that the term *gang* is regarded as a misnomer by members of street groups. In contrast, they see themselves as members of elite societies, as Katz (1988) has observed. Ethnographic reports show evidence that gangs, in claiming special status as street elites, call upon fragments of legends referring to historical elites or upon imaginations of mythical origin.

> Some [groups] track the status term of ancient and medieval royalty and aristocracy: Lords, Nobles, Knights, Pharaohs, Kings, Emperors, Viceroys, Crusaders, Dukes. Others pick up "classy" terms of style: Diplomats, Saints, and Savoys.

Another tradition of nomenclature ties ghetto youth to regal levels of the animal world: Lions, Eagles, Panthers, and Cobras. Still another points upward cosmologically, to Stars and Jets. Yet another turns toward the uppermost levels of the underworld: Satan's Angels and the Devil's Disciples. [Katz, 1988, cited by Sarbin, 1990, p. 58]

As described in this section, the Quixote principle may assume different manifestations and even more examples could be given. In essence, the principle shows that narratives guide actions. Narratives provide the characters, ideas, settings, instruments, and procedures that individuals or groups may take as models for shaping their own behavior. The Quixote principle also underlines the basic notion that the narrative approach is on the interface of individual and collective functioning.

2.3 The Constructive Potential of Emplotment

An essential feature of narrative is *emplotment:* constructing and interconnecting events in such a way that meaningful structures are developed. Emplotment marks the difference between a chronicle and narrative *construction.* As Polkinghorne (1988) has emphasized, a chronicle is a reflection of a purely chronological ordering of events taking the form: ". . . and then . . . and then . . . and then . . ." Narratives, however, have many ways of *combining* events and their relations. It is in the combination of events that narratives manifest their coherence. In other words, coherence is a feature of narratives, whereas chronological order is characteristic of a chronicle.

2.3.1 Ordering on the Basis of Relevance

One can only deviate from a purely sequential ordering of events if some events are considered as more *relevant* than other events. In order to clarify the term *relevance* (Prince, 1982), let us have a look at the sequence of events as reflected in the following sentences:

1. John had a good meal.
2. Then he went to his work.
3. He was very happy.
4. He met Bill who invited him for a drink.
5. Then he met Bob who said some very annoying things to him.
6. John felt very unhappy when he returned home.

Suppose one is asked to give a summary of this "story" by selecting not more than three sentences from the six mentioned above. It will come out then, that some combinations are a "better" summary than other ones. For example, the sentences 3, 5, and 6 form together a better summary than the combination of 1,

2, and 3 or the combination of 1, 2, and 6. Apparently, some of the sentences are more relevant than other ones as parts of the story as a whole.

Our preference for the combination 3, 5, and 6 as the best summary in the example above is conservative in one respect: It keeps the original temporal ordering of the events intact. That is, 3 precedes 5, and 5 precedes 6. A more rigorous way of restructuring is to start the summary with number 6 and then go back to some of the preceding sentences. The story can then be paraphrased as follows: When John came home, he was very unhappy (number 6), much in contrast with his good mood earlier in the day (number 3). The reason was that he met Bob, who said annoying things to him (number 5). This reordering of the original chronology makes sense if the narrator wants to emphasize some parts of the sequence more than others. Just in case the narrator wants to stress the unhappy mood of John as being in full contradiction to the way he knows John in ordinary circumstances, he or she has the liberty to start with this part and then to move backward in an attempt to find the *reason* for John's state of mind. Reversing the pure chronology of events is also used in the form of flashbacks in film making. The inclusion of flashbacks at the right moment may considerably enhance the dramatic quality of the plot.

The relevance of an event and the organization of the total frame of the story are not only dependent on considerations on the part of the narrator, but also on the perspective of the narratee (the person to whom the story is being told). When one tells a story, the selection and organization of events told will be guided by an assumed stock of common knowledge. When, for example, a man explains to his neighbor why one of the trees in his garden was blown down by a heavy storm the previous night, he will explain that the tree fell down because it was weaker than the other trees in his garden. However, when at a later time he looks to the same tree together with a visitor from another country, he will explain that the tree was the victim of a thunderstorm. Apparently, the narrator mentions different reasons for the falling of the tree, dependent on the knowledge and the interest of the narratee. In addressing the neighbor the thunderstorm was not mentioned as a cause, since this would be completely redundant in this conversation. In the contact with the foreigner, however, it makes sense to mention the storm because it fills a gap in the knowledge of the narratee and is, therefore, taken up as a relevant part of the story. (For an elaborate discussion of the concept of relevance in the field of causal attribution and causal explanation, see Hilton, 1990.)

The supposed knowledge and interest of the narratee function as criteria for the selecting and ordering of events as parts of a told narrative. The story includes events that are "nonobvious" and "worth telling" and these events are organized in such a way that the content and organization of the story are relevant in the eyes of the narratee. The real or imagined presence of a narratee may imply that some events are eliminated, whereas in another contact the same events may be included. Such restructuring of the original "real" sequence of events is rendered possible by the fact that a narrative as told is not simply an isolated chain of events permanently fixed. Rather, it is a flexible organization of events in which content and organization are dependent on the intentions of the narrator and the interest and questions of the narratee. This embeddedness of the story in social relationships makes it a true representative of the root metaphor of contextualism.

A pure description of a succession of "naked" events may even evoke a feeling of absurdity. As a clear illustration, Prince (1982) refers to the book *The Stranger* from the French existentialist Albert Camus. In the first part of the book the main character, Meursault, is successively engaged in the following situations: He attends the funeral of his mother, goes to the movies where he sees a comical film, goes to bed with his girlfriend, goes to the beach for a walk, and kills there an Arabian man, whom he never met before. The life of Meursault is depicted by Camus as a pure sequence of events resulting in the assassination of a man, whom he kills without an apparent reason. In the second part the judges attempt, as part of the charge, to reconstruct the events as parts of a *coherent* narrative (Why did he go to the movies on the day of the funeral of his mother? Why did he kill the Arabian?). It seems almost impossible to answer such questions because even Meursault himself was not able to see intelligible connections between the events. Camus makes literary use of this incoherence as an expression of his existentialist world view, in which the concept "absurdity" plays a central role. The successive events represent in their simple chronology the fragmented existence of Meursault as a representative of people of modern time. When events, as part of an individual life, become dispersed over time without any apparent direction or purpose, then, according to Camus, life becomes "absurd." From a narrative point of view, the fragmented existence is characterized by gaps. These gaps, however, are not in the lacking events themselves, but in their lacking coherence.

2.3.2 The Theme Makes the Coherence

The usual detective story deviates at least in one respect from the absurdistic novel of Camus. When a murder is committed, there is a killer. One of the tasks of the detective is to find the reasons or motives "behind" the deed. The detection of a meaningful relationship between the events and the intentions of the actors reveals the "point" or the theme of the story. When the detective, not yet knowing the guiding theme behind the actions, observes something unusual that he or she simply does not understand, it will, nevertheless, receive his or her careful attention. Although he or she does not understand it now, it may be a relevant detail because it may fit as a meaningful piece in the puzzle at a later moment. At this moment the detective is not yet able to tell us if the observation is "to the point" or not, but in the course of time, he or she *may* succeed in showing that this observation is part of a more elaborate pattern of events that form together an insightful plot.

The example of the detective story illustrates a more general feature of narratives, the dialectic relationship between event and plot. As Polkinghorne (1988) has argued, the meaning of a particular event is produced by a recognition of how event and plot interact, each providing form for the other. Events do not dictate any plot, and not every plot can order a set of events. An appropriate configuration emerges only after a moving back and forth between plot and events. A proposed plot structure is compared with the events at hand and revised according to the principle of "best fit." In this comparative process emplotment is not the imposition of a ready-made plot structure on an independent set of events. Instead, the dialectic process takes place between the events themselves and a theme which discloses their significance. This theme allows the grasping together of the events as interrelated parts of a story. The theme functions as a guide for the selection of certain events as relevant and other events as irrelevant. On the basis of a guiding theme, new events may even be generated (e.g., a detective sets a trap for the suspect in order to further validate the reading of the facts).

As suggested by the detective story, different plots may compete as best fitting to an existing set of events and the most appropriate plot defines the relevance of a particular event. For example, if in the case of murder the theme is jealousy, particular events are relevant. Other events, however, come into mind when the theme centers around an illegitimate heritage. The two themes will guide the detective's attention to different situations and persons and, accordingly, different information and facts will be collected. This procedure shows that the dialectical relationship between events and plot makes a narrative a highly dynamic and flexible process. The perfect certainty of a syllogistic reasoning is absent in a narrative account. The account is more or less probable, but never completely fixed. The "best fit" is never a perfect fit because the construction of a rival account can never be excluded entirely. The notion of emplotment implies that the database, the pool of available events, is never defined in any final way. Because the narrative mode is intrinsically context bound, and because contexts are always more or less changing, new plots or changes in existing plots can always emerge.

2.3.3 Basic Themes in Narratives

The highly dynamic relationship between plot and events, as described in the preceding section, does not exclude that culture provides us with a limited amount of basic themes that function as organizing frames for the understanding and interpretation of the events in our lives. Such themes, with changes in emphasis or interpretation in the course of history, offer a structure for understanding the events in the lives of many people. Let us give some examples.

A classification of themes in close relationship with nature was developed by Frye (1957) (see also White, 1973). Frye argued that themes in narratives are rooted in the experience of nature, and in the evolution of the seasons in particular. The uprising of nature in spring gives inspiration to *comedy*, expressing social harmony that people experience after the threatening winter. The calm and wealth of the summer give rise to the *romance*, which poetically describes the triumph of good over evil, of light over darkness, and of virtue over vice. (Note that the romance referred to here is not necessarily concerned with attraction between people.) Autumn confronts people with the contrast between the pining away of life and the coming death of the winter; this transition gives rise to *tragedy*. Finally, the winter makes people aware of the fact that one is ultimately a captive of the world, rather than its master. In this season *satire* is born, as people recognize that they are ultimately inadequate when confronted with the task of overcoming definitively the dark force of death.

Whereas Frye's classification was based on the cyclical movements of nature, Gergen and Gergen (1988) were more interested in developments of a more linear type. They classified narratives according to their movement over time toward a desirable end state. In a *progressive* narrative the individual links experiences in such a way that increments toward an end state are prevalent. An individual engaged in a progressive narrative might say: "I am really learning to overcome my shyness and to be more open and friendly with people." A *regressive* narrative, by contrast, tells about decrements in the orientation toward a desirable end state. Somebody might say: "I can't control the events of my life anymore." Finally, it is also possible that events are linked in such a way that the individual remains essentially unchanged with respect to the valued end point. This type of movement characterizes the *stability* narrative, and is expressed in a statement like "I am still as attractive as I used to be."

In his book *The Hero with a Thousand Faces*, Campbell (1956) argues that there is one *monomyth* representing a collective experience in various cultures. Myths of various kinds and cultures tell about the impressive figure of a hero, who has an important message to tell to the community. Overcoming personal and historical limitations, the hero has reached a transcendental understanding of the human condition. The hero typically retreats from the community and has extraordinary experiences far from daily life. After a period of meeting challenges, he or she returns, transformed, to convey the acquired wisdom to the community. Moses who climbed the mountain and returned with the Ten Commandments is a typical example. Also Buddha who, in the great renunciation, gave up his princely life and became a wandering ascetic represents a hero figure.

The studies described above show that different classifications of basic themes exist and that the number of themes is different for different authors (see also Polti, 1921/1977). Despite this variety, these studies suggest that behind the myriads of stories people tell one another, a limited amount of basic themes function to organize the stories in such a way that they become meaningful to individuals and communities.

2.3.4 Motives in Narratives

Whereas the examples of themes in the previous section are based on an analysis of the *content* of various stories, a variety of studies have made assumptions about the psychological *motives* of the actors. A classic example is Murray's (1938) system of needs and his use of the *Thematic Apperception Test* (TAT) as an assessment instrument. The underlying assumption is that the themes expressed in the stories reflect the more or less unconscious needs of the subjects. One and the same picture may invite subjects to tell different stories with different themes (e.g., achievement, affiliation, dominance, sex, etc.). In Murray's case we see that needs result in different themes that guide the plot. Subjects are usually able to develop plots relating the various items in the pictures presented to them in the assessment. Murray has inspired later investigators to use TAT procedures to analyze people's stories on the basis of motives or needs: achievement motive (McClelland, Atkinson, Clark, & Lowell, 1953), power (Winter, 1973), affiliation (Boyatzis, 1973), and the opposition of power and intimacy (McAdams, 1985a).

In our own work (Hermans, 1988; Hermans & Van Gilst, 1991), we have related psychological motives on the individual level to basic themes on the collective level. On the basis of an analysis of both collective stories and the self-narratives of a variety of clients, we distinguished between stories in which *self-enhancement* (i.e., self-maintenance and self-expansion) is the main theme and stories in which *contact and union* with the environment or other people is the guiding principle. In a study of Goya's serial painting *The Capture of the Bandit El Maragato*, it was observed that this painting expressed the polarity of winning versus losing, representing the theme of self-enhancement. It was found that the same theme was present in the self-narratives of clients: The experience of winning was expressed in such statements as "In my body awareness I feel very masculine," or "While playing tennis I can release myself." The experience of losing was expressed in statements like "Violence and aggression have knocked me down" or "I have the feeling that John can be strong by keeping me weak" (Hermans, 1988). A similar procedure was followed in a study of the Narcissus myth (Hermans & Van Gilst, 1991). It was demonstrated that the central part of the myth, Narcissus looking into the water, represents the experience of un-fulfilled love and can be interpreted as an expression of an existential longing for contact and union with other people and with oneself. A precious detail in Ovid's version of the myth is that Narcissus fell in love with the image of whom he considered to be somebody else before he discovered that the lover was his own mirror image, a discovery that did *not* change the nature of his longing. On the basis of affective patterns derived from the central part of the myth, we explored whether similar patterns exist in the individual narratives of clients. We found that the theme of unfulfilled longing was also present in the self-narratives of clients, in specific statements like "I think it's too bad that I couldn't remove some of my mother's loneliness when she was still alive with my cheerfulness" or "Dick's suicide: Failing to do anything for him; not being able to stop him; that I didn't see through it all." These studies suggest that basic themes, expressed in classic stories, are present in the self-narratives of ordinary people of our time as well.

In summary, the plot functions to transform a purely chronological listing of events into an organized whole, recognizing the contribution that certain events make to the development of a story. The theme of a story, playing a central role in the plot in individual or collective stories, serves as a criterion for highlighting certain events as more relevant than others. Story themes, and psychological motives, bring coherence in events and facts that are otherwise fragmented and dispersed over time.

Notes

1. One could object against the term *narrative thought* because it could suggest that it is simply "pure thinking." For a good understanding of Bruner's (1986) position, it must be added that he conceives an intrinsic relationship between story and action: ". . . the story must construct two landscapes simultaneously. One is the landscape of action, where the constituents are the arguments of action: Agent, intention or goals, situation, instrument, something corresponding to a 'story grammar.' The other landscape is the landscape of consciousness: What those involved in the action know, think, or feel, or do not know, or feel. . ." (p. 14). In other words, a narrative is a construction and, in this sense, more closely related to Vico's "to know is to make" than to Descartes' *Cogito*.

2. Sarbin (1989), in discussing the metaphor of the body as container, refers to the debate between Lazarus (1984) and Zajonc (1984). This debate centered on whether emotion was a happening unmediated by cognition (Zajonc's position) or one mediated by perception and cognition (Lazarus' position). Neither questioned the ontological status of emotion. Any question that leads to the study of emotion as isolated from the actor-in-a-setting leads to the reification of the emotion, a treatment more in line with mechanism than with contextualism.

CHAPTER 3

The Decentralization of the Self

The Descartean *Cogito*, supposing a highly centralized ego in full control of its own thoughts, has since its conception aroused vehement opposition. In the course of the history of psychology and philosophy, and particularly in recent years, there have been serious attempts to "dethrone" the father of philosophy. Scholars from psychology and other disciplines have become aware that the disembodied self, thinking in "splendid isolation," is more the product of a cultural bias than a universal phenomenon. In this chapter we will discuss several developments that have in common an emphasis, in one way or another, on the decentralization of the self. This will lead to a conception in which the decentralized self functions as a multiplicity of voices rather than as a unitary thought process. Finally, we will demonstrate, on the basis of the work of the Russian literary scientists Michael Bakhtin, that a narrative approach to the self results in a decentralized multiplicity of divergent and even opposed characters that are related to one another in a dialogical way.

3.1 The American Pragmatists and the French Structuralists

Recently, Colapietro (1990) compared the insights of two groups of thinkers, the classical American pragmatists, John Dewey, Charles Pierce, William James, and George Herbert Mead, with the modern French philosophers, Jacques Lacan, Michel Foucault, Jacques Derrida, and Francois Lyotard, often labeled as structuralists. Although these two groups of thinkers are situated at different places and times and show marked differences in their world views, they share a concern with the decentering of the person as a subject.

3.1.1 Dewey's Subject–Sufferer

At the center of the American pragmatists, Colapietro observes, is the felt sense that all discourse is a form of praxis and, in turn, all forms of praxis assume the existence of fallible agents taking part in complex, uncertain circumstances. These forms of practice are to be considered as interactions between the human

organism and its environment. For the pragmatists, it is discourse that transforms dumb and inarticulate creatures into thinking and knowing animals.
When Pierce, Dewey, and Mead deal with "discourse," they refer not only to
public exchanges but also to thinking, that, in Dewey's terms, was characterized
as a "preliminary discourse." Discourse must not be taken too narrowly, that is,
in terms of the phonic or graphic symbols of natural language. If one identifies
language with such symbols, there is, without doubt, thought apart from language. If, however, "language" is used to signify all kinds of signs and symbols,
then there is no thought without language. Along these lines Dewey concludes:
"Thought lives, moves, and has its being in and through symbols, and, therefore, depends for meaning upon context as do symbols" (quoted by Colapietro,
1990, p. 645). It is a general characteristic of the pragmatic idiom that they
insist upon the inseparability of thought and symbolization and, in addition, of
symbolization and context.

Context includes not only the enveloping situation but also the selective
interest of situated agents. Rather than in the abstract term *cognition,* Dewey is
interested in people's "cognitive struggles" that become associated with all kinds
of procedures and practices aimed at problem solving. Dewey sees all self-
reflection as setting out from the problematic and confused. Growing out of
problematic situations, reflection can ascend to ever higher levels of generality
and become ever more abstracted from the original problematic situation. The
more remote thinking is from the urgencies of the immediate situation, the more
likely it is going to convert a provisional disregard of context into a virtual
denial of this factor. Dewey considers this neglect of function of the concrete
situation "the besetting fallacy of philosophic thought" and the pragmatic idiom
as a design to counter this fallacy.

In marked contrast to the Descartean perspective, the world is not simply
beyond our consciousness in Dewey's view. The omnipresent world frustrates our
hopes and intentions, and the problematic situation is involved in the process of
thinking from the start. This intrinsic relatedness of organism and situation, and
their complexly organized interactions instigate Dewey to redefine the terms
subject and *object.* In traditional Western philosophical thinking, subject and
object as mutually exclusive entities have often been antithetically defined in
such a way that they can hardly have any transactions with each other. In an
attempt to restore their transactional character, Dewey defines "object" in a
twofold manner and "subject" in a similar way. An object is, in one sense, "that
which objects, that to which frustration is due." In another sense, it is "the
objective; the final and eventual consummation, and integrated secure independent state of affairs." Also in redefining the term *subject,* Dewey refers to its
etymological origin: "The subject is that which suffers, is subjected [thrown
under] and which endures resistance and frustration; it is also that which attempts subjection of hostile conditions; that which takes the immediate initia-

tive in remaking the situation as it stands" (quoted by Colapietro, 1990, p. 653). The subject is, so to say, an agent–sufferer: embodied and located in a problematic situation the subject is susceptible to suffering and resistance from the part of the situation, and at the same time capable of opposition, exertion, and innovation. Dewey's view of the subject as an embodied agent, continuously involved in innovative action, is not far removed from Vico's basic concept of "corporeal imagination," as discussed in Chapter 1.

By conceiving the subject not simply as "above" the situation, but in terms of "subjected to," and the object not as a thing "in front of me" but as an active force capable to "object against" me, Dewey creates a framework in which the transactional relation between the two entities is restored and their complex interrelatedness admitted. To see practice as a transaction between organism and environment is, Colapietro concludes, a way of decentering the subject. As agent–sufferer, the subject is living between two centers: the subject as acting upon the world and the world acting upon the subject. The interaction is so complex that the environment is in a way *in* the subject.

3.1.2 The Play of Signifiers of the French Structuralists

Most French philosophical thinkers today are highly skeptical about conceiving the subject in the solitary and disembodied sense of Descartes. The main shift has been from a paradigm centering on consciousness to one focusing on language. In this new paradigm, conscious subjectivity (the *I* as aware of itself) is not seen as given at the outset of human condition, but as constituted only in and through language. The origin of subjectivity is not to be traced in the workings of the individual mind, but in the pervasive influence of symbolic systems. In this view the subject is deprived from its status as source and master of meaning. The subject is more a result of systems of convention than an origin of personal creativity. The *I* is not supposed as something that has an existence prior to discourse, but is called into being as one who is addressed by others. The stability of the subject, or the fixity of the *I*, is largely, if not totally, illusory. In the structuralist view, the identity of the subject is essentially a series of positions evoked as a response to the discourse of others. An important implication of this view is that I am, in principle, not able to find out *who* I am, because who I am has been and continues to be determined by how I am addressed by others, both by other human beings and my own immanent other (i.e., the unconscious in Lacan's view). For example, when structuralists are interested in gender identity, this identity reflects the way people address one another in a particular society. My personal construction of this identity, that is, the way I give meaning to my gender identity in a personal and creative way, is rather beyond the scope of the structuralists' view.

The specific position of the French structuralists becomes particularly evident in their view of language. In the tradition of the classic work of De Saussure, language is above all a play of signifiers. We certainly use language to refer to the world, but the referents of our utterances are highly dependent on the linguistic context. The linguistic sign (like all other signs) is an arbitrary correlation of a *signifier* and a *signified.* However, the status of anything as signified is not fixed once and for all. What is at one moment signified can readily become at a later moment a signifier. For example, when somebody says: "Look at that tree," the tree is the object signified. But this object can itself function, in another situation, as a signifier of, say, strength or fertility. Sometimes a tree is just a tree, but the tree is always potentially more than a tree. The potentiality of anything whatsoever to operate as a sign within some system of signs refers to changing contexts in which the "same" sign may assume different and ever-changing meanings. In this play of signifiers there is no ultimate signifier. The meaning of signs emerges as part of ever-changing discourses in ever-changing historical circumstances.

3.1.3 Comparison of the Pragmatists and the Structuralists

In his comparison of the American pragmatists and the French structuralists, Colapietro concludes that both movements represent a radical criticism of Descartes' *Cogito* and that both are concerned with the decentering of the subject. The difference, however, is that, whereas the structuralists emphasize impersonal structures and processes, the pragmatists stress intersubjective transactions and practices. For the structuralists, language is above all a play of signifiers, whereas for the pragmatists language is a set of practices by which embodied agents establish shared frameworks of ongoing activity. Because of their rather impersonal view of language, the structuralists tend to leave aside the status of the self as agent and see the self mainly as a passive construct of social forces. The pragmatists, however, decenter the disembodied *Cogito,* precisely to recover the embodied agent.

Both groups, the American pragmatists and the French structuralists, are, in their treatment of language, concerned with the decentralization of the subject. The pragmatists, however, in treating human selves as embodied and, thus, embedded agents, with innovative potentials, are more in the tradition of Vico than the modern French structuralists. For precisely this reason we subscribe to Colapietro's (1990) thesis that a "translation" of contemporary French discourse into a more pragmatic idiom is required.

3.2 Decentralization in Contemporary Conceptions of the Self

The trend toward decentralization, present in the grounding work of the American pragmatists, is also marking more recent psychological and linguistic developments. In order to give an impression of this trend, five examples, mainly of American and French origin, will be briefly discussed: (1) the growing emphasis on the multifacetedness and possibilities of the self, (2) deconstructionism in literary criticism, (3) the notion of subpersonality, (4) the concept *imago* as a character in self-narrative, and (5) the structural analysis of myths and folktales. Despite how different these developments may be from one another, they converge in the trend toward decentralization of the human mind.

3.2.1 The Multifacetedness and Possibilities of the Self

The emphasis on the complexity of the self that was already present in the views of the American pragmatists is strikingly present in recent developments in the psychology of the self. In their review of developments in self-research, Markus and Wurf (1987) argued that one of the most dramatic changes in the last decade has been in the structure of the self. They criticize the earlier conceptualization of the self as only generalized or "average," (e.g., labels as "positive" and "negative" self-concept referring to a person's self *as a whole*). The answer has been to view the self as a *multifaceted* phenomenon, as a set of images, schemas, conceptions, prototypes, theories, goals, or tasks. A similar movement has occurred among sociologists, for whom it is now commonplace to refer to the "multiplicity of identity." Typical of this movement is that identity is described as including one's personal characteristics and feelings as well as one's social roles and status. Apparently, psychologists and sociologists are converging in conceiving of the self as a highly complex but organized phenomenon (see also Rosenberg & Gara, 1985). Note that already in 1890, James in his *Principles* considered the self not as a unitary but as a multifaceted phenomenon when he discussed the "rivalry and conflict of the different selves" (p. 309).

Another progression, also in full agreement with the action-oriented conception of the American pragmatists, is the growing tendency to conceive of the self as a highly *dynamic* process, and to emphasize its *possibilities*. Higgins (1987), for example, distinguishes between several domains of the self: the actual self (i.e., attributes one actually possesses), the ideal self (i.e., attributes one ideally possesses), and the ought self (i.e., attributes one should or ought to possess). Discrepancies between these domains are associated with different kinds of emotional vulnerabilities. A discrepancy between the actual and ideal self is related to dejection (e.g., sadness), whereas a discrepancy between the actual self and the ought self results in agitation (e.g., fear). A highly dynamic view of the self was also presented by Markus and Nurius (1986), who argue that some selves are not actual but simply possible selves—the self one would like to be or is afraid of becoming. These selves function as motivating forces, providing images of desired or undesired end states. The increased interest in potential selves (see also Schlenker, 1985) is, again, in agreement with James' basic insights. He even used the term *potential self* in order to emphasize its dynamic quality (James, 1890, p. 396).

Developments toward a dynamic and multifaceted conception of the self, and the increased interest in the concept of the possible self in particular, can be seen as an important step in the direction of decentralization. When the self is multifaceted in such a way that discrepancies between subsystems are emphasized (Higgins) or past and future states function as possibilities of the mind (Markus), then the emphasis is shifting from one center of organization to two or more such centers. The focus on one locus of organization gives way to the *relation* between different loci.

3.2.2 Deconstructionism and Texts as Open Systems

In a provocative paper, Sampson (1985) argues that the ideal of personhood in our Western culture can be qualified in terms of a "centralized, equilibrium structure." The ideal self is seen as a centralized ego forming a singular unit of mastery and control rather than a pluralistic, decentralized "manyness." The centralized ego lives in a state of equilibrium with the environment by having the environment under control. This conception suggests that order and coherence necessarily go together with centrality and equilibrium. The association between order and equilibrium, however, is more a cultural bias than an intrinsic necessity. It is Sampson's purpose to show that, in marked contrast to this association, order and coherence can also be achieved under decentralized and nonequilibrium circumstances. For the sake of argumentation he discussed recent developments in physics, literary criticism, and political theory which all challenge our existing concept of order. We will—keeping close to Sampson's review—discuss the development that has the most direct relevance to our present purpose, that in the area of literary criticism.

Our traditional conceptions of personhood are challenged by recent notions about texts and authorship (e.g., Bruns, 1982; Derrida, 1978; Ricoeur, 1970). What is commonly labeled deconstructionism questions the idea that a text is a fixed entity with a singular meaning that can eventually be deciphered. In fact, deconstructionists reason, the text as an autonomous body of knowledge is actually a relatively recent and culture-specific innovation. The invention of the printing press and the capacity to duplicate writings have given texts the appearance of being fixed. Before this invention, however, scribes laboriously copied each text by hand and embellished it as they went along. Each work was in a sense a new text.

Rejecting the notion of fixity now associated with texts, deconstructionists argue that texts have as many meanings as there are times and places in which to be read. Derrida (1981) has challenged the entire notion of authorship by holding that every text suffers from textuality; writings get their meaning only in the context of the discourse dominant in a particular era. The same text is read and reread as part of a changing play of signifiers that is prevailing in the meaning system of a certain period of history. [For a critique of Derrida's neglect of the individual subject as an agent, see Colapietro's (1990) discussion of the French structuralists at the beginning of this chapter.]

The conception of a text as an act of dialogue between author and reader was espoused by Garfinkel (1967), who argued—from an ethnomethodological perspective—that the understanding of the interaction between two actors is not fixed but varies with the unfolding of their encounter. In the course of a conversation, the meaning of earlier items changes and is continually reframed by what is currently expressed. Similarly, Cicourel (1974) found that later encounters with tapes or transcripts of previously completed interactions generate new meanings, even among the original participants. Deconstructionists and ethnomethodologists, therefore, are on common ground in emphasizing that people telling their life story to another person are not the *exclusive* authors of their story since each life story is told in a social context. Subjects or clients telling the stories of their lives to a psychologist are not telling a fixed text, but a text that is continuously interpreted and reinterpreted and thereby reordered in changing social contexts.

Developments in literary criticism and other fields are for Sampson (1985) reason to conclude that neither textual reality nor other forms of reality have an unchangeable, absolute base. The fact that reality cannot be grasped in any absolute or final form, however, does not warrant the conclusion that our world is chaotic or incoherent. Rather, order and coherence emerge from the continuous interplay between the open system and its environment. Texts are also to be viewed as open systems.

3.2.3 The Play of Subpersonalities

Most of us know the experience of being taken over by a part of ourselves which we did not know was there. We then say "I don't know what got into me." Often this is a negative experience, although it could potentially be positive as well. We find ourselves acting in ways which seem to be unusual or which go against our interests, as if we were at that moment another person. This may last as long as the situation lasts—perhaps a few minutes, perhaps an hour, perhaps a few hours—and then it changes when we go into another situation. Rowan (1990) describes this as the working of a subpersonality, which he defines as "a semi-permanent and semi-autonomous region of the personality capable of acting as a person" (p. 8). Subpersonalities are characterized by a certain degree of dissociation, that Rowan, along with Beahrs (1982), considers not as an either/or phenomenon, but as a phenomenon that exists along a continuum. Subpersonalities have a range of relative dissociation in that they take us over sometimes gently and sometimes more forcefully. A description provided by Marie-Louise von Franz, a Jungian psychotherapist, clearly expresses the phenomenon of relative dissociation:

> I could give you a whole list of the persons I can be. I am an old peasant woman who thinks of cooking and of the house. I am a scholar who thinks about deciphering manuscripts. I am a psychotherapist who thinks about how to interpret people's

dreams. I am a mischievous little boy who enjoys the company of a ten-year-old and playing mischievous tricks on adults, and so on. I could give you twenty more such characters. They suddenly enter you, but if you see what is happening you can keep them out of your system, play with them and put them aside again. But if you are possessed, they enter you involuntarily and you act them out involuntarily. [Rowan, 1990, p. 9]

Rowan gives an extended review of a diversity of psychological theories and psychotherapeutic systems that are more or less related to the concept of subpersonality. For the sake of illustration, we give, keeping close to Rowan's discussion, an impression of one of the oldest systems that is still popular nowadays, psychosynthesis.

The founder of psychosynthesis, Alberto Assagioli, introduced his system in the years after 1910 in Italy. Publication of his works in English started in the 1960s and culminated in Vargiu's (1974) workbook on subpersonalities. Psychosynthesis assumes that in each of us a diversity of subpersonalities is striving to express themselves, and growth can be facilitated by knowing them: the hag, the mystic, the materialist, the idealist, the claw, the pillar of strength, the sensitive listener, the religious fanatic, the doubter, the frightened child, and others. Psychosynthesis allows for a considerable degree of individual variation. There is no particular cluster or combination of subpersonalities that is central to everyone, although certain patterns are quite common.

In the therapeutic working with subpersonalities, a five-phase process has often been found to be useful. In the first place, a particular subpersonality has simply to be *recognized* as it emerges from an internal conflict, dream, vision, or fantasy.

In the second phase, *acceptance,* the therapist explores to what extent the client is willing to work with the subpersonality. The client may see it as an enormous risk to enter into contact with the very thing he or she has most feared or hated for many years.

After several subpersonalities have been recognized and accepted, the working through of the relationship among the subpersonalities is central in the third phase, labeled as *coordination.* If there are interpersonal difficulties between two or more subpersonalities, some process of conflict resolution may be needed.

In the fourth phase, *integration,* the purpose is to enable the subpersonalities to work together in a harmonious way rather than being fragmented or disjunctive.

The fifth phase is one of *synthesis,* that leads to the discovery of the so-called "transpersonal self." This self functions as a unity in which the different subpersonalities are merging into an integrative whole. This phase marks the highest level of growth in human existence and is the final truth of the person.

The final synthesis is certainly not typical of all the other systems working with subpersonalities. There are systems in which the subpersonalities are not supposed to give up their position of relative autonomy. In *Voice Dialogue,* for example, devised by Stone & Winkelman (1985), there is no final fusion or mergence of the different subpersonalities. In this system an "aware ego" is supposed to be which is conscious of all the subpersonalities at work (e.g., "the protector/controller," "the pusher," "the critic," "the perfectionist," and others). This ego functions as a central reference point in which all the information produced by the successive subpersonalities comes together. This reference point is certainly not a center where the subpersonalities are fused or merged together. Rather, it is a center of intense awareness of what is going on in the psychological regions of the different subpersonalities, which remain intact in their position of relative autonomy.

3.2.4 Imagoes as Personified Images

In the course of the history of psychology, many scholars have realized that the self is far from a unitary construct closed off from images of other people. A classic example is the Freudian notion of introjection, resulting in internal images of the parents and their standards that may even suppress the individual's emotional impulses. A serious attempt to integrate earlier psychoanalytic notions with more recent developments in narrative psychology was made by McAdams (1985b). In an attempt to demonstrate the integrative power of the narrative approach, McAdams conceived the self as composed of a number of affect-laden imagoes, with the term *imago* defined as "an idealized and personified image of self that functions as a main character in an adult's life story" (p. 116). In his search of conceptual precursors of his concept of imago, McAdams referred to the psychoanalytic object-relations approach to personality theory, represented in the writings of Klein (1948), Fairbairn (1952), Jacobson (1964), and Guntrip (1971). In this approach the *internalization* of significant objects (e.g., the father, the mother) is considered the basis of interpersonal relationships. Fairbairn (1952), for example, assumed that the ego is object seeking from birth and that, in the process of social interaction, external objects are invariably internalized to become personified parts of the self. Once internalized, moreover, such objects come to influence these same relationships.

Another forerunner of McAdams' concept of the imago was Sullivan's (1953) notion of *personification.* Personified images of the self—such as the "good me" and the "bad me"—and personified images of others—such as the "good mother" and the "bad mother"—are, according to Sullivan, brought together into the child's self-system. Once organized and stabilized, such personified self-images construct and orchestrate the child's interactions with the environment in such a way that anxiety is minimized.

It is one of McAdams' (1985b) purposes to demonstrate that his concept of imago concurs with the recent "cognitivization" of personality and social psychology. He argues that imagoes function in a manner similar to self-schemata

(Epstein, 1973; Markus & Sentis, 1982)—as knowledge structures that guide the processing of information. Imagoes also function as "hot" cognitions, that are associated with highly emotional issues and experiences. Imagoes as the main characters in a person's life story, complementing and sometimes even opposing each other, play an important part in the processing of information and are thus responsible for the organization of the self.

3.2.5 Structural Analysis of Myths

A notable figure in the tradition of the French structuralists is Claude Lévi-Strauss (1958/1972) who, like the French philosophers mentioned earlier in this chapter (Lacan, Foucault, Derrida, and Lyotard), was strongly influenced by the founding linguistic work of De Saussure. Lévi-Strauss studied myths of diverse origin and considered them as expressions of a small number of basic structures. He believed that underlying the immense diversity of myths are certain constant universal structures that are the same for all people. He assumed that myths can be broken down into specific units (mythemes) that, like the basic sound units of language (phonemes), acquire meaning only when combined together according to certain rules. Along these lines, Lévi-Strauss conceived of a grammar with mythemes as basic units, with explicit relations beneath the surface of the narrative. The true meaning of a myth was not constituted by the consciously experienced surface level or the content of the story as told, but by the elementary rules that generate the story below the level of awareness. Generally, Lévi-Strauss was more interested in these rules as universal mental operations than in the incidental variations of the narrative content of the myths as highly dependent on local situations. Conceived in this way, myths are models for resolving the basic contradictions of life and ways of classifying and organizing reality.

In his discussion of Lévi-Strauss' work, Polkinghorne (1988) observes that the mind that does all this thinking and organizing is not the mind of the individual subject. Myths have no origin in the mind of any particular person. Instead of people thinking through myths, myths think themselves through people. Myths are not the product of an individualized mind that has particular purposes in telling a story. Rather, the individual tells or listens to a myth as part of an impersonalized discourse. In this way structuralism results in a far-reaching de-centering of the individual subject. Myths have a quasi-objective collective existence, and the individual is no longer to be regarded as the source and end of meaning. From the structuralist perspective, myths, as a rule-governed impersonal body of thought, exhibit an obvious disregard for the vagaries of individual thought and reduce any particular consciousness to a mere function of the structures (Polkinghorne, 1988, p. 83).

Prior to the structural analysis of Lévi-Strauss, another pioneer, Propp (1928/1968), analyzed Russian folk tales in the first decades of this century. He also was looking for a deep structure laying beneath the immense diversity of tales and took grammar, as the "abstract substratum" of living language, as a model for his study. As Polkinghorne (1988) explains, Propp's model can be understood through the analogy of the sentence. In the simple sentence, "The bear ran fast," three functional units can be distinguished: The subject ("the bear"), the verb ("ran"), and the predicate or adjective ("fast"). In each of these functional units, various terms can be substituted (for the subject, for example, "the boy," "the dog," or "the river"). The fact that this vertical substitution is still creating a meaningful sentence means for Propp that the structural force of the sentence is located on the level of the functional units rather than on the level of the substitutions. For example, a folktale may have the following structure: "The villain causes harm or injury to a member of the family." In this sentence the dramatic quality does not depend on the specific substitutions. The villain may be, for example, a robber, an ex-lover, or a banker, and the injury may be as divergent as the dramatis personae are. The central thesis is that the basic meaning is in the deep structure more than in the surface tale. [For a critical discussion of Propp's analysis, see Ricoeur (1986); for more recent developments expanding on Lévi-Strauss's and Propp's structural approaches, see Polkinghorne (1988, pp. 85–99).]

In sum, we have drawn on developments of divergent origin in order to demonstrate the basic trend toward the decentralization of the mind. These developments have in common that, in marked contrast to the Descartean *Cogito*, they question the existence of a unitary, closed, highly centralized subject or self, as an entity in itself, having an existence "above" or "outside" the social environment. Rather, the developments converge in considering the human mind as a multifaceted phenomenon, with other individuals not outside but *in* the self. An important distinction can be made between developments in the tradition of the American pragmatists and those in line with the French structuralists. Although both converge in moving toward decentralization, the structuralists go so far as to consider the subject as merely subjected to an impersonalized discourse. The pragmatists, and also present-day conceptions of the self (e.g., possible selves, imagoes, subpersonalities), have in common that they keep intact the subject as agency. The advantage of this point of view is that it takes the decentralization seriously *without* neglecting the potentials of the individual as an agentic force. Moreover, the pragmatists' conception of the subject as an embodied agent, in line with the Vichean notion of corporeal imagination (Chapter 1), will keep our vivid attention, also in the coming analyses.

3.3 The Polyphonic Novel: A Multiplicity of Voices

The decentralization of the self can be further expanded by referring to the original work of the Russian literary scholar, Mikhail Bakhtin (1929/1973). His book *Problems of Dostoevsky's Poetics*, originally published in Russian, is of particular importance. The relevance of this work for psychology has recently been discussed by Vasil'eva (1988) and Florenskaya (1989). We will first demonstrate that Bakhtin's ideas represent a significant contribution to understanding the dialogical nature of the self and then translate his ideas into the Jamesian concepts of *I* and *Me*.

3.3.1 The Polyphonic Novel

It is Bakhtin's thesis that Dostoevsky—one of the most brilliant innovators in the history of literature—created a new form of artistic thought, the polyphonic novel. The principle feature of the novel is that it is composed of a number of independent and mutually opposing viewpoints embodied by characters involved in dialogical relationships. On the stage of mutually interacting characters, the author, Dostoevsky himself, is only one of many. Each character is "ideologically authoritative and independent," that is, each character is perceived as the author of his or her own legitimate ideological position, not as an object of Dostoevsky's all-encompassing artistic vision. The characters are not "obedient slaves" in the service of Dostoevsky's intentions, but are capable of standing beside their creator, disagreeing with the author, even rebelling against him.

In Dostoevsky's novels there is not one single author, Dostoevsky himself, but several authors or thinkers, Raskolnikov, Myshkin, Stavogin, Ivan Karamazov, the Grand Inquisitor, each having their own voice and telling their own story. The hero is not simply the object of Dostoevsky's finalizing artistic vision, but comes across as the author of his own ideology. There is not a multitude of characters within a unified objective world, subordinated to Dostoevsky's individual vision, but "a plurality of consciousness," represented by voices who ventilate their own ideas. As in a polyphonic composition, moreover, the several voices or instruments having different spatial positions and accompany and oppose each other in a dialogical relation.

3.3.2 Logical versus Dialogical Relationships

The notion of dialogue can only be properly understood by establishing the difference between logical and dialogical relationships. Bakhtin gives the following examples (see also Vasil'eva, 1988). Take two phrases that are completely identical, "life is good" and again "life is good." From the perspective of Aristotelian logic, these two phrases are related in terms of *identity;* they are, in fact, one and the same statement. From a dialogical perspective, however, they may be seen as two remarks expressed by the voices of two spatially separated people in communication, who in this case entertain a relationship of *agreement.* Here we have two phrases that are identical from a logical point of view, but different as utterances: The first is a statement, the second a confirmation. In a similar way the phrases "life is good" and "life is not good" can be compared. In terms of logic, one is a *negation* of the other. However, as utterances from two different speakers, a dialogical relation of *disagreement* exists. In Bakhtin's view, the relationship of agreement and disagreement is, like question and answer, basically dialogical. For a good understanding of Bakhtin's position it must be added that he certainly does not reject the rules of logic: "Dialogical relationships are totally impossible without logical and concrete semantic relationships, but they are not reducible to them; they have their own specificity" (Bakhtin, 1929/1973, p. 152).

Logical relationships are "closed," in so far as they do not permit any conclusion beyond the limits of the rules that govern the relationship. For example, once the identity or negation thesis has been applied to a set of statements, there is nothing left to be said, nor is an opening created to the domain of the unexpected. In Bakhtin's (1929/1973) dialogical view, however, "consciousness is never self-sufficient; it always finds itself in an intense relationship with another consciousness. The hero's every experience and his every thought is internally dialogical, polemically colored and filled with opposing forces . . . open to inspiration from outside itself. . ." (p. 26). The openness of consciousness in Dostoevsky's heroes is continuously resisting any final conclusion: "His self-consciousness lives on its unfinalizedness, its open-endedness and indeterminacy" (Bakhtin, 1929/1973, p. 43), and "every thought of Dostoevsky's heroes . . . feels itself to be a speech in an uncompleted dialog" (p. 27). Openness is an intrinsic feature of dialogue and its recognition a necessary condition for the understanding of individual life: "The genuine life of the personality can be penetrated only dialogically, and then only when it mutually and voluntarily opens itself" (Bakhtin, 1929/1973, p. 48).

Bakhtin's conception of dialogue is not only open, and "unfinalized," but also highly *personal*. He observes that Dostoevsky's world is "profoundly personalized" and that each character is a "concrete consciousness, embodied in the living voice of an integral person" (Bakhtin, 1929/1973, p. 7). A particular utterance is never isolated from the consciousness of a particular character. And because one particular character is always implicitly or explicitly responding to another character, "a dialogical reaction personifies every utterance to which it reacts" (p. 152). In this view the context of a particular utterance is always highly personalized.[1]

3.3.3 Spatialization of Characters

For Bakhtin the notion of dialogue opens the possibility to differentiate the inner world of one and the same individual in the form of an interpersonal relationship. By transforming an "inner" thought of a particular character into an utterance, dialogical relations spontaneously occur between this utterance and the utterance of imaginal others. In Dostoevsky's novel *The Double*, for example, the second hero (the double) was introduced as a personification of the interior voice of the first hero (Golyadkin). The externalization of the interior voice of the first hero in a spatially separated opponent instigates a full-fledged dialogue between two independent parties. In Bakhtin's (1929/1973) terms: "This persistent urge to see all things as being coexistent and to perceive and depict all things side by side and simultaneously, *as if in space rather than time,* leads him [Dostoevsky] to dramatize in space even the inner contradictions and stages of development of a single person. . ." (p. 23, emphasis added). In this narrative spatialization, Dostoevsky constructs a plurality of voices representing a plurality of worlds that are neither identical nor unified, but rather hetero-geneous and even opposed. As part of this narrative construction, Dostoevsky portrays characters conversing with the devil (Ivan and the Devil), with their alter egos (Ivan and Smerdyakov), and even with caricatures of themselves (Raskolnikov and Svidrigailov).

The spatialization of dialogical relationships allows for the treatment of a particular idea in the context of both interior and external dialogues, in this way creating ever-changing perspectives:

> The intersection, consonance, or interference of speeches in the overt dialogue with the speeches in the heroes' interior dialogs are everywhere present. The specific totality of ideas, thoughts and words is everywhere passed through several unmerged voices, taking on a different sound in each. The object of the author's aspirations is not at all this totality of ideas in and of itself, as something neutral and identical with itself. No, the object is precisely the act of passing the themes through many and varied voices, it is, so to speak, the fundamental, irrescindable multivoicedness and varivoicedness of the theme. [Bakhtin, 1929/1973, p. 226]

As in a musical polyphonic composition, a particular idea or theme (e.g., aggression, love, jealousy) has not a fixed, self-contained, unchangeable mean-ing. Instead, by leading the theme through the various voices, its many-facetedness and potentials can be brought to expression.[2]

3.3.4 The Simultaneity of Voices

Closely related to the spatialization of dialogical relations is the principle of simultaneity, as characteristic of Bakhtin's thinking. In Dostoevsky's novels, utterances are concentrated, even if they are successively uttered, as being coexistent at one point in time, as if in space rather than time. This perceiving of utterances side by side underlies Bakhtin's thesis that every word, as soon as it enters in a dialogical relationship, is "double voiced." A word has always two directions: both toward the object of speech and toward another word, originating from another person's speech. In the conversation with a real or imagined other, the word of the other is present in the act of speaking and contributes to its form and content. In Bakhtin's terms, "the author's intention makes use of another person's word in the direction of its own aspirations" (1929/1973), p. 160).

The "double voicedness," as organizing the speech of a single speaker, is even present when the words of the other are omitted. This is what Bakhtin means when he uses the phrase "hidden dialogicality": "The second interlocutor is invisibly present, his words are absent, but the profound traces of those words determine all of the first interlocutor's words. Although only one person is speaking, we feel that this is a conversation, and a most intense one, since every word that is present answers and reacts with its every fiber to the invisible interlocutor. . ." (1929/1973, p. 163–164). The influence of the invisibly present locutor clearly demonstrates that for Bakhtin the notion of dialogue is not identical with explicitly spoken conversation. Dialogue is at the heart of every form of thought.

The simultaneous presence of the words of two interlocutors is also reflected by Bakhtin's analysis of "microdialogues," the interior dialogues in which the other is present even when the thinker is "alone." In *Crime and Punishment*, for example, Raskolnikov recreates not only the words of another character, Dunya, but even the intonations through which she seeks to convince, and adds to them his own ironic, indignant intonations: "Well, after all, this is her Rodya, isn't it, her precious Rodya, her firstborn!" (Bakhtin, 1929/1973, p. 61). Such observations reflect for Bakhtin the idea that dialogue penetrates every word, giving rise to conflicts and interruptions of one voice by another, even if the other person is not actually talking.[3]

3.3.5 The Relativity of Meaning

In his book *Dialogism* (1990), which is based on Bakhtin's oeuvre as a whole, the literary scholar Holquist presents a comparison between Einstein's relativity theory and Bakhtin's world view. Although not directly related, Einstein's thought experiments in some ways correspond to Bakhtin's attempts to use the situation of dialogue as a means for avoiding the pitfalls of traditional ideas about the subject as an isolated being. Einstein invented several situations in his attempts to tackle problems in perception raised by the speed of light. For example, if light travels at a certain velocity in one system and at the same velocity in another system, moving without acceleration relative to the first, then the observer's ability to see motion depends on one body changing its position vis-à-vis other bodies. From such thought experiments and other evidence, we have learned that motion has only a relative meaning: One body's motion has meaning only in relation to another body. Similarly, meaning in dialogue is always of a relative nature:

> Dialogism argues that all meaning is relative in the sense that it comes about only as a result of the relation between two bodies occupying *simultaneous but different* space, where bodies may be thought of as ranging from the immediacy of our physical bodies, to political bodies and to bodies of ideas in general (ideologies). [Holquist, 1990, pp. 20–21]

The spatiality inherent in dialogue leads Holquist to conclude that dialogism is a form of architectonics, the general science of ordering parts into a whole. A relation is something that always involves ratio and proportion. In this view on meaning, we see that the coherence of the self is not restricted to the individual per se, but is the result of a dialogical relationship between the individual and other persons. In other words, the self is not a given but an emergent.[4]

3.4 The Self as a Multiplicity of *I* Positions

One of the main representatives of American pragmatism, William James (1890), devoted a whole chapter in his book *Principles of Psychology* to the concept of self. In his treatment of the subject, he made a distinction that, according to Rosenberg (1979), is classic in the psychology of the self: between the self-as-knower (or the self as subject) and the self-as-known (or the self as object). Let us first consider what James means with these terms and then continue by translating them into narrative psychology and into the conceptual framework of the polyphonic novel in particular.

3.4.1 *James' Distinction between* I *and* Me

The terms *I* and *Me* were discerned by James (1890) as the two main components of the self. The *I* is equal to the self-as-knower and continuously organizes and interprets experience in a purely subjective manner. Three features characterize the *I*: continuity, distinctness, and volition. The *continuity* of the self-as-knower manifests itself in a "sense of personal identity" and "the sense of sameness" through time (p. 332). A feeling of *distinctness*, of having an own identity, an existence separate from others, also characterizes the *I*. Moreover, a sense of *personal volition* is expressed by the continuous appropriation and rejection of thoughts by which the self-as-knower manifests itself as an active processor of experience. Implicit in the experience of each of these features (continuity, distinction, volition) is the awareness of self-reflectivity that is essential for the self-as-knower (Damon & Hart, 1982).

In defining the *Me*, James (1890) was aware that there is a gradual transition between *Me* and *Mine*, and therefore he identified the *Me* as the empirical self that in its broadest sense is described as all that the person can call his or her own, "not only his body and his psychic powers, but his clothes and his house, his wife and children, his ancestors and friends, his reputation and works, his lands and horses, and yacht and bank-account" (p. 291). James called these primary elements the constituents, and they indicate a basic feature of the self, that is, its extension. The self is not an entity, closed off from the world and having an existence in itself, but, rather, extended toward specific aspects of the environment (Rosenberg, 1979).

James distinguished three kinds of constituents of the self-as-known: material characteristics (body, clothes, possessions), spiritual characteristics (thoughts, consciousness), and social characteristics (relations, roles, fame). The extension of the self in terms of these constituents precludes the misunderstanding of considering the interplay between *I* and *Me* as a process taking place only within the individual person, separate from the thought process of other people. The inclusion of the social self that, in terms of Mead (1934), has the capacity of "taking the role of the other," accounts for the fact that the perspective of the other can be incorporated into the self, so that it becomes an integral part of the self. In this way James escapes from what usually has been described as the objection of solipsism, as inherent in all those forms of thinking that, in the line of Descartes, assume the existence of an individual consciousness, defined as essentially separated from the existence of other people. In James' solution of this problem, the self is—as *I*—distinct from other people, but —as social *Me*— the perspective of the other is included *in* the self.

Another feature that distinguishes James' self from the Descartean *Cogito* is the inclusion of the body as part of the (material) self. The *I* can never be dissolved from the *Me* (and *Mine*), and, consequently, the *I* cannot be thought of as separate from the body. The intrinsic relation between *I* and *Me* precludes the supposition of a completely separated *I*, and the same is true for the relation between the *I* and the body. The *I* is, therefore, always bound to the existence of "my body."

In sum, James' distinction between *I* and *Me*, and the way he elaborates on this distinction, implies that two objections against the Descartean *Cogito*, discussed in Chapter 1, are met. First, the problem of the mind–body dualism has received an answer by the intrinsic relatedness of *I* and (material) *Me*. Second, the problem of solipsism or self–other dualism has been answered by the relatedness of *I* and (social) *Me*. The *I–Me* relation can be considered, in Colapietro's (1990) terms, as a way of decentering the subject, typical of the American pragmatists. We recall that the decentering of the American pragmatists keeps intact the personal position of the subject as an original source of meaning production. In James' (1890) conception, the *I* as a personal activity is represented by its volitional capacity. The *I*, capable of appropriation and rejection of thoughts as part of the capacity of self-reflection, functions as an original source of thinking and production of ideas.

3.4.2 I as Author/Me as Actor

Mancuso and Sarbin (1983) and Sarbin (1986) have made a valuable contribution to the psychology of the self by translating the *I–Me* distinction into a narrative framework. They argue that the uttered pronoun *I* stands for the author, the *Me* for the actor or narrative figure. With the self as author, the *I* can imaginatively construct a story in which the *Me* is the protagonist. Such narrative construction is possible because the self as author can imagine the future and reconstruct the past and describe himself or herself as an actor. Moreover, narrative construction is a means for *organizing* episodes, actions, and the significance of the actions; it is an achievement that brings together different facts and fantasies that otherwise may be spread across both time and space (Sarbin, 1986, p. 9).

Jaynes (1976) has also used the distinction between the *I* and the *Me* in describing the self as a "mind space." The *I* constructs an analog space and metaphorically observes the *Me* moving in this space. For example, we plan to visit somebody, imagine the house where we are going, and see ourselves talking to a friend. In the dynamics of consciousness, the *I* is always seeing the *Me* as the main figure in the story of one's life. Narratization underlays all our activities. Seated where I am, Jaynes (1976) explains, I am writing a book and this fact is imbedded in the story of my life: "time being spatialized into a journey of my days and years" (p. 63). Not only the structuring of our behavior, but also the assigning of causes to our behavior is part of narratization. Consciousness is ever ready to explain anything we are doing. Thieves may narratize their act as due to poverty, poets theirs as due to beauty, and scientists theirs as due to truth, "purpose and cause inextricably woven into the spatialization of behavior in consciousness" (Jaynes, 1976, p. 64). For Jaynes the conscious mind, and the self in particular, is a spatial analog of the world, and mental acts are analogs of bodily acts. The self functions as a space where the *I* observes the *Me* and relates the movements of the *Me* as parts of a narrative construction.

Referring to the work of Jaynes (1976) and others, Smith (1985, 1991) argues that the meaning of basic concepts in a particular culture (e.g., mind, time, love) "inheres primarily in the network of its metaphorical affinities, which characteristically can be described as connotationally coherent rather than logically consistent" (1985, p. 73). Smith also emphasizes that the spatialized and narratized construction of experience demands respect for the "as if" and not debunking of it. Our value-laden world is richly metaphoric and in this condition lies its tragedy, comedy, and glory (Smith, 1985, p. 75).

3.4.3 The Multiplicity of I Positions: Theoretical Integration

The metaphor of the polyphonic novel expands on the narrative conception of the *I* as an author and the *Me* as an observed actor and has, therefore, the potential of advancing beyond existing conceptions of the self. Whereas in Sarbin's (1986) version of the self-narrative a *single* author is assumed to tell a story about himself or herself as an actor, the conception of the self as a polyphonic novel goes one step further. It permits the one and the same individual to live in a multiplicity of worlds with each world having its own author telling a story relatively independent of the authors of the other worlds. Moreover, at times the several authors may enter into dialogue with each other. The self, conceptualized as a polyphonic novel, has the capacity of integrating the notions of imaginative narrative and dialogue.

In the polyphonic translation of the self there is not an overarching *I* organizing the constituents of the *Me*. Instead, the spatial character of the polyphonic novel leads to the supposition of a decentralized multiplicity of *I* positions that function like relatively independent authors, telling their stories about their respective *Me*'s as actors. The *I* moves, in an imaginal space, from the one to the other position, from which different or even contrasting views of the world are possible. Moreover, like the authors in Dostoevsky's novels, the different authors, localized at different positions in the imaginal landscape, may enter into dialogical relationships with one another, agreeing or disagreeing with each other. In this highly open and dynamic conception of the self, transactional relationships between the different *I* positions may lead to the emergence of meanings that are not given at one of the available positions.

Before we elaborate the dialogical view presented above, we will first discuss some developments in twentieth century novelistic literature that expand on some of the notions inherent in Bakhtin's polyphonic novel.

Notes

1. Bakhtin, in his insistence on personalized discourse, identifies De Saussure as the leading spokesman for "abstract objectivism," a linguistic tendency that he strenuously opposes. Abstract objectivism treats language as a pure system of laws governing phonetic, grammatical, and lexical forms that confront individual speakers as norms over which they have no control. Another tendency opposed by Bakhtin is "individual subjectivism," that can be considered as the polar opposite of the first. It denies preexisting norms and holds that all aspects of language can be explained in terms of the individual speaker's voluntarist intentions. Note that each of these tendencies can be distinguished on the basis of the self–other distinction. In "abstract objectivism" the otherness is so dominant that it obliterates all possibility of subjectivity. In "individual subjectivism," on the contrary, it is the individual *I* who is in full control of meaning. It is the prospect of the notion of dialogue that it acknowledges both the existence of preexisting structures and the subject as an innovative agent (Holquist, 1990).

2. Marvin Rosenberg (1983) also uses the term *polyphony* in order to describe the complexities of the protagonists of great tragic drama, with their multiplicity of often contradictory roles, drives, impulses, and traits. A tragic character represents, in Rosenberg's view, a polyphony of voices, some harmonious, some dissonant, some nuclear, some peripheral. The combinations of tones are perceived in mixed chords that change as the character's complexities shift and develop. However, as Rosenberg demonstrates in the case of Shakespeare's *Macbeth*, the most distinctive melody of tragedy is dissonance.

3. In line with Bakhtin, Holquist (1990) explains that the utterance represents not only the direct communication between the locutors, but is also on the border between what is said and what is not said.

The simultaneity of the said and the unsaid is most apparent in the area of intonation, where the utterance is "stitched" to the social situation in which it is spoken. Intonation is the immediate interface between the said and the unsaid. In the words of Voloshinov (1976): "It pumps energy from a life situation into verbal discourse. . ." (quoted by Holquist, 1990, p. 61).

4. The description of dialogical meaning in terms of part–whole relationships is well in agreement with narrative meaning that can be understood in these terms as well. Polkinghorne (1988), for example, holds that "Narrative creates its meaning by noting the contributions that actions and events make to a particular outcome and then configures these parts into a whole episode" (p. 6).

CHAPTER 4

Developments in Modern Novelistic Literature

We are all framed of flappes and patches, and of so shapelesse and diverse a contexture, that everie piece, and everie moment playeth his part. And there is as much difference found betweene us and our selves, as there is betweene our selves and others.
Montaigne (1580/1603, pp. 196–197)

Bakhtin's conception of the polyphonic novel is certainly not an isolated phenomenon in the novelistic literature. On the contrary, much of the twentieth century's literature is strikingly similar to central ideas in the work of Dostoevsky, upon whose work the term *polyphonic novel* was based. We will discuss in this chapter two main trends typical of twentieth century novelistic literature: (1) the spatialization of time, and (2) the retreat of the omniscient author. Since these notions are intimately related to Bakhtin's thesis, they will be discussed in some detail. Finally, we will relate these concepts to recent psychological conceptions of self-narrative and argue that the dialogical self assumes a view of the term *narrative* that is largely in agreement with what is generally called the modernist movement in literary science.

4.1 The Spatialization of Time

In 1945, Joseph Frank published his classic essay *Spatial Form in Modern Literature*, that introduced the concept of "spatial form" into literary discussion. Since then it has been accepted as one of the cornerstones for a theory of modern novelistic literature (reprinted in 1991 together with Frank's responses to his critics). As an example of historical significance, Frank took Flaubert's famous county fair scene in *Madame Bovary* as a starting point in his analysis. The scene depicts the romantic rhetoric by which Rodolpho woos the sentimental Emma.

As Flaubert sets the scene, action is going on simultaneously on three levels. On the lowest plane, there is the surging and jostling mob in the street, mingling with the cattle brought to the exhibition. Slightly above the street on a platform are the speechmaking officials, in front of the attentive crowd. And on the highest level, from a window overlooking the spectacle, Rodolpho and Emma are watching the fair and carrying on their amorous conversation. This scene illustrates what Frank means by the spatialization of form in a novel. For the duration of the scene the time flow of the narrative is halted; attention is fixed on relationships within the immobilized time-area. As Flaubert later wrote, in commenting on this scene: "*Everything should sound simultaneously* . . . one should hear the bellowing of cattle, the whispering of the lovers, and the rhetoric of the officials all at the same time" (quoted by Frank, 1991, pp. 16–17). The relationships between the parts of this composite whole are juxtaposed independently of the progress of the narrative and "the full significance of the scene is given only by the reflexive relations among the units of meaning" (p. 17).

In a similar vein, Frank (1991) examined Proust's oeuvre and observed that Proust does *not* follow any of his characters *continuously* throughout the entire course of his novel. Instead, they appear and reappear in various periods of their lives. Hundreds of pages sometimes go by between the time they were last seen and the time they show up again. When they reappear, the passage of time has invariably changed them in some decisive way. Rather than following a character in a continuous line of development, the reader sees various snapshots of the characters "motionless in a moment of vision" (Frank, 1991, p. 26). Proust had learned that, in order to experience time in a more pronounced way, it was necessary to rise above it and to grasp both past and present simultaneously. By the discontinuous presentation of character, Proust forces his readers to juxtapose disparate images spatially, in one moment of time, so that the passage of time is communicated directly to their sensibility. In this way Proust tries to break through the habit, which ordinarily conceals the passage of time: At any one moment of time the changes are so minute as to be imperceptible. However, one has only to look at two photos taken at different moments in time, close enough together that they reflect their contrasts, and the difference between the two photos reveals the *discontinuous* change the pictured person has undergone.

The experience of discontinuous change is also created in Virginia Woolf's novel *To the Lighthouse* (1927/1990), a narration of the events of 2 days, separated by a period of 10 years. The first part is about the family Ramsay, who planned a visit to the lighthouse that had to, however, be cancelled due to bad weather. The expectations and disappointments of the children are described with great care. The second part is about how the family has become a victim of the passage of time: One of the sons was killed in the war, one daughter died in the childbed, and also Mrs. Ramsay, the binding figure in the family, passed away. Finally, the father and one of the sons actually make the travel to the lighthouse, that now assumes a strongly symbolic character. The light symbolizes the past and, at the same time, the contrasting worlds of the parents: the earthly and emotional world of the mother in opposition to the intellectual world of the father who was always looking for a higher, abstract truth. The dramatic and symbolic quality of the travel, and the lighthouse in particular, are strongly enhanced by the description of the present against the background of a highly discontinuous, but simultaneously present past. [1]

4.1.1 The Architectonic Novel: Literature, Painting, Film

In her study of twentieth century novelistic literature, Spencer (1971) introduced the concept of the "architectonic novel." With this term she describes such divergent works as Nin's *Cities of the Interior*, Döblin's *Berlin Alexanderplatz*, Fuentes' *Change of Skin*, Robbe-Grillet's *In the Labyrinth*, Lowry's *Under the Vulcano*, and other image-evoking titles. The most conspicuous feature of architectonic novels is their abandonment of the traditional principle of narration as a coherent and continuous ordering of events from the predominant perspective of one single author. Instead, the architectonic novel adopts the procedure of construction by means of *juxtaposition*, that is, the setting beside one another of story parts that may seem to be unrelated if one sticks to one and the same perspective. The most typical representative of the architectonic genre is the novel with an "open structure," allowing multiple perspectives, some of which are actually contradictory. The purpose is to expose a subject from different and even opposed angles, that is, fact *and* fiction, or observation *and* imagination, and to bring together these perspectives in such a way that an impression of simultaneity is produced.

In the architectonic novel, Spencer observes a loss of interest in the description of character "for its own sake," as having an existence in itself, with an emphasis on coherence of the successive story parts and continuity over time. The architectonic novel, on the contrary, and the open-structured novel in particular, embody multiple perspectives and break with the traditional conception of a story as having a beginning, a middle part with a developing intrigue, and an ending with a "solution." Instead, the concentration of multiple perspectives at one moment in time allows one to make completely new combinations of story parts that give a clear sense of discontinuity. In this discontinuity, new fields of meaning are disclosed.

Spencer observes that architectonic novels have much in common with cubist painting. Picasso, who is together with Braque the founder of Cubism, has deliberately decomposed his object in order to make a new construction on the basis of the fragmented pieces. [2] As Diehl (1977) explains, Picasso looks to his object from different angles and juxtaposes these perspectives in one and the same painting. In this way his well-known multileveled faces and multiple profiles appear. Parallel to the open structure of the architectonic novel, we find in Picasso's oeuvre a breaking down of the sharp separation between the painting and the environment, as expressed in the dissociation of the contours of his painted people and objects:

> . . . his [Picasso's] main interest is in the major problem of creation which he instinctively chose: Combine and assemble various pictorial elements, obtain their true junction on the canvas, attain the internal unity of painting (which Cézanne already defined) and achieve a degree of cohesion which enables him closely to associate the whole universe, throwing down frontiers or traditional distinction between man and all that surrounds him. [Diehl, 1977, p. 46][3]

The creators of Cubism were convinced that the frame of a painting creates an artificial boundary between the artwork and reality. An illustrative example is George Braque, who in 1910 deliberately called attention to his painting *Still Life with Violin and Pitcher* as a "real" painting by including at the top of the canvas a naturalistically rendered nail. In this way the artist shatters the illusion of the artistic work as separate from everyday life.

Similarly, the frame of a narrative can easily serve as a boundary that restricts the audience's attention exclusively to what is inside the frame. The open structure of the architectonic novel combines fact and fiction in such a way that the fictive elements of the novel are open to the realities of everyday life and form new meaning structures in their combination. Spencer refers to the example of Anaïs Nin, who made no distinction between her diaries and her fiction. Nin collected observations and impressions of her friends, analyzed her own thoughts and emotions, and gave these observations and analyses a place in the fiction of her books. Her assumption was that the maintenance of a formal boundary between the novel and its surrounding environment—life—is an anachronistic formality without meaning in our time.

A technique frequently used by Picasso and Braque is collage. It is a pasting together of fragments of newspapers, photographs, wood, glass, etc. as part of a painting or drawing for the purpose of creating a new relationship between basically disparate materials (Myers, 1979). As Spencer (1971) argues, the architectonic novel is often constructed as a collage as well. Alfred Döblin's *Berlin Alexanderplatz* (1929/1961), for example, may be compared to a massive collage. It is the story of Franz Biberkopf's struggle to survive on the streets of Berlin between the two world wars. The story consists of an assemblage of very diverse components: a large group of scarcely individuated characters that represent well-known social types, snapshot-like descriptions of street scenes, lyrics from ballads, patriotic songs, hymns, references to Old Testament tales, Greek myths, quotations from advertisements, newspaper poems, mathematical formulas, and nursery rhymes.

In the way that the several fragments are composed, the basic rhythm of the architectonic novel can be felt. In this genre the quality is more to be found in the rhythmic patterns of the combined fragments than in the narrative coherence of the events. The emphasis on rhythm is another similarity between the architectonic novel and the Cubist painting. Picasso achieves a "melodious architecture of fragmented shapes" (Diehl, 1977, p. 47) that expresses certain rhythmic patterns:

> . . . another factor also emerges with the utmost efficacy: His desire to integrate movement into composition, frankly to set down the problem of rhythm and enrich the work of art with the qualities of a real live organism . . . rhythm is the master, punctuating each work with a discreet pounding by the play of orthogonal criss-crosses, less frequently oblique, which go quicker and soon extend into multiple echoes, thanks to their clever repetition up to infinity . . . Picasso . . . demands the utmost autonomy for both line and coloured splash in order to obtain an intensive suggestion of movement by the simple alternated juxtaposition of planes and the free fragmentation of shapes. [Diehl, 1977, p. 48]

The architectonic novel has a clearly pictorial quality: It invites the reader to see reality as exposed at a glance. It *varies* appearances in order to amplify the limited distances of the human visual field. The juxtaposition, so typical of the architectonic novel, is called "montage" in film. Every piece of film embodies a perspective and different or even contrasting pieces are presented without transitions or explanatory passages. The argument for this construction is certainly not to give a truly successive account of facts, but rather to *enhance the quality of the relationship between the pieces.* In this way it is possible to fix the attention on the interplay of different story parts within a limited time area. This attention is of a highly dynamic nature because one can move back and forth between the different pieces of a composition.

The technological advances of film and television in the twentieth century certainly have had a strong influence on novelistic literature. Spencer argues that the swift language of visual images in film and television have shown us new ways of organizing what our senses receive: We take in sensations and words all at once instead of sequentially. Indeed, the traditional novel is more of a temporal kind, whereas film is more of a spatial kind. Pictures have no tenses and, therefore, give the impression of continuous presentness, although they are less suited than the novel to the exploration and projection of inner states of consciousness. The camera eye can alternate between different and contrasting spatial perspectives; it can, by the use of flashbacks, alternate between past and present, and even can visualize imaginations of the future. It is, therefore, not surprising that this medium, with its capacity for clear, powerful, and immediate visualization, has attracted many inventive novelists (Spencer, 1971).

The writer of an architectonic novel, the Cubist painter, and the filmmaker have in common that they all make use of an essential difference between "lived time" and "lived space," originally formulated by Bergson (1907, 1934): Relationships in time are irreversible; relationships in space are reversible. From the perspective of the passage of time, it is impossible to go back to an earlier point in time. From the perspective of space, however, one can move from point A to point B and from point B back to A again. By the transformation of temporal relations into spatial relations, elements of past, present, and anticipated future can be brought together by the procedure of juxtaposition, in an attempt to create new relationships. The reversibility inherent in juxtaposition represents a basic structure that also underlies the notion of dialogue, which assumes the existence of an *inter*subjective exchange.

With the spatialization of time and the architectonic quality of modern novelistic literature, we are far from Descartes' *Cogito* and close to Vico's constructionism. In plugging his ears, Descartes could never hear a polyphonic composition and in closing his eyes he could never enjoy the beauty of architecture. One would expect Vico, however, to understand the structure of the modern novel, because it would call on the creative force in human nature, which he called *ingenium*. With this force humans, as embodied creatures, can alter their world by inventions and move things into "new relationships." And the principle of juxtaposition may function as a poetic or artistic means for the exploration of meaning structures emerging from these relationships.

4.2 The Retreat of the Omniscient Narrator

The spatialization of time is closely related to another development in modern literature, the retreat of the omniscient narrator. Spencer (1971) holds that there is a definite influence of modern physics in literature, in that everything in space is conceived as relative to a moving point of reference and that such a view renders obsolete the convention of the *exclusive* perspective of one and the same author. The issue of relativity played a major role, for example, in Sartre's criticism of the position of the author in the work of the French novelist Mauriac: "He [Mauriac] has tried to ignore, as have most of our authors, the fact that the theory of relativity applies to the world of the novel, and that, in a true novel, there is no more place than in the world of Einstein for the privileged observer" (quoted by Spencer, 1971, p. 76).

A first step in the process of retreat is made in those books in which the teller is not the author but another person. An illustrative example is Gertrude Stein's book *The Autobiography of Alice Toklas* (1933), a work that made her a well-known and even notorious figure in literary circles. The work contains her ideas about modern literature and relates to the main people who played a significant role in her life. The person who tells all these things, however, is Alice Toklas, her partner, housekeeper, typist, and editor of her books. Stein thus writes her autobiography in the third person, creating an "external" perspective, revealing the way she sees herself viewed by other people. This external perspective is, within the same work, combined with her internal perspective, from which she tells how she sees herself. Together the two angles allow a more complete picture of the person Stein is. In dialogical terms, two *I* positions are assumed, allowing the possibility that the one position—implicitly or explicitly—responds to the other position, complementing it and agreeing or disagreeing with it. [For another example of an "external" perspective, see Fitzgerald's *The Great Gatsby* (1925/1992), in which the protagonist's neighbor functions as the narrator.]

Whereas Stein's *Autobiography* is structured on the basis of two positions, William Faulkner goes a step further by introducing in his novel *The Sound and the Fury* (1929) a multiplicity of positions. In this book, that breaks away from the tradition of the chronologically ordered story, the decline of the family Compson over a period of 30 years is related to from four angles. The Compson brothers (Benjy, Quentin, and Jason), and the black housekeeper Dilsey tell, each from their specific position, about a number of important events in the family. One of the brothers, Benjy, is feeble minded and tells his story in a rather confusing way, leading to considerable jumps in his train of thoughts. The differences in the positions (e.g., white versus black and high versus low intelligence) allow for considerable distances between the perspectives, thus producing a juxtaposition of highly divergent views on the same subject.

The retreat of the author is also very convincingly portrayed in Pirandello's *Six Characters in Search of an Author*. Six characters enter a theater in an attempt to find an author who will help let their suffering be known: a father and his stepdaughter involved in a deep emotional conflict, a mother, and three children. In an earlier stage, the father had left the mother because she loved another man. But the man died and she returned to her husband. Then she discovered that the father and the stepdaughter had an incestuous encounter in a brothel. The family relationships had reached the stage of intolerable stress. The situation was so complex that nobody, not even the author, could tell the story of the family as a coherent narrative. Instead, the different characters, arguing with each other in very emotional ways, told their stories in fragments, faced with their apparent inability to communicate their concerns. The different fragments could only be put together by the public and the author in the course of the play. The characters challenged the author to give an answer to *their* problems.

By retreating from the omniscient position, the author has certainly acknowledged the inadequacy of one sole position. This step toward a more modest, relativistic stance is not to be considered simply as resulting from mere ignorance. On the contrary, characters are often chosen or invented because they are capable of providing various masks *for the author*. What captures the excitement of the novelist is the possibility of a character as "a voice" through which the author may express a special attitude toward reality. Disguised as a character, the author enters the novel and in doing so he or she not only has the possibility of using the specific characteristics of the role in question but also of using different or even contrasting roles in an attempt to juxtapose different viewpoints.

4.2.1 James Joyce's Ulysses

A novel with far-reaching influence on modern twentieth century literature was certainly Joyce's *Ulysses*, a work conceived as a modern epic (Frank, 1991). Whereas it took the Homeric Odysseus many years to return from Troy to Ithaca, Joyce exposes the wanderings of his characters from morning till night in *one* day in Dublin. He views the city life mainly through two characters, Stephen De-dalus, a young, somewhat arrogant intellectual, and Leopold Bloom, a humble advertising salesman. It was Joyce's aim not only to depict the outer life of his characters, often with minute and shocking details, but also their inner lives, bringing together seemingly unrelated and illogical thought patterns. The two characters are contrasting in a number of ways: Stephen is young, interested in philosophy and intellectual affairs, a son without a father, and Catholic. Bloom is older, preoccupied with body and sex, a father without a son, and Jewish. After having moved through Dublin independently for a great part of the novel, they meet one another at the end of the brothel scene and then go to the house of Bloom where "the duumvirate" have a conversation, comparable to the con-tact between Odysseus and Telemachus in Ithaca. In this scene, Joyce allows his characters to agree on certain matters *and* disagree on others. For example, after it was described that Stephen and Bloom "both were sensitive to artistic impres-sions, musical in preference to plastic or pictorial," it was revealed that "Stephen dissented openly from Bloom's views on the importance of dietary and civic selfhelp while Bloom dissented tacitly from Stephen's views on the eternal affirmation of the spirit of man in literature. . ." (Joyce, 1922/1986, Chapter 17, lines 20–30).

As already mentioned, both modern literature and Cubist painting make extensive use of the principle of juxtaposition. Joyce's (1986) use of unusual linguistic constructions, in an attempt to bring his otherwise contrasting charac-ters together or to combine them in specific ways, is exemplified by the following passage: "Substituting Stephen for Bloom Stoom would have passed successively through a dame's school and the high school. Substituting Bloom for Stephen Blephen would have passed successively through the preparatory, junior, middle and senior grades of the intermediate and through the matriculation, first arts, second arts and arts degree courses of the royal university" (Chapter 17, lines 549–554). Similar substitutions take place when Joyce examines the relation that exists between their ages: "16 Years before in 1888 when Bloom was of Stephen's present age Stephen was 6. 16 Years after in 1920 when Stephen would be of Bloom's present age Bloom would be 54. . ." (1922/1986, Chapter 17, lines 447–449).

Like many other twentieth century novelists, Joyce makes use of the so-called "stream of consciousness" technique. The associative thought process, in all its illogical, instantaneous, and whimsical jumps, is revealed as directly as possible, without interference by the author. Instead of ordering the thoughts of the characters from an authorial "super position," explaining to the reader what happens in the mind of the character, the author allows the character to speak or think spontaneously on the spur of the moment. This implies that the train of thought of a character is not only determined from within (i.e., as purely internal associations), but also, intermittently, is influenced by sensations and perceptions of the immediate environment (sounds, smells, words, visual stimuli). Sometimes the impact of the stream of consciousness technique is enhanced by adapting form to content. That is, the author takes the freedom to violate grammatical rules in order to express the immediate experiences of the subject more directly. An example of the stream of consciousness technique is the famous "monologue intérieur"[4] of Molly Bloom at the end of Joyce's *Ulysses*. In this case the author deletes all interpunction in order to let the character speak from her *own* world as freely as possible:

> Yes because he [her husband] never did a thing like that before as ask to get his breakfast in bed with a couple of eggs since the City Arms hotel when he used to be pretending to be laid up with a sick voice doing his highness to make himself interesting for that old faggot Mrs Riordan that he thought he had a great leg of and she never left us a farthing all for masses for herself and her soul greatest miser was actually afraid to lay out 4th for her methylated spirit telling me all her ailments she had too much old chat in her about politics and earthquakes and the end of the world let us have a bit of fun first God help the world if all the women were her sort down on bathingsuits and lownecks of course nobody wanted her to wear them I suppose she was pious because no man would look at her twice I hope. . . [Joyce, 1922/1986, Chapter 18, lines 1–11][5]

The stream of consciousness technique gives the author a great liberation from the strict chronological ordering of events. It allows a character to make discontinuous, unexpected, sudden jumps to other moments in time, similar to flashbacks and flashforwards in film. It also renders the possibility of introducing other characters in seemingly unrelated ways and of juxtaposing them in order to create unusual and original structures. Implicit in the stream of consciousness technique is that the author takes a step back and lets the characters speak for themselves, without molding them into a single unifying framework.

To summarize, the spatialization of time in modern novelistic literature fits together with the retreat of the omniscient author. The principle of juxtaposition, so characteristic of novels with spatial form, is also applied to the relation between author and character. The author, becoming part of the text and thus giving up his or her privileged and centralized position, may take the role of one or more characters, often with contrasting world views. These characters may at times enter into dialogical relations of question and answer, agreement and disagreement, and their features may be combined into new constructions in which fact and fiction go together or even fuse.

With reference to the previous chapter, Bakhtin's (1929/1973) polyphonic novel can be compared to the spatial novel in at least three ways: (1) as multi-voiced and embodied, the characters in the polyphonic novel represent two or more spatially different positions that are related according to the principle of juxtaposition; (2) the omniscient author retreats and takes a position as one or more characters in the novel itself; and (3) by entering the novel the author has the opportunity to entertain, in the position of a character, dialogical relationships with other characters.

4.3 Self-Narrative in Psychology: Time and Space

Prevailing conceptions of narrative and self-narrative in psychology are strongly biased to its temporal dimension, with the spatial dimension rather neglected. Sarbin (1990), one of the main advocates of a narrative approach in contemporary psychology, concludes: "The temporal context of experience and action is what makes the narrative a congenial organizing principle. Action, and the silent preparation for action, because extended in time, is storied. We live in a story-shaped world. Action takes on the narrative quality, the familiar beginning, middle, and ending" (pp. 61–62). The organizing influence of the ending was also emphasized by Mancuso and Sarbin (1983): ". . . we remind the reader that the ending of the story is always implicated in the story's construction" (p. 251).[6]

Gergen and Gergen (1988) also see time as *the* defining characteristic of narrative and not space: "We shall employ the term self-narrative . . . to refer to the individual's account of the relationship among self-relevant events *across time*" (p. 19, emphasis added). In line with their emphasis on the temporal dimension, Gergen and Gergen (1988) emphasize the *coherence* of stories: Events are combined into "goal-directed, coherent sequences" (p. 19).

Drawing on Bakhtin's polyphonic novel, and developments in twentieth century novelistic literature, we emphasize *time* and *space* as the two basic notions that are of equal importance in the organization of narrative (space may even be considered as more basic in so far as time is "spatialized"). This results in a conception of story that recognizes not only *continuity* but also *discontinuity*, and not only *coherence* but also *separateness* of the different story parts as intrinsic features of the narrative mode. Our proposal is not only to acknowledge the essential role of coherence in the self, but also to place strong emphasis on the intrinsic separateness of different or contrasting *I* positions. As such the self functions as a multiplicity of positions that are located at different places in an imaginal landscape. At the same time, however, the self is multivoiced, and the different voices may enter into dialogical relationships with one another. It is in the dialogical relation that the possibility of coherence is given. The different positions cohere as far as they are dialogically related; they are separate as far as one and the same person is like "different characters," resisting any final unification.

The supposition of a basic continuity of the story mode could easily suggest the existence of one and the same I moving through time with a high degree of sameness and identity. This view, however, is based on a unified view of the self, that is able to provide a narrative account from a centralized position. It is one of the groundbreaking developments in modern novelistic literature, that the absolute position of the omniscient author is challenged. Correspondingly, one may, within the psychological realm, question the existence of an omniscient self as representing a highly centralized position from which the self as a whole could be organized and perceived. Such an omniscient, centralized view would certainly run the serious risk of neglecting the diversification, conflict, and contradiction that, once faced, may extend the experiential field of the person and contribute to its richness.

The dialogical view of the self can be further clarified by taking seriously the notion of emplotment. Recently, Polkinghorne (1988) proposed that a "plot" combines two dimensions, one chronological, the other nonchronological. The chronological dimension shows that the story is made up of events along the line of time. The nonchronological dimension "lifts the events into a *configuration* so that, scattered though they may be, they form a significant whole" (p. 131, emphasis added). In other words, emplotment liberates a narrative account not only from the pure time sequence, but also allows for a construction in which parts and wholes are to be discerned. In the line of modern novelistic literature, the principle of juxtaposition is a form of configuration in which the notion of space is given priority over time. This means that the chronological ordering in terms of a beginning, a middle, and an ending is not the final word of emplotment. The constructive activity of emplotment allows for a juxtaposition of events, in which the original time sequence is changed or even reversed, in the service of finding new configurations. Moreover, different moments or periods in a person's life may produce different characters that may be combined in particular configurations of *I* positions.

Emplotment as a construction of part–whole configurations allows, moreover, for the simultaneous existence of coherence and separateness. The different characters in a story retain, as *parts* of a whole, their position of relative autonomy. As dialogically related, they form new combinations that function as coherent *wholes*. An implication of this view is that the characters do not give up their separateness. However, this separateness keeps the characters from dissolving into fragmentation, since the notion of dialogue is a guarantee for their coherence as parts of an organized whole.

Emplotment, as a liberation from the constraints of chronology, does not allow the ending to play a central role in the construction of a story. Such a dominant role would be in sharp contradiction to Bakhtin's thesis of "unfinalizibility" that gives a narrative, conceived as a polyphonic novel, an open-ended character. Narrative, conceived as a multiplicity of *I* positions, means, in fact, that *each I*, as an author, has its own story to tell. This implies that there is not a single and final ending. Rather, a complex narrative with ongoing dialogical relationships between several positions assumes an open process that resists not only a final unification, but also a final completion.

Notes

1. The concentration of disparate elements in one and the same object or word is for modern novelists a useful procedure to enhance its symbolic quality. A classic example is Joyce's title *Finnegans Wake* (1939), that refers to a popular folktale in which the bricklayer, Tim Finnegan, falls in a drunken state from a ladder and lies on the floor for dead. During the wake he becomes alive again when by accident some whiskey falls on his lips. The Irish word for whiskey is *uisce beatha*, which means elixir. In this way the title refers to the theme of death and rise, and to the fall at the same time. Moreover, the title includes the word *fin* (end, as part of "final") in combination with *again* (new beginning). Also the main protagonist of the book, indicated by the initials HCE, functions at two levels of interpretation. HCE refers to the pubkeeper Humphrey Chimpden Earwicker, who lives with his wife and children in the Irish *Chapelizod;* at the same time the initials stand for *Here Comes Everybody.* The work can be read at two levels, on the personal level of a particular person, and on a more universal level, with the focus on general themes such as life and death, guilt and innocence, past and present (Teleac Coursebook, 1991).

2. For Picasso, a (cubist) painting can be considered "a sum of destructions." By breaking down the elements of a naturalistic form, a new synthesis can be achieved that represents the original form more truly (Spencer, 1971).

3. Seemingly unrelated things may, nevertheless, be intriguing just because their gap functions as a deeper source of meaning. In his study of allegory, Fletcher (1964) says: "The silences in allegory mean as much as the filled-in spaces, because by bridging the silent gaps between oddly unrelated images we reach the sunken understructure of thought" (p. 107).

4. The frequently used term *monologue intérieur* might suggest that such an account is not dialogical. On the contrary, monologues are typically filled with perspectives of others and echo the words or intonations from other people, with the personal attitude of the speaker added. In this quotation this becomes apparent in fragments such as "telling me all her ailments . . ." and "help the world if all the women were her sort. . . ."

5. In a study of Joyce's method, Litz (1961) concluded that one of Joyce's major artistic techniques could be described with the notion "expressive form." This technique seeks to establish a direct correspondence between substance and style. The form imitates or expresses qualities of its subject or

the setting of action. Thus an episode which takes place in a newspaper office is cast in the form of a newspaper, or a section on sentimental girlhood is written in a "namby-pamby jammy marmelady drawersy (alto lá) style" (Litz, 1961, p. 44).

6. Whereas many writers of literary modernism attempt to evoke the experience of simultaneity by juxtaposition of narrative fragments, Joyce does the same by giving his works a circular structure. The last sentence of *Finn Wake* (1939), for example, is incomplete: "A way a lone a last a loved a long the." The last word *the* can at the same time be read as the first word of the same work that begins with a sentence in which the first word is omitted, ". . . riverrun, past Eve and Adam's, from swerve of shore to bend of bay, brings us by a commodius vicus of recirculation back to Howth Castle and Environs." Note that dreams and myths, that are an important source of inspiration for modern novelists, are often incomplete and open ended.

CHAPTER 5

The Dialogical Self: Tension between Dominance and Exchange

In fact, our conceptual explorations are based on the assumption that two concepts, "self" and "dialogue," can become meaningfully combined into a third concept, the dialogical self, in such a way that in their theoretical integration, new relationships, or even new vistas, are disclosed. The questions that remain to be answered then are about what the dialogical self really is, what its defining characteristics are, and how it functions in the everyday life of people. These questions can only be answered if we take the social nature of human life into account. In the process of socialization the person's self, and the potential range of *I* positions in particular, is organized not only by the person himself or herself, but also by the social environment. Therefore, we will start this chapter by studying in some detail some of the precursors of the mature self, in close correspondence with the first signs of dialogue. Then we will focus on the questions of when and how the social environment, and institutions in particular, begin to mold, organize, and restrict the range of potential positions.

5.1 The Development of the Self and Dialogue from Birth

One of the major assumptions of the concept of dialogical self is the existence of a relationship between self and other, which requires some degree of differentiation between these two poles of communication. All evidence suggests that *some* differentiation is present from birth on.

When mother and infant first look at each other, they are not really strangers. They have been intimately connected for the infant's entire existence in the womb and have only recently been *separated*. When they meet face to face, the mother gets to know the new arrival by looking, touching, and talking with the infant (Klaus, Kennel, Plumb, & Zuelke, 1970). Most mothers follow a similar pattern in getting to know their newborn infants. They reach out and tentatively touch the infant's fingertips, arms, and legs. Within a few minutes, they place their palms on the infant's trunk and massage and stroke the tiny body. They look, and their eyes meet. Even right after birth infants will follow the mother's general gaze. Mothers of blind infants report that they feel "lost" because their infants cannot return their gaze (Fraiberg, 1974).

In the first hour after birth the infant is alert, and the mother's receptivity is intensified. The two "converse" in some sense: The mother talks to her infant and the infant moves to the *rhythm* of the mother's speech (Condon & Sanders, 1974). Seeing the infant move and look at her face encourages the mother to keep on speaking, touching, and looking.

5.1.1 Conversational Turn-Taking

In their study of early mother–child interaction, investigators have been able to use stop-frame and slow-motion microanalysis of films and videotapes. They have observed that mothers and infants begin to take turns from the moment the infant is born. (See Clarke-Stewart *et al.*, 1988, for a review). From birth, babies suck in a regular pattern of bursts. Mothers are sensitive to this pattern and act in correspondence to it: When the baby sucks, the mother is quiet; when the baby pauses, the mother touches it and talks to it. In this early stage the baby sucks and pauses, independent of whether the mother responds or not. However, a mother treats the baby's bursts of sucking as a "turn," and this rhythm creates a highly structured pattern of interaction (Kaye, 1977). In fact, mothers act *as if* the baby were taking turns in actual "conversations." In this process of turn-taking, a mother will generally wait the length of a conversational pause and listen for an *imaginal* response from the baby before continuing on (Stern, 1977). Later, these pauses are filled in by the infant's babbling, and contingent responding to this babbling by the mother tends to increase the incidence of babbling (Bloom, Russell, & Davis, 1986). As Clarke-Stewart *et al.* (1988) observe, mother and child can be considered at this point to be participating in a *pseudodialogue*. Although the child is still too young to engage in a real dialogue, the fact that the responses of mother *and* child are highly contingent upon each other makes them appear as real communicative interactants.

By the time the baby is a year old, he or she is generally able to give some real responses. When there is an expectant pause, the baby vocalizes, and pseudodialogues soon develop into more developed speech acts (Newson, 1977):

Baby: (Looks at a toy top)
Mother: "Do you like that?"
Baby: "Da!"
Mother: "Yes, it's a nice toy, isn't it?"
Baby: "Da! Da!"

When 2 to 3 years of age, children have been found to converse not only with their parents and siblings, but also with an *imaginal* interlocutor (Garvey, 1984).

The young child is not yet able to "think" silently in words, as most adults do, and therefore uses language to rehearse or rework a prior conversation. In a familiar surrounding children may take the opportunity to express certain ideas, amuse themselves, and use language to direct their own actions. Garvey (1984) recorded the variety of vocalizations and speech that emerged from 28-month-old Sarah's room during a nap period. They ranged from quiet murmurs to grunts, squeals, and intoned babbles; from humming to snatches of songs, rhymes, and counting. Sarah talked to a doll, had a "telephone conversation," described her own activities (e.g., "I'm putting my socks on"), and gave accounts of her searching for and playing with toys.

The sounds that emerge from Sarah's room lead us to draw at least two conclusions: (1) she echoes or imitates events that happened at earlier moments, which supposes the working of *memory;* and (2) she brings a divergence of events and impressions together that were scattered over a longer period of time, in an act of *imagination,* juxtaposing them on the spot of the moment. This developmental account rephrases an insight of Vico, when he said: ". . . imagination is nothing but extended or compounded memory" (1744/1968, p. 75).[1]

5.1.2 Self with Other

In his research on infant development, Stern (1983) proposes that the "self" and the "other" are differentiated affectively, perceptually, and cognitively from birth onward. He argues that Mahler, Pine, and Bergman's (1975) notion of an early postnatal symbiotic state has not been confirmed by research. Rather, argues Stern, developmental research has indicated that the child is "an avid learner from birth." Even the very young infant is competent, predesigned to perceive the world in a highly structured fashion, mentally active in constructing a variety of concepts of which visual schemata and the recognition of the mother's face are the most important. In other words, mother and child are separate entities who nevertheless enter into a close interaction from birth on.

The interaction that Stern (1983) assumes to characterize mother–child contacts, called "state sharing," includes such events as mutual gazing, vocalizing together, interactional synchrony, and stereotyped games (e.g., pat-a-cake). State sharing also covers such simple mother–child interactions as smiling, in which the smile of the one evokes the smile of the other.

Moments of state sharing, Stern (1983) argues further, are the first glimpses the child receives of intersubjectivity. During moments of state sharing the infant is ". . . engaged in the slow and momentous discovery that his experience which he already senses is distinctly his own, is not unique and unparalleled but is part of shared human experience . . . he is establishing subjective intimacy" (p. 77).

The developmental picture gets complicated here, however, because recognition of the infant as a "separate self" does *not* make the baby a completely autonomous individual. In fact, the early need for attachment and the later loosening of this attachment are two of the major milestones in childhood (Ainsworth, Blehar, Waters, & Well, 1978).[2]

5.1.3 Self against Other: Personal Space and Stranger Anxiety

The notion of dialogue requires not only an orientation to the other, but also a separation from the other: Somebody tells something *to* somebody else from his or her *own* perspective. Therefore, a growing autonomy may be considered an indispensable precondition of mature communication. The phenomena of "personal space" and "self-boundary structures" can be considered early manifestations of the child's striving for autonomy. There is growing evidence for a relation between the development of a self-boundary structure and the onset of what has been called "stranger anxiety" during the second half of the first year of life. At some point a young child realizes that a stranger has the potential to intrude on his personal space and therefore becomes fearful of all strangers, particularly in the absence of a caretaker (see Horner, 1983, for a review).

Psychologists have regarded the concept of personal space as relevant to interactions with others and as an integral component of the self for both children and adults. Personal space differs from territory in that it accompanies the individual's movements. Thus, Burgoon and Jones (1976) describe it as "the invisible volume of space that surrounds an individual . . . an invisible, dynamic, and transportable space the site of which is governed by the individual . . . at any point in time" (p. 131). Sommer (1959) originally specified four defining characteristics of personal space: (1) it is portable; (2) its geographical and psychological center is the individual's body; (3) it is demarcated from the rest of the environment by invisible boundaries; and (4) intrusion into it by others arouses discomfort, causing the individual to withdraw. Based on various studies of ego and body boundaries, Horner (1983) added two characteristics: the actual size of the individual space and the degree of intimacy existing between the interactants. Personal space fluctuates according to various social, psychological, and organismic conditions, with the boundaries becoming semipermeable when a certain degree of familiarity exists.

A psychological parallel of personal space is the self-boundary structure. Formulations concerning the functional significance of self-boundaries are quite similar to those made concerning personal space. Fisher and Cleveland (1968) have claimed that people collect their assumptions about life into a "behavioral space" that separates the individual from what is "out there." The self-boundary structure can be understood as a screen, which people carry with them at all times and can at any time interpose between themselves and the outer situation.

Of the many methods that have been used to study personal space and self-boundary phenomena in humans, most have focused on various aspects of interpersonal proximity and nonverbal interaction (e.g., gaze interaction), with special attention to spatial invasions (e.g., an experimenter or confederate moves close to an unsuspecting subject). The use of various "distancing" techniques and the point at which these are used are then measured as an indicator of when and how much discomfort is aroused. As already mentioned, the actual comfort-able distance is determined by several factors, including age, gender, degree of acquaintance, friendship, personal attraction, cultural background, need for affiliation, and psychopathology. (See reviews by Evans & Howard, 1973; Hay-duck, 1978; Sundstrom & Altman, 1976.)

The first signs of stranger anxiety can be observed when the child is 4 to 6 months old. When an unfamiliar person appears, the baby studies the person's face intently, frowns, takes a deep breath, and usually looks or turns away, or may even cry (Bronson, 1972). This wariness of strangers is an important new development that demonstrates the infant's growing awareness of the social environment. It also indicates, as suggested by Horner (1983), that *active* (as opposed to purely reactive) behavioral processes are now at work, which directly correspond to later adult patterns for maintaining personal space. Between 6 and 12 months, as cognitive awareness increases, the likelihood that the infant will be wary increases (Decary, 1974). Sometimes during this period infants become not only wary but also fearful. They cling to their parents, burst into tears, scream, or scoot away from the stranger. Apparently, the intensity of the infants' reactions will depend on their interpretation of the stranger and the situation (e.g., Who else is present? How does the stranger act?). Safe in mother's arms, an infant may be wary but will usually not cry out of fear; when alone, upset, or in an unfamiliar place, the infant is likely to react fearfully; and if the stranger looks too serious, looks scary, approaches too quickly, comes too close, or doesn't back away when the infant indicates some wariness (e.g., looks away from the stranger), then the infant is likely to react with even more overt fear (Bronson, 1978).

Interestingly enough, the human infant is capable of making perceptual discriminations between mother and nonmother long before it reacts to a strang-er with some hesitancy. The baby differentially recognizes the mother on the basis of olfactory information already in the first weeks after birth (Cernoch & Porter, 1985). This suggests that it is *not* the differentiation of mother from nonmother that determines the onset of stranger anxiety. It is, rather, a growing awareness of one's personal space and the establishment of self-boundaries that appear to motivate the child's sudden perception of a stranger as an intruder.

As we have seen, there is an initial differentiation between the self and the other in early infancy, which manifests itself, at the end of the first year, as fixed boundaries for a stranger and semipermeable boundaries for a familiar person. This differentiation, however, does not mean that the many experiences of the child are in any way integrated; that is, the child's various contacts with people or other significant experiences are not ordered in such a way that new experiences can systematically be assimilated. Of major importance for the integration of experiences is the emergence of some point of reference to function as a center around which the "blooming buzzing confusion" confronting the infant can be organized (James, 1890; Burns, 1979). From this perspective, the emergence of self-recognition and the increasing capacity for language are major milestones in the child's development.

5.1.4 Self-Recognition in the Mirror

Recognition of the self in the mirror has received a great deal of attention as an index of self-awareness, self-consciousness, and social development in humans and infrahumans (Damon & Hart, 1982; Lewis & Brooks-Gunn, 1979, 1984; Loveland, 1986). The mirror method has been used with infrahumans to explore the presence or absence of *any* self-awareness in such species. It has been used with babies, who cannot tell us what is in their awareness, making it difficult to determine *when* some element of consciousness or self-awareness appears to develop.

A number of studies have used the "marked-face technique" originated by Gallup (1968) and by Amsterdam (1972), independently. In this procedure the infant is unobtrusively marked with a spot of rouge or dye on the face (usually the nose). The child is then placed before a mirror and observed to see whether he or she proceeds to examine the spot or not. Amsterdam found that from about age 6 months to 1 year the subjects only behaved "socially" toward the mirror, sometimes trying to "find the actual baby" by looking behind the mirror. Many of the infants in this age group also enjoyed observing their own movements in the mirror, but they demonstrated *no* spot-directed behavior. After about 14 months of age, the search for "the baby in the mirror" declined rapidly and withdrawal from the mirror became increasingly evident. Of the older, 21- to 24-month-old, subjects, however, 63% evidenced self-recognition (indicated by mark-directed behavior).

A more refined series of studies was reported by Lewis and Brooks-Gunn (1979) in which the acquisition of more specific self-knowledge was examined using measures of visual self-recognition in a mirror, a videotape, and a photograph. These investigators also used the marked-nose technique, including an unmarked condition in which no rouge was applied. In children older than 18 months, nose-directed behavior was rarely seen in the no-rouge condition but increased markedly in the rouged condition. As before, the infants under 1 year of age enjoyed the mirror more than the older infants, often touching, kissing, and smiling at the image in the mirror and bouncing before the mirror. Older infants were more likely to touch *themselves* or to act coy and silly before the mirror, although they were overall less likely to show sustained attention to the mirror image. The investigators concluded that "other-directed behavior" was more characteristic of infants in the first year and "self-directed behavior" of infants in the second year. (See Anderson, 1984, and Loveland, 1986, for reviews.)

5.1.5 Proper Names and Pronouns as Points of Self-Reference

Some time after solution of the marked-face task, children begin to identify the self-image in the mirror by name or with a pronoun (Zazzo, 1979). More generally, children around 2 years of age start using language to identify themselves and express the fact that they are distinct from others. A little boy may see his photograph and pipe up "Me!" Similarly, he may define his self-boundaries by grabbing a toy and insisting "Mine!" or asserting "I Micky," "I boy," or "I a baby."

Learning to use personal pronouns correctly is a difficult task. Children's initial use of "I," "You," "Me," and "Mine," is confused. They hear their mother use the word *you* when speaking to them and may therefore address themselves as "you" instead of "I." They may speak of themselves in the third person instead of the first person, as in, "Pete (I) is hungry." And they may also use the object instead of the subject form of the pronoun: "Me (I) want it." Ordinary words such as *apple* or *doll* can be easily imitated, whereas words like *You* or *I* must always be reinterpreted by the child rather than imitated directly (in linguistic terms they are "shifters," because their referents shift depending on who is speaking). Correct use of pronouns is difficult because it requires perspective taking and this capacity has not yet fully developed. In addition, increasing accuracy in the use of pronouns may also be dependent on children's maturing conception of their *own* individuality. Finally, the child's use of the pronouns themselves may also stimulate further differentiation of the self and the other (Burns, 1979), although very little research along this line has been done.

The child's name itself also functions increasingly as a reference point for the organization of self-relevant experiences. Children hear their names repeated over and over again by others who accompany the name with appropriate gestures, actions, and words, which, in Mead's (1934) terms, indicate the feelings of the others for the child and their beliefs about her or him. The child's name can be associated with both positive and negative gestures or words: "Oh, Bobby sweet" may be uttered when the child has hugged someone or given someone something, and "Bad Bobby!" may be screamed when he has just thrown his cereal bowl on the floor. This link between the child's name and the contexts in which it regularly gets used may be of direct relevance to the child's developing self. If children hear their names persistently used within a context of appreciation, their self-feelings will be rather positive. In contrast, if their names are used within a depreciating context, where children are persistently disapproved or rejected, their feelings about themselves will presumably be negative.

Once children have their names and the various pronouns in their linguistic repertoire, a variety of actions, features, and traits can be associated with the name *by the children themselves.* They can also now begin to formulate, as an *I* about their *Me,* their own self-narratives, although they will still be highly dependent on the nature of their interactions with their parents in particular and the parents' appreciations of them. These narratives may be quite fragmented due to lack of temporal organization, but they will nevertheless contain some of the earliest reflections on the self: "Tommy eaten up everything . . . Tommy big boy."

5.1.6 Early Forms of Role Playing

As Piaget and Inhelder (1969) have argued, symbolic play is a major expression of cognitive activity in the years from ages one to four. Examples of the simplest kinds of play are pretending to be an animal, that a chair is a car, or that a wooden block is a person. The first forms of playing with objects progress to the child's pretending that he or she is another figure. For example, a child may act like a grown-up, that is, like a mother, father, policeman, or doctor. An even higher level of organization is achieved when the child announces to play a particular role ahead of time: "Let's play . . ." (called "announced fantasy play;" see Field, DeStefano, and Koewler, 1982). In this stage children may be involved in a play in which they act as if they are that particular character, acting similarly and even imitating its tone of voice.

At the age of 2 to 3 years old, children are progressively able not only to play the role of a particular character, but also to reverse roles. For example, they may say: "I am the doctor, you are the child," and at another moment propose: "I am the child, you are the doctor." Here we see an analog of the use of shifters like *I* and *you:* The doctor who is *I* at one moment in time is *you* at another moment. By changing roles and correspondingly shifting the pronouns, children are taking different or contrasting *I* positions and experience these positions *in their mutuality.*

In the same period in which they are involved in role playing, children begin to be fascinated by fairy tales and other stories that strongly appeal to their vivid imaginations. Those stories often impress children and adults by their dramatic confrontations between protagonists and antagonists and by the strong discontinuities of the plot. Little Red Riding Hood finds herself confronted with the big wolf, who suddenly eats her grandmother. Snow White becomes the victim of her jealous stepmother and is later poisoned by her, but finally awakens from her deathlike state by the arrival of the prince. Tom Thumb, the smallest of the family, is threatened by the giant but, clever as he is, he steals the giant's boots and escapes moving with big steps, with his brothers safe in the boots.

Fairy tales and the great variety of other tales in books, films, and television provide a great heterogeneity of possible positions that are partly in the realm of fantasy (e.g., fairy-tale figures), partly in real life (e.g., doctor, policeman), and on the interface of both (e.g., stories of good or bad parents, happy or unhappy children). Altogether the child's world becomes populated by a multiplicity of positions, forming a mixture of fact and fiction. At the same time, developments in memory, imagination, and role taking enable the child to imagine himself or herself not only *in* these positions, but also to shift from one position to the other. In this way the child comes to know these positions in their (often contrasting) relationships and in their mutuality.

5.1.7 Imaginal Dialogues in Adult Life

Imaginal dialogues play an important role in adult life on the interface of fact and fiction. In her book, *Invisible Guests,* Watkins (1986) observes that in most psychological theories imaginal phenomena are most often approached from the perspective of the real. "Reality" and "fact" have a clear ontological priority, and imaginal others are seen as a derivative from and subordinate to real others. Nevertheless, imaginal dialogues influence our daily lives to a significant degree. They exist *beside* actual dialogues with real others and constitute, *interwoven* with actual interactions, an essential part of our narrative construction of the world. We find ourselves, for example, communicating with our critics, with our parents, with the photograph of someone we miss, with a figure from a movie or dream, with our consciences, with our gods, with our reflection in the mirror, with our babies, or with our pets. Imaginal dialogues have had a significant influence on the work of historical figures. Machiavelli had imaginal conversations with historical personages. Petrarch wrote letters to the eminences of classical antiquity; Landor wrote volumes of imaginal dialogues between the sages of different centuries, and Pablo Casals said: "Bach is my best friend." Watkins (1986) adds to these examples that imaginal others affect our interactions with "actual" others just as surely as the other way around (p. 69).

Despite their invisible quality, imaginal others are typically perceived as having a spatially separated position. This applies not only to our own culture (e.g., imaginal contact with a deceased parent or friend, with a wise advisor, with an ideal lover), but also to non-Western communities. Referring to the work of Warneck (1909), Watkins gives the example of the Bataks of Sumatra, who believed that the spirit, who determines the character and fortune of a person, is like "a man within a man." Such a spirit does not coincide with his or her personality and can even be considered as an opponent. It is experienced as a special being within the person, with its own will and desires. Cassirer (1955) also emphasizes that in mythical consciousness a tutelary spirit is *not* conceived as the "subject" of someone's inner life but as something objective, "which dwells in man, which is spatially connected with him and hence can also be spatially separated from him. . ." (Cassirer, 1955, p. 168, cited by Watkins, 1986).

Caughey (1984), a social anthropologist, has also studied the role of "imaginary social worlds," both in Western and in non-Western cultures. He did fieldwork on Fáánakker, a pacific island in Micronesia, and in the Margalla Hills of

Pakistan. When he compared these cultures to North American culture, he found that imaginal interactions are in no way restricted to non-Western cultures. His estimation was that the "real" social world of most North Americans includes between 200 and 300 people (e.g., family, acquaintances, friends, colleagues). In addition, a number of imaginal figures populate their everyday world, that can be divided into three groups: (1) media figures with whom the individual never had face-to-face contact, but with whom the individual nevertheless engages in imaginal interactions; (2) imaginal replicas of parents, friends, family members, or lovers who are treated as if they were really present; and (3) purely imaginary figures produced in dreams and fantasies. Like Watkins (1986), Caughey holds that imaginal dialogues and interactions exist side by side to real interactions (e.g., "If my wife could see me now. . .") and may or may not have a direct link with reality.

Not surprisingly, both Caughey (1984) and Watkins (1986) object to the identification of "social relationships" with only "actual social relationships." Caughey considers this conception as incomplete and actually representing "an ethnocentric projection of certain narrow assumptions in Western science" (p. 17). For the same reason he prefers to speak of an (imaginary) "social world" rather than a purely "inner world" in order to emphasize the interaction with somebody who is felt to be "there." From this perspective, there does not exist a "private" world as distinguished from a "public" world, because each world is populated with imaginal or real people.

5.1.8 Four Developmental Prerequisites for the Dialogical Self

The foregoing observations can be summarized by assuming four developmental prerequisites that precede the emergence of the dialogical self: (1) act, (2) memory, (3) imagination, and (4) language.

From birth onward mother and child interact. The child's acts have, in the first weeks of life, mainly the character of biological impulses (e.g., sucking behavior) that, however, are taken up as inputs for pseudodialogues. If the baby is approached as if he or she can converse, impulsive behavior is potentially dialogical. The same is true for the baby's first spontaneous movements. First they are undirected and unintended, but they can be treated by the parents as if the baby is orienting toward the social environment. Only later spontaneous movements develop into meaningful gestures (e.g., pointing). The child is treated as if it is able to do something which it cannot at that particular moment, but by pretending that the interaction is dialogical, the mother *makes* it dialogical in the long run. Biological impulses and movements are typically human by their dialogical potential.

By developing a *memory*, the child is able to do more than live purely in the moment. Because events are stored in memory they can influence the child's experience, even when the event remembered is not perceptually present. Memory makes it possible not only for the child to bring events of the past into the present situation, but also to contract events originating from divergent situations or scattered at different moments in time. The contraction of divergent events into one moment in time is a precondition for establishing relations among them.

Imagination provides the possibility of combining real events in such a way that new structures emerge that are not simply a copy of perceived reality. Imagination is, as we have already discussed, a typically constructive activity that uses realistic elements but combines them so that new meaning structures are produced. All products of human imaginations, from giants in fairy tales to revolutionary scientific discoveries, make use of realistic elements that are combined or transformed into something new.

The acquisition of *language* means an enormous step in the process of maturation, since it enables the child to exchange the things remembered and the products of imagination and to share them with other human beings. Moreover, the child identifies himself or herself as *I*, and has from then on a reference point available for the organization of information and knowledge about the world. By the specific combination of language and imagination, the child and the adult have the possibility to construct a narrative about the world, and a self-narrative in particular, in which other people play their roles as if they were other *I*'s. Language is indispensable for telling and understanding the stories told from these divergent positions.

5.2 Dominance in Dialogical Relations

When children have reached the stage at which they are able to talk and think about themselves, in James' terms, as *I* about *Me*, they have reached a period in which society begins, more than before, to influence and organize their world. Since the *Me* is also a "social *Me*," they are not able to think, feel, or act in isolation from the community in which they participate. They are continuously involved in dialogues in which representatives of the community (mother, father, aunt, uncle, teacher, peers) place them in particular positions (child, pupil, friend) that can vary according to the social situation the child is part of. Moreover, the child is addressed not in a neutral or abstract way, but rather in an approving or a disapproving way. He or she is a "good" child or a "bad" child, a "diligent" or a "lazy" pupil, and a friend you can "trust" or "not trust." Moreover, the child is able to transform "you are. . ." utterances from the community to "I am. . ." utterances in constructing a self-narrative. These positions, however, are not simply "copies" of the views of others, but imaginatively constructed and reconstructed in the course of development. In other words, the other's view does not determine the child's self but certainly influences it in the sense that it is taken up in a continuous process of symbolic interaction in which the child, and later the adult, "answers" to these influences.

If we define the self as a multiplicity of *I* positions, the community is not only able to address the child in a variety of social positions, but also to let the child know how these positions, and the way the child functions in them, are approved. In Mead's terms, people make use of a broad array of gestures, words, and sentences to let children know how they perceive them in the varying positions occupied. Because the children are increasingly able to "take the role of the other," they address themselves as they are addressed by others and organize, at least to some degree, the possible array of positions accordingly. This means that particular positions assume a more powerful place than others and that some of the positions become neglected or even suppressed.

In order to explore the influence of the community on the organization of the self, we will in the coming sections argue that dialogues, as they organize the contact among people, have the capacity to make some positions more dominant than others. It will be argued that dominance, as an intrinsic feature of dialogue, not only organizes but also restricts the multiplicity of possible positions in the process of socialization.

5.2.1 Power in Dialogue: Symmetrical and Asymmetrical Relationships

In a study of dialogue as the interplay of participants' initiatives and responses, Linell (1990) observed emergent patterns of symmetry versus asymmetry (or dominance). He argued that such emergent patterns can be partly understood as reproductions of culturally established and institutionally congealed provisions and constraints on communicative activities. In the tradition of authors like Bakhtin and Vygotsky, who were concerned with the reproduction of intersubjectivity in a cultural and historical perspective, Linell emphasized that meanings are not entirely constructed *ab novo* in interaction. Rather, they belong to a cultural capital inherited and invested by new actors through history. This means that the microcontext of concrete dialogical relationships cannot be understood without some concept of macroframes (organizational and ethnographic context). Every utterance has a history in preceding discourses and an embeddedness in situation and culture.

Along with Wrong (1968), Linell even holds that asymmetry exists in *each* individual act–response sequence. The speaker has a certain privilege in being able to take initiatives and display his or her view. However, in the continuous reciprocity of influence, the actors continually alternate the roles of "power holder" and "power subject" in the course of their interaction. As institutionally structured and prescribed, dialogical relationships characteristically differ in these role alternations, in that one party comes out as more dominant than the other. It is therefore instructive to study how and by whom the dialogue is driven forward in different situations. Linell (1990, p. 155) gives an example from a radio phone-in on the Swedish network, in which listeners are invited to phone the program presenter. The excerpt below is taken from a conversation between the program presenter (P) and a 10-year-old boy, the caller (C):

1. P: Are you interested in being busy working with your hands, can you do woodwork and such things?
2. C: Yes, a little.
3. P: Mm, have you ever made a bark boat?
4. C: No.
5. P: You haven't, no, but you do other things perhaps?
6. C: Yes.
7. P: What then?
8. C: Well, now that I have woodwork at school, then I have made some dice and such things, pencil stands and . . .
9. P: I see . . . , etc.

This conversation is a very asymmetrical one: The programmer asks the questions and holds the initiative, whereas the caller's role is reduced to one of responding to initiatives from the interlocutor, with a few voluntary expansions. This type of exchange seems quite typical of a child's conversation with an adult stranger. In the above interview the subordinate party, the child, does little more than what is minimally required, given the other party's questions. For a good understanding of dialogue, it is important to note that the above interview is the product of both parties, although the one takes a much more active role than the other. The program presenter certainly dominates the boy by forcing him to answer rather specific questions, but without any doubt the child's passivity also contributes to this pattern. Without the presenter's persistent questioning, the dialogue would come to a complete standstill. In other words, both parties are intercursively defining conditions for each other's contributions.

Let us now look, for the sake of comparison, at another piece of conversation, as discussed by Linell (1990, p. 151). It is taken from a casual exchange between two strangers who met at a recreation center. They have a short talk about running at a nearby running track:

1. A: How long does it take to run the 10 kilometer track?
2. B: Up to an hour. That's what it usually takes.
3. A: I see. [pause] Six minutes per kilometer.
4. B: Yes, but the kilometers are not equally long on that track.
5. A: Oh, well, the ground varies like that.
6. B: Yes, that too, but then the distances aren't equally long between the markings [i.e., kilometer markings].

In this excerpt A takes the initiative, whereas B is put under the obligation of answering. B gives a response (No. 2), although it is hardly more than a minimal one. B does not take any independent initiative of his own, which leaves A with the opportunity, and even an implicit responsibility, to accept and give some credit to B for his response ("I see"). At the same time A uses his turn to add a reflection, which displays A's understanding of B's response. In utterance No. 4, B reacts to A's interpretation in No. 3, carrying on the dialogue by taking a new initiative. B, on his turn, is not quite sure how to interpret A's remark. Accordingly, he takes a new initiative, requesting more information. B gives this and takes the opportunity to explain what he meant by his preceding remark (No. 4).

The above excerpt shows clearly how the dialogue is, in a cooperative way, brought forward by the interlocutors responding to each other and taking new initiatives. The initiative is not continuously on the part of one interlocutor, but alternates, and in this alternation the speakers contribute to a mutually constructed interpretation of the situation at hand. The second excerpt (about the jogging track) is certainly more symmetrical than the first one (the radio interview) and makes more use of the combination of the two points of view. As a consequence, the actors display their unfolding understanding of the joint discourse on a play-by-play basis. That is, understanding is not something that is necessarily "there" before verbalization. Rather, the symmetrical dialogue should be considered as a construction, even a co-construction, of the two parties involved. It is certainly not, in terms of Schegloff (1982), borne out of the speaker's forehead as the delivery of a cognitive plan.

One of Linell's (1990) purposes is to demonstrate that dominance in interaction is multidimensional. There are many ways in which a party can be said to "dominate," that is, to control the "territory" to be shared by the interactants in communication. The territory is then the jointly attended and produced discourse. There are at least four different dimensions involved in dominance in interaction: interactional dominance, topic dominance, amount of talk, and strategic moves.

As demonstrated in the two excerpts above, *interactional dominance* deals with patterns of asymmetry in terms of initiative–response structure. The dominant party is the one who makes the most initiatory moves: the contributions that strongly determine the unfolding local context. The subordinate party allows, or must allow, his or her contributions to be directed, controlled, or inhibited by the interlocutor's moves. *Topic dominance* applies if one party predominantly introduces and maintains topics and perspectives on topic. By determining the topic of a conversation, an interlocutor may achieve a high degree of dominance that may be visible not only in the content of the talk, but also in the direction that the conversation takes as a whole. The person who makes up the agenda determines not only the topics that are at the center of the attention of the interlocutors, but may also have a strong influence on the topics that are kept outside the conversation, or are even concealed (e.g., a chairman who deliberately avoids putting a particular topic on the agenda). The *amount of talk* also reflects dominance relationships. A person who talks a lot in a conversation prevents, as long as he or she talks, the other party from taking a turn. The subordinate party is especially restricted in those situations in which the dominating party requires only a "yes" or "no" answer. In a cross-interrogation a suspect may be forced to answer with only "yes" or "no." Such a restricted answering may also be the result of the high prestige or the style of questioning of the interlocutor. When, for example, Socrates wants to prove that an ignorant slave knows the thesis of Pythagoras, he asks him a series of suggestive questions that need only a short affirmation by the slave. Finally, *strategic moves* function as a special type of dominance device. It is not necessary to talk a lot in a conversation or discussion to have a strong impact on the discourse. When one says few, but strategically really important, things, the direction and the resulting insights may be heavily influenced.

Parents are in a position to use extensively the dominance aspects of the dialogue so that children do not have much opportunity to express their views themselves. Linell refers to the work of Bruner (1985), who notes that in adults' conversations with small children, "the adult serves almost as the vicarious consciousness of the child in the sense of being the only one who knows the goal of the activity the two of them are engaged in." It is quite easy for parents to "steal" the child's turn or to reformulate or correct the child's contribution. In a study of pediatric consultations in an allergy clinic, Aronsson & Rundström (1988) observed that parents routinely stepped in as the spokespersons for their children (aged 5 to 15 years). Even when the doctor addresses the child, mothers simply grasp their children's turn or come in right after, ratifying and reinforcing what the children said and explaining what they meant, implying that they could not, or did not get the opportunity, to express it properly themselves (Linell, 1990, p. 162).

5.2.2 Ventriloquation and Types of Speech Events

In a discussion of Bakhtin's contribution to a sociocultural approach, Wertsch (1990, 1991) argues that an individual speaker is not simply talking as an individual but that in his or her utterances the voices of groups and institutions are heard. Wertsch explains that, for Bakhtin, dialogicality includes, but also extends far beyond, the process whereby one speaker's concrete utterances come into contact with another speaker. Dialogue is more than face-to-face contact and interaction between individuals. Bakhtin was also concerned with the dialogic orientation among "social languages" (e.g., languages of particular groups) within a single national language (e.g., Russian, English) and among different national languages within the same culture. From the perspective of contextualism, it is relevant to note that Bakhtin made here a switch from dealing with unique speech events (i.e., individual utterances) to dealing with categories, or types of speech events (i.e., types of utterances produced by types of voices). Wertsch notes that Bakhtin provides relatively little concrete detail on how national languages enter into dialogical contact. With regard to social language, however, he was more specific. Let us follow some of Wertsch's observations.

For Bakhtin, a social language is a discourse peculiar to a specific stratum of society (e.g., age group or professional group) within a given social system at a given time. Within a single national language, there exist a multitude of social languages. This implies that national languages and social languages can, at least to some extent, vary independently of one another. Examples of social languages are social dialects, characteristic group behavior, professional jargons, languages of generations and age groups, languages of the authorities of various circles and passing fashions, and languages that serve the sociopolitical purposes of the day.

Bakhtin holds that speakers always speak in social languages when producing unique utterances, and thus social languages shape what the individual voices can say. This process of producing unique utterances, whereas at the same time the speaker is speaking a social language, involves a specific kind of multivoicedness that Bakhtin terms *ventriloquation*. With this term he meant the process in which one voice speaks through another voice or voice type as found in social language. The term *multivoicedness* (that we discussed extensively in Chapter 3) thus refers not only to the simultaneous existence of different individual voices, but also to the simultaneous existence of the voice of an individual and the voice of a group.

Although Linell's (1990) analysis of dominance, including his excerpts of talks and discussions, referred to explicit utterances with turn-taking behavior, it also applies to the more implicit manifestations of dialogue. That is, the voices of groups or institutions may, more or less, dominate individual speech acts. People, who are educated according to the articles of faith and dogmas of a particular religion, may reflect in their individual speech acts the words they have heard so often in the past. As generally known, institutionalized religions vary greatly according to the degrees of freedom they permit to their members. In traditions that have a more strict and orthodox character, individual interpretation and freedom of action are rather limited. A special case are sects with an authoritarian cult that may even assume, in Goffman's terms, the character of total institutions. In that case, the individual voice is dominated by the authority of the leader in a rather extreme way, and the freedom of individual speech may be seriously restricted.

According to Bakhtin, it can be maintained that each word that is spoken by an individual speaker is "double voiced": A word has always two directions, both toward the object of speech and toward a word originating from another person's speech. As we have seen in Wertsch's analysis of Bakhtin's work, "the other word" may also be the word of a group or an institution. Those groups and institutions may vary greatly in the extent to which they dominate the individual's word. Consequently, people's view of the world and of themselves may be more or less dominated by the voices of the groups (e.g., religious, socio-economic, racial, political, educational, etc.) to which they belong.

What are the implications of the foregoing considerations for the self? This question can only be answered if we realize that the dialogue has two main features, "intersubjective exchange" and "dominance." In their combination, these features imply that dialogue is the activity of co-construction of reality, in which at any moment in time one party is more dominant than the other. The more symmetrical the dialogue is, the more it provides opportunity for mutual influence; the more asymmetrical it is, the more it constrains the exchange of views and experiences.

In the concept of "dialogical self" the notions of intersubjective exchange and dominance as the main features of dialogical relationships are applied to the self, considered as a multiplicity of *I* positions. This means that a more or less intensive exchange between positions is supposed, with explicit attention to the relative dominance between positions. Although any rigid boundary "inside" and "outside" would be highly artificial, there are positions that function mainly in the outside world (e.g., parents, family members, friends, teachers, colleagues, judges, enemies) and positions that belong mainly to the inside world of the individual (e.g., imaginal lovers, deceased parents, wise advisors, critics, or enemies with whom the person imaginatively interacts). The inside and the outside world function as highly open systems that have intensive transactional relationships. The self, as a highly contextual phenomenon, is bound to cultural and institutional constraints. Dominance relations are not only present in the outside world but, by the intensive transactions between the two, organize also the inside world. This implies that the possible array of imaginal positions becomes not only organized but also restricted by the process of institutionalization (e.g., in family, school, church, military service, community life). Some of the possible positions are approved; others are disapproved or even rejected. An important implication is, finally, that, depending on the extent of dominance in the dialogical relationships, some positions are strongly developed, whereas others are suppressed or even dissociated.

Notes

1. Imitation can be considered as a rudimentary form of dialogue. The imitator simply replicates the form or movement of the other, as young children can do when they are answering the good-bye movements of the adult. Also the first echoing of words (e.g., *mamma, bye-bye*) is a rudimentary form of dialogue. Bakhtin's "double-

voicedness" finds its origin in echoing the words of the other. Note also that the first form of polyphonic music is the canon, in which two people or groups sing the same song but start at different moments, the second singer answering the sounds of the first one.

2. Ainsworth's distinction between the need for exploration and the need for attachment can be considered as a developmental precursor of the striving for autonomy and the longing for contact and union in adulthood (a review of studies will be presented in Chapter 9).

CHAPTER 6

Dynamics and Synthesis of the Self

It is a major achievement,
believe me, to act as one person.
Seneca (circa 65/1965, p. 516)

When the self is conceived of as a multiplicity of positions, and when, moreover, there exist dominant relationships among those positions, the question of synthesis must be posed. The mere existence of a multiplicity of positions could easily suggest a fragmented individual wandering in a jungle, moving from one position to another without any meta-view on the self as a whole. When, moreover, one of the positions in the self is very dominant, other positions that belong to the realm of possibilities of the self are neglected or even suppressed, and are, therefore, prevented from playing an active role in the synthesis of the self.

In this chapter a case study is presented as a starting point for a discussion on the dynamics of the self and the necessity of synthesis. The subject was followed for 3 weeks, a period in which she devoted herself to an intensified self-reflection which had particular implications for her behavior. The case study not only demonstrates that certain parts of the self dominate other parts, but also the importance of achieving a more symmetrical or synthesized self. The discussion following this case presentation leads us to the basic question: What exactly do we mean by the term *synthesis?* (This term can only be properly understood if the relative autonomy of the different and contrasting positions is taken seriously.)

6.1 The Case of Alice: Traits as Dynamic Characters

Alice, a 28-year-old woman working part-time as a teacher, participated in a research project on the dialogical self at the University of Nijmegen. She belonged to a group of students who cooperated in response to a presentation on the project by the first author of this book to a class of students who were engaged in a part-time training in social sciences.

6.1.1 Valuation of Past, Present, and Future

The investigator invited the subjects, each individually, to tell their self-narratives in terms of valuations of specific aspects of their own past, present, and future. The concept of *valuation* (Hermans, 1987a,b, 1988, 1992b) refers to any unit of meaning that, in the process of self-reflection, receives a positive or negative value in the eyes of the person: a precious memory, a bad experience with a teacher, a good talk with a friend, an unsolvable problem, an intriguing dream, a moral dilemma, a future goal, or an unreachable ideal. The term *valuation* is the central concept in valuation theory, that views the self as an organized process of valuation. The *process* aspect refers to the historical nature of human experience and implies a spatio–temporal orientation: The person lives in the present and is, from a specific point in space and time, oriented toward the past as well the future. The *organizational* aspect emphasizes that the person not only orients successively to different aspects of his or her spatio–temporal situation but also, through the process of self-reflection, brings these aspects into a composite whole (a valuation system). In other words, the self is conceived of as a developing narrative of personal meanings attributed to events considered as relevant in one's individual history.

In order to describe the procedure as concretely as possible, we describe Alice's case step by step. First, the investigator asked her to mention two parts of her personality that she herself saw as opposites, with one part more or less dominating the other part. Alice then described that she saw herself mainly as an "open" person and added that other people saw her as open ("friendly," "helpful," and "sociable") as well. (Note that Alice impressed the investigator as open, in her way of talking, smiling, laughing, and easiness and directness of contact.) She added, however, that there was another part, less acceptable to herself, and less visible to others, that often conflicted with her open part. This part she labeled as "my closed side."

Next, the investigator asked Alice to concentrate, successively, on her open side and on her closed side, and to tell her self-narrative, first *as an open I* and then, separately, *as a closed I*.[1] In order to evoke Alice's self-narrative, the investigator provided her with some open-ended questions (see Table 1). These questions, an integral part of the self-confrontation method (Hermans, 1987a,b, 1988), are intended to bring out important units of meaning for the past, present, and future. The questions invite subjects to reflect on their life situations in such a way that they feel free to mention those concerns that are most relevant from the perspective of the present situation. The subjects are free to interpret the questions in any way they would like. The subjects are also encouraged to phrase the valuations in their own terms in order that the formulations are as much as possible in agreement with the intended meaning. The typical form of expression is the sentence (i.e., the basic unit of text). In a sentence the

Table 1

Questions of the Self-Confrontation Method

Set 1: *The Past*

These questions are intended to guide you to some aspect of your past life that is of great importance to you.

Was there something in your past that has been of major importance or significance for your life and which still plays an important part today?

Was there, in the past, (a) person(s), an experience, or a circumstance that greatly influenced your life and still appreciably affects your present existence?

You are free to go back into the past as far as you like.

Set 2: *The Present*

This set is also composed of two questions that will lead you, after a certain amount of thinking, to formulate a response:

Is there in your present life something that is of major importance for, or exerts a great influence on, your existence?

Is there in your present life (a) person(s) or a circumstance which exerts a significant influence on you?

Set 3: *The Future*

The following questions will again be found to guide you to a response:

Do you foresee something that will be of great importance for, or of major influence on, your future life?

Do you feel that (a) certain person(s) or a circumstance will exert a great influence on your future life?

Is there a future goal or object which you expect to play an important role in your life?

You are free to look as far ahead as you wish.

---

subject brings together those events that he or she feels belong together as elements of a personal unit of meaning. Although each of the questions in Table 1 may evoke a greater number of valuations, it was decided to limit them to two for the past, two for the present, and two for the future. This was done for each *I* position, (open and closed), so that Alice produced six valuations from the position of the open *I,* and another six valuations from the position of the closed *I* (see Table 2).

Although responding to the same set of questions (Table 1), Alice constructs from the two positions two completely different sets of valuations, referring to different memories of the past, different concerns in the present, and different and even contradictory plans for the future (compare, for example, nos. 6 and 11). The valuations from the open *I* are mainly organized around her mother, indicate her familiar way of life, and represent a fairly optimistic outlook on the

Table 2

Alice's Valuations from Her Open and Her Closed Position

Valuations from the open *I*
Past
    1. My mother, open and cheerful, has always been like a friend to me.
    2. In the past many friends visited our house: everything was allowed.
Present
    3. The contact with my boyfriend: I'm always listening to him, I'm always there for him.
    4. When there are problems in our family, I'm the one who is called, because I listen and am prepared to help.
Future
    5. In the future I want to meet lots of people, get to know lots of people.
    6. In the future I want to travel together with my partner; that makes me feel free.

Valuations from the closed *I*
Past
    7. When I was 12 years old, my father left the house; I know so little about that period; I think there is much pain and sorrow during that time.
    8. I have the feeling that I have never had a father.
Present
    9. In the contact with my father I must show my limits; otherwise he completely overruns me; that makes me sad, but it is also good learning experience.
    10. My partner and I have both had a broken relationship in the past: I do not want to lose myself again in another relationship.
Future
    11. I would like very much to have children, but this is suppressed by other things (traveling, studying, work, freedom).
    12. I need rest, no musts, would like to have just once an empty agenda.

world. The valuations from the closed *I*, on the other hand, center around her father, disclose a less familiar way of life, and are associated with more negative feelings. Considered this way, the valuations are not simply "different" as the valuation systems of two unrelated people may be different. Rather, the *I*'s oppose one another, sometimes even disagreeing with each other (e.g., Nos. 6 and 11).

6.1.2 Changes in Dominance and Meaningfulness

Next, the investigator invited Alice to concentrate on the last week and rate (on a 0–9 scale) each of the 12 valuations of Table 2 according to two dimensions: (1) how *dominant* the particular valuation had been in her thinking, feeling, and action; and (2) how *meaningful* the particular valuations had been for her thinking, feeling, and action.[2] Moreover, Alice agreed that she would, at the end of each *day*, concentrate for a while on the two sets of valuations in their combination, in order to bring the two *I* positions together, and to relate them to the events of that day. At the end of the *week*, she again rated all valuations on dominance and meaningfulness, and this continued for a full 3 weeks after the self-investigation. After these 3 weeks, we received from Alice her diary (with her self-reflections at the end of each day) and four measurements on dominance and meaningfulness (the first was a baseline and the second, third, and fourth were successive measurements, each at the end of a week of intensified self-reflection). Figure 1 compares mean dominance ratings for the six valuations of the open position with mean dominance ratings for the six valuations of the closed position at four successive measurements (Times 1–4). Figure 2 shows the mean ratings for meaningfulness at the same four measurements (Times 1–4).

Figure 1 confirms the expectation that *at Time 1* the valuations of Alice's open *I* are, as a group, higher in dominance than the valuations of her closed *I*. This result, representing the baseline, was expected because Alice herself had selected the two positions as differing in dominance. The differences are in the expected direction for thinking, feeling, and acting, although the differences are largest for acting. The extremely low dominance level of the closed position for action at Time 1 suggests that Alice did not express the closed part of her self in her behavior. It suggests also that her use of the term *closed* has primarily the connotation of "closed from behavioral expression."

Following the ratings for dominance over time, we see that the closed position has an upward tendency, whereas the open position shows a clear downward tendency, with a crossing of the lines between Times 2 and 3. These tendencies

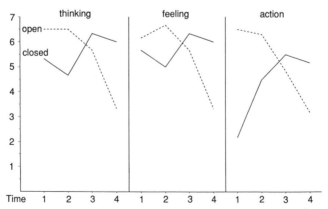

Figure 1   Dominance ratings of thinking, feeling, and action for the open and closed position at Times 1–4.

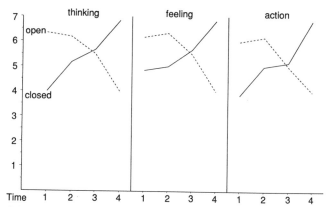

Figure 2 Meaningfulness ratings of thinking, feeling, and action for the open and closed position at Times 1–4.

and crossings are consistently found for thinking, feeling, and action. In the period of study, Alice transforms the initial dominance of her open position to successive dominance of her closed position.

The results for meaningfulness, as pictured in Fig. 2, are basically the same as for dominance. Again, we see an increase for the closed position, a decrease for the open position, and a crossing of the two lines between Times 2 and 3. At Time 1 Alice was aware that her open position was until that moment more meaningful to her than her closed position. During the process of intensified self-reflection, however, her ratings indicated that the valuations of her closed position were increasingly meaningful. At the same time, she experienced the valuations of her open position, *although they were highly meaningful at Time 1*, as decreasing in meaning over time.

6.1.3 The Phenomenon of Dominance Reversal

The apparent decrease in the ratings of the open position, both for dominance and for meaningfulness, is perhaps the most significant finding of this "exercise in dialogue." Why should Alice need this decrease in her open position? This question becomes even more relevant when we note that the valuations of her open position were generally positive valuations (see the formulations in Table 1). Moreover, the valuations of the open position were experienced as highly meaningful at Time 1. So, why decrease their meaningfulness? Why not increase the meaningfulness of her closed position *only*? In that case she would gain meaning from her increasing closed position, while at the same time *maintaining* the level of meaning of the open position, resulting in a combined increase of the two positions together that would be higher than the gain in meaningfulness that was actually achieved.

In order to understand the phenomenon of decreasing meaningfulness of a meaningful position, as found in Alice's case, we must point to the workings of the dominance feature of dialogue. This leads to the interpretation that Alice, in order to free the originally suppressed (closed) position, needs a "reactive dominance" of this position. It is as if Alice says to the closed *I* position: "Now it's your turn," with the consequence that the position that originally had the loudest voice has to hold itself back, at least temporarily. What has happened in this case can also be described as a figure–ground reversal. By transforming background to figure, one changes figure to background at the same time. In musical terms, when one hears two voices and concentrates on one of them, one pushes the other voice, deliberately or not, to the background.[3]

6.1.4 *Some of Alice's Reflections and Estimations*

At the end of the 3-week period of investigation, the results were discussed with Alice, who then permitted the investigator to read her diary. This provided additional information about the process of self-reflection over the period of 3 weeks. We present some of her own observations with reference to her thoughts, feelings, and actions:

Thoughts: ". . . I think that I sometimes flee to that side [open side] . . . Then I'm floating away from myself . . . I become aware that an important part of myself is in that closed side . . . I'm also beginning to see that when I express my vulnerable parts, I get much closer to other people, and then, it goes better with me too."

Feelings: "I've more sad moments than I used to have . . . still it feels okay, I don't put the brakes on it anymore . . . There is a norm that you may not be sad . . . my mother was my great example: Always being cheerful . . . When I can also express my closed side, I begin to feel more confident, I feel more something of a firm basis . . . when I express my closed side, I feel more calm, but there are also some guilt feelings."

Action: "I decided to visit my father for one day, as a consequence of this investigation . . . our contact was good . . . However, I must draw clear boundaries . . . till here and not farther . . . For the first since a long time, I've also phoned my brother, and asked him for advice . . . the fact that I asked him for help, whereas usually other people ask me, gives me a good feeling. Also I let people know that I have no time for hour long talks, when I am busy with something . . . I'm able to say 'no' more often, and I see that this works well. Also in my study: I used to be the first to start with things in a group . . . Now I'm holding myself back more often . . . "

Altogether, Alice's observations suggest that she is involved in a process of actively contrasting the open and closed parts of herself. Although the growing admission of her closed part is associated with sadness and feelings of guilt, she feels more confident and calm, knowing and feeling that she is involved in a process of redressing an unbalanced situation. Moreover, this self-in-process is certainly not purely an "inner" development. Rather, she takes new initiatives in the contact with significant others, both in her family situation and in study.

In order to further probe the relative autonomy of the two positions, the investigator finally asked Alice to give an estimation of the *subjective ages* of her two *I* positions. This was done by asking her how old she *feels* as an open *I* and how old as a closed *I*. Alice indicated that the age of her closed *I* felt considerably younger than that of her open *I*. She estimated the age of the closed *I* as 4 to 5 years old, whereas the open *I* felt as 35 years old (recall that her chronological age was 28).[4]

6.1.5 Theoretical Analysis of Alice's Case

Alice's case can be better understood by considering it from the perspective of several concepts and notions discussed in the foregoing chapters. Alice was invited to tell some relevant parts of her self-narrative, from the perspective of two contrasting *I* positions. In each position the *I* told as an author of a relatively autonomous world, a specific story, with different valuations of the past, present, and future. The two narratives were juxtaposed in one and the same self-investigation in such a way that their relationships and contrasts could be made visible. Moreover, the two narratives were brought into contact with her everyday situation, so that an optimal situation for dialogical contact between positions and the actual characters of her everyday life was established. In other words, the investigation was arranged in such a way that the fictive characters (open and closed *I*'s) playing a central role in her inside world were brought into contact with the real characters of her everyday situation. From that moment on, an intensified self-reflection started, and dialogical contact among the various characters was stimulated.

At the beginning of the self-investigation, the two main characters (open and closed) were quite asymmetrical in social power, with the open character more dominant. Finally, the dominance ratio was reversed in favor of the closed character. These results illustrate a phenomenon, dominance reversal, that is of peculiar relevance for the study of dialogical processes, and for the functioning of the self in particular. The phenomenon of dominance reversal points not only to the relevance of the notion of symmetry/asymmetry, but also to the very dynamic nature of the dialogical self. The activity of dialogue may reorganize the self and create a high degree of discontinuity over time. By the nature of its dialogical potential, the self is equipped to confront the "inside" characters with one another, but also, by the nature of an open transactional relationship, to confront the internal and the external characters with one another. Finally, temporal differences were spatialized by asking Alice to estimate the subjective ages of her two characters. Although they were localized in quite different periods of her life span, the characters nevertheless were juxtaposed by bringing them together in one and the same self-investigation. This bringing together of different characters, who then start to actively relate to one another, results in a self that is, in fact, a co-construction.

The presented case study also demonstrates that traits, particularly as opposites (e.g., open versus closed, active versus passive, ambitious versus lazy, serious versus playful, masculine versus feminine), can be studied as protagonists and antagonists in a dramatic narrative. As discussed in Chapter 2, traditional trait theories function as typical representatives of the root metaphor of formism. In this quality traits are thinglike features that people use to label themselves and others. When, however, traits are translated into the idiom of contextualism, and as parts of a dialogical self in particular, they function as if they are characters who have their own story to tell about their past, present, and future, and who are able to exchange information and knowledge. Conceived in this way, we are far from traditional notions of cross-situational consistency of traits and test–retest reliability. Rather, the contextualization in the form of relatively autonomous authorial positions dynamizes the self in a process of confrontation, with the phenomenon of dominance reversal as a possible result.

It is certainly not our intention to make any generalizing statements based on only one case, nor is it presumed that the phenomenon of dominance reversal can be found in every individual. Our purpose is merely to point to the *existence* of a phenomenon and to describe it as an indication of dialogical dynamics *par excellence*.

6.2 Synthesis as a Process

In Alice's case only two traits were studied, as opposed characters in a narrative. When we use the term *multiplicity*, or Bakhtin's *multivoicedness*, a greater number of possible positions is supposed. The reason that the "open" and "closed" characters were invited to speak was that these traits played a significant role in *this* period of the life of *this* person. However, even when we limit ourselves to this particular period in Alice's life, it would certainly be possible to distinguish other traits, that would perhaps also be organized in oppositional ways. The open and closed parts of Alice's self were *selected*; they certainly did not cover all of her possible positions.

The term *multiplicity* is well applicable under the assumption that the self is populated to a greater or lesser degree by different characters or can be imaginatively constructed in this way. If multiplicity is doing justice to a person's actual experiences (e.g., the existence of a multiplicity of imaginal figures) or to a person's capacity for imaginative constructions (e.g., translating traits as characters), the question of synthesis is unavoidable. Until now, we have used two terms that theoretically prevented the self from falling apart into pieces. First, the notion of *relative* autonomy of the *I* positions, and second, the notion of dialogue.

If the positions would be entirely autonomous, there would be no way to approach them as a whole. The existence and functioning of entirely autonomous characters would lead to a fragmentation of the self, as can be found in the dysfunction that is commonly called "multiple personality." There is, however, a clear distinction to be made between "multiplicity of characters" and "multiple personality." Watkins (1986) was sharply aware of this distinction when she said:

> Contrary to fearful expectation, this multiplicity of characters in an individual's experience would not resemble a pathological state of "multiple personality." In the latter there is no imaginal dialogue, only sequential monologue. The person identifies with or is taken over by various characters in a sequential fashion. The ego is most often unaware of the other voices. It is paradoxical that the illness of multiple personality is problematic precisely because of its *singleness* of voice at any one moment, not because of its multiplicity. Improvement starts when dialogue and reflection between the selves begins to happen, when there is multiplicity in a single moment of time, rather than multiplicity over time . . . [pp. 104–105]

Apart from the problem of fragmentation, there is an additional question that also emphasizes the necessity of any form of synthesis. Given a multiplicity of characters, this question may be posed this way: Who is responsible for the organization of the self as a whole and, in particular, for the reorganization of the self in the case of dominance of one of the characters? In Alice's case, for example, the open character was highly dominant at the start of the period of investigation. At the end, however, the closed character was rather dominant. What reason could the open character have to give up its relative position of dominance? As the formulation of the valuations suggested, the open character was not only open, it *wanted* to be open. Moreover, Alice got positive reactions from her environment for being such a pleasant and sociable person, from her parents, friends, and colleagues at work and school. The open character would not have many convincing reasons to give up its dominant position and share power with the rather antagonistic closed character. On the other hand, the closed character was, at the beginning of the period of investigation, in an underdog position and had not much opportunity to express itself in Alice's behavior. What could this closed character do to increase its power within the realm of the self? Given the existing power differences and the contradictory interests of the two positions, the open character would not have much reason to become more modest. Rather, it had something to lose. The closed character, on the other hand, would have the greatest difficulty becoming more dominant, simply because it lacked power to change its position. Moreover, the closed character was by its nature less sociable and, if expressed to the outside world, would probably receive less approval than the open character. (At least there would be the risk of disapproval because other people only knew Alice as an open person.)

In spite of the above considerations, we have seen in Alice's case a strong change in the form of a complete dominance reversal within a relatively brief period of time. How can we account for such a change if we cannot account for it as long as we restrict ourselves to the two characters in question? It seems that this question can only be satisfactorily answered if we assume the existence of a *third position,* that is of a different nature than the other two and plays a major role in the synthesis of the self. We will discuss the topic of synthesis in some detail because it is here that there is a risk of misunderstanding. We will treat the issue of synthesis by thinking along similar lines as Schwartz (1987) did in his paper on "multiple selves" and discuss some of his proposals for the sake of argument.

6.2.1 The Modular Brain

One of Schwartz's (1987) purposes is to demonstrate that the mind consists of parts that function in a rather autonomous way and that, given this relative independence, the notion of synthesis deserves attention as a main function of the self.

Schwartz refers to recent developments in brain research that show striking parallels with developments in the study of the self. An example is the book *The Social Brain* by Gazzaniga (1985), a scientist who was in the 1950s and 1960s engaged in investigating the different functions of the left and right brain. His later research led him to conclude that the original distinction between left and right hemisphere function was simplistic. He discovered that the brain actually consists of an undetermined number of independently functioning units or "modules" that have specialized functions (see also Fodor's 1983 view on the modularity of mind). As we go through our daily lives, different modules (for processing visual, auditory, tactile, and other information) are made accessible without these shifts becoming part of our conscious awareness or control. Our emotional life, Gazzaniga continues, is as shaped by the relationship among modules as our cognitive functioning. The life of an individual consists of a group of "modular selves," clusters of related beliefs, feelings, and expectations about the world. These modular selves, like cognitive modules, function to some degree beyond our control. A familiar experience for many people is, for example, that, in becoming sad or angry, they behave toward another person in a way that they are sure is going to make things worse, but still they are unable to stop. In these situations people may have the impression that something or someone has taken control of them.

Another work that addresses the implications of the brain's modularity is Ornstein's (1986) book *Multimind: A New Way of Looking at Human Behavior.*

Ornstein considers the mind not as a single, unified entity, but rather as diverse and complex. The mind contains different kinds of "small minds" that are temporarily employed, wheeled into consciousness, and then returned to their place after use.

Schwartz refers also to the fields of computer science and artificial intelligence, where in the original models information was stored and processed in a serial manner, that is, information was stored in one area and processed in another. Only one cluster of information could be processed at a time, and the whole worked like an assembly line in a factory. More recently, however, researchers have developed parallel computers which allow many different processors to work side by side. As part of this constellation, computers communicate with but remain largely independent of one another. Computers can jointly solve a problem by individually and simultaneously addressing separate aspects of it. Computers "think" in a way that approximates human intelligence much more than the earlier, serial computers.

The mind can even be considered as working like a society or democracy argued Hofstadter (1986), a computer scientist involved in the field of artificial intelligence. A brain with its billions of neurons resembles a community made up of smaller communities, and so on. In this hierarchy of communities, the highest-level communities, just below the level of the whole, Hofstadter calls "subselves" or "inner voices." He considers these subselves as competing facets that try to commandeer the whole.

Schwartz concludes that these developments, at the cutting edge of psychoneurology and computer science, are converging on a new, multiself view of people. He continues his review of the literature by referring to a number of developments in psychoanalysis and psychotherapy that are greatly in support of the view that the self is composed of a number of relatively independent subselves or subpersonalities. Finally he arrives at the central question: "Who runs the show?"

6.2.2 The Third Position as Metaperspective

As a family therapist, Schwartz (1987) worked with a bulimic client who could easily identify several voices that regularly participated in heated conversations with each other. One voice was highly critical of everything about her, particularly her appearance. Another voice defended her against this criticism. Another voice made her feel sad, hopeless, and helpless, and still another kept directing her to binge. Listening to these voices, the therapist became aware that, in addition to the voices that interacted with one another, there was another state of consciousness that interacted with the parts, but in a different way. When he asked, for example, "Sally, how do you like the sad part of you?" it was this special state that would answer as Sally, and it seemed to be able to achieve a perspective that was more balanced than that of the subparts. The difference was also that this special state allowed the client to take a meta-perspective: It was not at the same level as the other parts, but it represented a perspective in which some kind of overview of the parts could be achieved. Schwartz called this state the (capital) Self in order to distinguish it from the great variety of subselves. The Self offers a perspective from which one begins to see oneself as a field wherein various subselves interact. From the perspective of the Self, one does not rigidly identify with any particular participant of one's internal community, but with the interacting nature of the system itself. From a theoretical point of view it is important to note that the Self, more than the subparts, is concerned about *relationships* and not so much about one particular part of the self.

Schwartz's observations are highly similar to the observations of the investigator whose work with Alice was reported in the first part of this chapter. When Alice talked about her two characters, the open and the closed, at the end of the 3-week investigation, she did not give the impression that she completely identified with just one of them. Rather, in her answers she was "moving" from the one position to the other and moving back again, which gave the impression that she was concerned about the way the two were related to one another. The investigator also observed that he too was, while interviewing Alice, interested in her opinion from a *relative* point of view. The discussion about Alice's experiences and the study of the changes over time were at no point completely absorbed by one of the specific positions.

On the basis of the above observations, we assume with Schwartz that, in the simplified case of two positions, there is a third position possible that has the character of a metaperspective. This position is, therefore, labeled as Self and has to be distinguished from the self as the usual broader term that comprises all *I* positions that play a role of significance in the person's world. The Self can certainly be considered as an *I* position too, but it is of a special nature. It has the capacity to juxtapose and interrelate the other positions that neither apart nor in their incidental relationships can achieve any synthesis of the self as a whole.

6.2.3 Synthesis as Activity in a Field of Centripetal and Centrifugal Forces

The Self as we view it, would, however, be misunderstood, if it were considered as a metaperspective that as some kind of "observer on a mountain" permits an overview of the self as a whole. This depiction would neglect the role of the Self as a synthesizing *activity,* that is, as a continuous attempt to *make* the self a whole, despite the existence of parts that try to maintain or even to increase their relative autonomy. The nature and function of this synthesizing activity can best become understood if we discern two antagonistic forces in the self, one centrifugal, another centripetal. The centrifugal force refers to the tendency of the different parts to maintain and increase their autonomy: The lover wants to love, the critic to criticize, the artist to express, and the achiever to excel. As long as these characters are involved in their activity, they are not concerned with the strivings and longings of the other characters. Their intentions require a certain degree of autonomy. The centripetal force, however, attempts to bring these tendencies together and to create a field in which the different characters form a community. For the establishment and organization of this community, the synthesizing quality of the Self is indispensable.

The phenomenon of "dominance reversal," discussed earlier in this chapter, can only be understood as emerging from a field of centrifugal and centripetal forces. The fact that one of the positions is dominant in a particular period points to the workings of the centrifugal force. This force permits a character to achieve a rather independent position that, in satisfying its specific strivings and longings, more or less suppresses the other positions. The act of reversal, however, reducing the power of the dominating position and enforcing the power of the weaker position, is an expression of the centripetal force. What is meant by "synthesis" is, in essence, the centripetal force in the self, that can never be considered in isolation from the opposing, centrifugal force.

6.2.4 The Illusion of Final Unification

In a thorough discussion of the nature of "opposites," Guardini (1925) argues that in the case of opposites, the two opposing states are related in such a way that one is neither deduced from the other nor reduced to the other, and that they can never be fused. Given these characteristics of opposites, there can be, as long as life is organized according to oppositional characteristics or states, no *final* unification of the mind.

The issue of final unification touches a vivid controversy between Bakhtinian and Hegelian views of opposites. As Holquist (1990) explains, Bakhtin vehemently objected against the Hegelian idea that the evolution of the mind went through a fixed sequence of stages in order to result finally in the "absolute mind," in which all prior opposites were "resolved." Dialogue, Bakhtin insists, does not know such a final resolution, nor in the history of humanity, nor in the particular history of the individual. For him it is imperative that differences cannot be overcome: Separateness, simultaneity of differences, and opposites are basic conditions of existence. In Bakhtin's view of history, the criteria by which higher degrees of consciousness can be judged are not singularity and unity, as is the case with Hegel, but rather multiplicity and variety. Therefore, Bakhtin and Hegel differ greatly on the notion of progress. Hegel envisions a constantly upward-moving surge of progressive consciousness, whereas Bakhtin conceives history as a constant contest between self and other. In dialogical relationships, the tension between self and other is never resolved in any final way. This insight applies not only to the history of humanity, but also to the life of the individual person (Holquist, 1990).

In the line of Bakhtin's view, we see the Self not as a capacity to integrate the "subparts" in any final way. This point of view could rather be labeled as "the illusion of final unification," because it denies both the intrinsic separateness of dialogical positions and the existence of relative dominance. Moreover, such a final unification would result in a gross overestimation of the workings of centripetal forces and an underestimation of centrifugal forces.

6.2.5 Part–Whole Confusion

In discussing the relationship between the Self and subselves, Schwartz (1987) points to the fact that each subself has its own goals and intentions. For example, many people may have a strongly developed inner voice or thought pattern that pushes them to do their work rather than watch TV. When these people are not active, this voice becomes activated in an effort to gain their attention and motivate them with messages like "Why are you so lazy?" or "You will not amount to anything." When this part becomes extreme, it may dominate the other parts and take control of the self as a whole. Finally, this person may act, think, and feel like a type A personality. It may happen, at times, that another part directs the person's attention with the message "Stop and smell the roses," or "Take a day off." If, however, the achievement-oriented part is particularly harsh, the person may feel guilty when complying with this message and may even proceed to "shut the mouth" of the opposite part. There may at the same time be a vague feeling of sadness as a result of blocking the needs of the part of the self that wants to relax.

In the above example, the achieving character is not only dominating the others, but is also polarizing in such a way that the relaxing character is considered as somebody that is merely interfering with the plans of the active part. The character that wants to counterbalance the dominating one is merely considered an adversary, so that there is no cooperation among the two characters at all. A true cooperation is only possible if the two characters could, for example, complement one another in doing one and the same activity. Such cooperation can be found in people who are involved in a creative process and who may use moments of complete relaxation in the service of production of ideas, or for those who enjoy moments of relaxation most intensely after periods of hard working or even as a reward for it.

In the case of the type A personality, with one dominating, achieving character, the question may be posed as to how the Self is organized and if there is any synthesis at all? This question can only be answered if we assume that the Self also, in its synthesizing aspirations, can be dominated, temporarily or more constantly, by one of the characters of the self. The point is that the Self is subjected to the same centrifugal forces that also work on the other parts of the self. This means that, with the change of situation, and even under the pressing influence of the situation, one part may become so dominant that it is impossible for the Self to counterbalance this particular character.

The situation has the power to evoke a particular character in the self and can even reinforce this character so that it becomes dominant. In the interaction between self and situation there is, however, the possibility for the person to engage in some situations and not in others or to feel attracted to some people or groups more than to others, so that the preferred situations reinforce existing dominance relations in the self.

The self–situation interaction can also account for the fact that people may feel that they achieve in some situations a much greater degree of synthesis than in other situations. For example, at work a person may feel highly dependent upon others' opinion of his or her achievements and thus become increasingly involved in conforming to specific external expectations and even feel incapable of escaping these normative expectations that are felt to restrict the self as a whole. In another situation, however, the same person may achieve—often at specific times or at specific places—a considerable liberation from these norms and feel stimulated by the environment to listen to "other voices" of the self and experience the deep enjoyment (with painful shadings) of being rooted in one's center. People may, of course, greatly vary in the nature of those situations (e.g., conversing with a good friend, listening to music that is moving, wandering in nature, being immersed in writing, being "alone" late at night).

In sum, the Self represents a metaposition that is actively oriented to synthesize the self as a whole. In this process, the different characters never give up their relative autonomy and, therefore, resist any final unification. Moreover, one of the characters may, in the course of the self–situation interactions, become so dominant that even the Self is, temporarily or more permanently, under its control. In other words, the Self is always threatened by the dominant aspect of dialogue.[5]

6.2.6 Searching for a Metaphor: Conductor or Composer

In an attempt to find a metaphor, Schwartz (1987) imagines that the Self and its parts operate as a kind of orchestra in which the individual musicians are analogous to the parts and the conductor to the Self. A good conductor has a sense of the value of each instrument and the ability of each musician. The conductor is uniquely able to sense the best point in a symphony to draw out one section and to mute another. Good musicians, on the other hand, are not only able to play a melody skillfully, but also to silence their instrument at the right time. Schwartz (1987) proceeds:

> Each musician while wanting to spotlight his or her own talent or have the
> piece played in a way that emphasizes his or her section, has enough respect for the

conductor's judgement that he or she remains in the role of following the conductor yet playing as well as possible. This kind of a system is (literally) *harmonious*.

If, however, the conductor favors the strings and always emphasizes them over the brass, or if the conductor cannot keep the meta perspective of how the symphony as a whole should sound, or if he or she abdicates and stops conducting all together, the symphony will become *cacophonous* . . . [p. 31, emphases added]

However clarifying and suggestive the metaphor of the conductor may be, one may wonder if it is the metaphor that is most suited to depict the relation between Self and positions. The main objection that can be raised in the context of the dialogical self, is that the function of a conductor as described above represents a highly centralized position. The conductor is, from a central position, leading the performance and his or her movements are giving directions to the individual musicians. The function of the conductor, as depicted above, seems particularly incompatible with the "retreat of the omniscient narrator," as discussed in Chapter 4, in the broader context of the decentralization of the self. The analog with the conductor is certainly doing justice to the metaposition of the Self, but insufficiently acknowledges that particular positions may not only influence the Self, but may even alter it. Such positions may take initiatives that are, certainly in early stages of development, not under the control of the Self, although the Self may be enriched by these initiatives. In short, the conductor of the symphony orchestra provides a metaphor that emphasizes the centripetal forces more than the centrifugal.

In the light of the above considerations, we propose that the Self can be better compared with a composer than with a conductor. In particular, we have in mind a composer of contemporary music who invents new music by letting himself or herself be inspired by a vast array of sounds, intonation of voices, folk melodies, visual impressions, music from other composers, music from previous eras, other styles, etc. A typical example of someone who brings together highly different and contrasting styles in one and the same musical work is the Russian composer Alfred Schnittke (born in 1934), who enjoys a growing recognition in the West. One of the most spectacular features of this composer is the fact that he brings together musical traditions that are perceived as completely different and contrasting in many respects. He combines, among others, tonal and atonal music, classical music and jazz, and he incorporates particular melodic structures from, for example, Beethoven or Mozart. He develops these musical forms into more complex, amelodic structures of a more contemporary kind. He can be considered a typical twentieth century composer who has practiced modern styles as dodecaphony and seriality, yet they do not prevent him from including the popular tunes of a brass band in one and the same composition. An important feature of his music is its unpredictability and discontinuity. In a recent interview he spoke of his first symphony:

It includes, for example, very long, hard agressive variations on the Dies Irae. In the beginning it is not very clear that this variation principle is at work. Later the variations gain in clarity, they become the framework for a twelve-tone series. When, finally, these Dies Irae tones can be heard very clearly, I suddenly select two tones from it that incidentally resemble a popular hit, the hit appears, the total construction falls down, and banality is ruling—something that is even not very inapplicable because Dies Irae and devilish banality are closely related. [Van Rossum, 1992, p. 38][6]

A composition in which disparate elements are brought together is certainly not a musical construction that only includes "harmonious" constructions (see preceding citation from Schwartz, 1987). On the contrary, disharmonic structures are essential elements that bring the composer's intention to full expression. There is an additional reason that Schnittke's work is at odds with the conception of the traditional classical symphony. When disparate or divergent musical elements sound simultaneously or are in a phase of transition, the music as a whole gives, at times, the impression of a cacophony. Such a cacophony is, again, the intended result of a juxtaposition of heterogeneous musical material. This juxtaposition leads much of twentieth century music to depart from traditional notions of coherence and continuity, giving way to structures that incorporate incoherence and discontinuity.

To put it another way, the relation between composer and music is not different from that between writer and book. The scientist, for example, who is writing a book never does this in complete "social" isolation. He or she has read, or is reading during the writing process, a host of other authors or has discussions with interested colleagues. The writer reacts, answers, agrees, and disagrees with these colleague thinkers who, on their turn, may answer questions that the writer is posing. They may even present *new* thoughts and ideas that the writer has not asked for but that inspire him to continue his search in new directions. At times the colleague authors may bring in such a multitude of divergent and conflicting thoughts and ideas that the whole scene becomes chaotic and "sounds like a cacophony." As many authors know, these moments of chaos are particularly productive, because they may open unexpected realms of thought. It is at these moments that the synthesizing capacities of the writer are challenged to the utmost.

6.2.7 Some Conceptual Distinctions

In summary, there are two reasons why the relation between composer and music is a better analogy for the relation between self and parts than the relation between conductor and orchestra. First, the composer allows himself or herself to become inspired by other composers and voices who may take initiatives in bringing new musical material. In so far as the composer listens to these voices, he or she takes a decentralized position. Second, the (contemporary) composer combines a great heterogeneity of musical material in one and the same composition, so that in juxtaposing this material, new musical structures are produced and unexpected relationships emerge.

The relevance of the notion of decentralization, that led us to question the metaphor of the conductor, is also reason to prefer the notion of "position" over the terms *subselves* or *subpersonalities*. Such terms suggest a hierarchical organization that supposes the existence of some superstructure that is "above" the multitude of subselves. As we have argued in the previous chapter, the self is a dialogical phenomenon that works according to the principles of intersubjective exchange and dominance. There are dominance relationships not only among the different positions, but also among the positions and the (synthesizing) Self. This implies that at times the Self may be dominated by one or more of the specific positions. In that case the dominating "subself" is, from a perspective of power, not "under" (sub), but "above" (supra) the Self. Therefore, it seems, in a dialogical view, better to consider the Self as a (special) position, that is, in principle, able to juxtapose the other positions and place them in a particular structure. This conception places the Self in the middle of a highly dynamic field of criss-cross dialogical relationships among possible positions, subjected to influences from all sides. This highly dynamic field of energy, that is continuously dependent on expected and unexpected changes in the situation, leads us to reject the existence of any final unification. Therefore, it is more reasonable to conceive of a *synthesizing activity* in which the struggling individual is continuously involved than of a (final) *synthesis* that may suggest the achievement of an end state.

The notion of dominance may also create a misunderstanding if it is solely interpreted in a negative way. Although it may sound negative, it is, from a conceptual point of view, certainly not something "undesirable." First of all, turn taking, as an intrinsic aspect of dialogue, requires a temporary dominance of one voice in order to make exchange possible. Second, a position, in the form of a speaking character, may only let its voice hear when it has the opportunity to take a turn. This turn taking applies not only to short-term conversations, but also, as we have seen in the case of Alice, over a longer period of time. A character that has been denied a voice for a long time may take the chance to temporarily dominate the scene in order to fully express itself. Moreover, the Self may agree and even foster such a temporary dominance in order to express and balance the possibilities of the self as a whole.

6.3 Self as a Nonlinear System

The dynamic quality of the self as a whole, and of the synthesizing Self in particular, can be further clarified by describing it as a nonlinear system. As

Schwalbe (1991) has recently argued, nonlinearity is a key term for understanding the activity of self-organization.

Nonlinear dynamical systems, Schwalbe explains, are not the closed systems of interacting that are the concern of Newtonian mechanics. Rather, these systems are open to their environment and act iteratively on their own output. Studies of such systems in physics and other branches of science led to the development of what has been called the self-organization paradigm (e.g., Jantsch, 1980; Prigogine & Stengers, 1984). The paradigmatic shift here is the view of structural features of open systems as manifestations of the tendency of matter to self-organize when it is caught up in an energy flux. The stability of such systems is manifested in what have been called "dissipative structures," "process structures," "dynamic regimes," and "dynamic patterns," terms that have in common that they capture stability in process terms. They are synonymous for temporally enduring configurations of matter sustained by the flow of energy through a dynamical system. Examples of such stable dynamic states are the pattern of vortices in a turbulent stream, the flame of a candle, or a human body.

The nonlinearity of dynamical systems is described by Schwalbe (1991) as follows:

> Such systems operate iteratively on the information they generate and recapture, and are able to recapture information through *multiple, simultaneous* feedback channels. What this means is that small fluctuations in energy flows through one part of the system can sometimes be radically self-amplifying such that discontinuous changes in system states occur. This characteristic also produces the phenomenon known as the butterfly effect . . .
>
> The butterfly effect is a shorthand term for the idea that the outcome states of nonlinear dynamical systems are sensitively dependent on initial conditions. The term derives from the suggestion that since weather is the result of the operation of a nonlinear dynamical system, it might be dramatically affected by a small perturbation, such as the flapping of a butterfly's wings. The fascinating implication of this feature of nonlinear dynamical systems is that even though such systems operate deterministically, their outcome states are *not predictable*. [p. 275, emphases added]

So far nonlinearity is applicable on physical processes like the weather. Living organisms, however, are a special case in that they can be described as selective systems. Such systems have the capacity to incorporate special feedback mechanisms that function as internal channels of information flow. Via these channels, the system can react to the effects of its own action. Feedback mechanisms are also used for recapturing some of the information it produces. They selectively reduce and amplify information in such a way that the stability of the system is preserved. Selective systems have thus the special capacity to be indefinitely self-renewing (or "autopoetic"), as long as they remain open to their environments and the flow of energy through them stays within critical limits.

In describing the genesis of the self in selective systems terms, Schwalbe emphasizes the role of what he calls "imagery." Once infants have developed the brain architecture to enable memory, he explains, they begin forming internal representations of elements of the external world. The information captured in this form can now begin to functionally substitute elements from the world. As soon as imagery is formed, infants can use this capacity to create information in the form of stabilized patterns of energy dissipation. Imagery thus creates a new kind of feedback channel enabling the brain to regulate and maintain a regular pattern of information flow within itself.

Imagery also increases organization by linking distinct rhythms of energy dissipation. An important feature of imagery is that it can represent more than one aspect of an object. It can "answer to" more than one simple impulse. One may, for example, imagine the face of an old friend, the smell of a hospital, or the sound of an auto crash. Each of these images probably evokes more than one response. In fact, one word evokes in the imagery a multiple response. In Schwalbe's (1991) terms: ". . . imagery synthesizes rhythms of energy dissipa- tion into meta-rhythms and thus further complexifies the self" (p. 283).

The significance of imagery, Schwalbe continues, is that it renders possible the emergence of an autonomous consciousness capable of sustaining its own development. When imagery evokes elements of the world and combines them into new configurations, this can give rise to new experiences. The very pres- ence of information, selected and combined in the form of imagery, thus en- genders further self-organization. In short, imagery is an essential capacity for understanding the functioning of the self as a nonlinear, selective system.

Although Schwalbe does not explicitly deal with the notion of dialogue and self-narrative, his treatment of the self as a nonlinear system and the role of imagination contribute significantly to the understanding of self-organization. In the course of development, a child "selects" particular information from the outside world and, by the act of imagination, forms a number of positions. This imaginative capacity is combined with an impressive acquisition of language, and this combination enables both external and internal communication among I positions. These positions are synthesized in a metaposition in which the diversity of the specific positions is juxtaposed in such a way that processes are stimulated that can be described in terms of nonlinearity. By concentrating on a diversity of often opposing and conflicting positions, the Self becomes a center of "dialogical juxtaposition," that is, in the high density of dialogical positions, "combined forces" emerge that give the self, as a whole, its self-renewing vital- ity. In accordance with the nonlinearity of such a system, the meaning structures (such as self-narratives and valuation processes) are to a large degree unpredict- able.

Notes

1. In giving the instructions the interviewer encouraged Alice to think and feel as an open *I* and as a closed *I*, respectively. The interviewer also asked whether Alice felt able to make a clear transition from the open to the closed position. Such a transition deserves great care by the investigator, because the dominant position (the open *I*) may prevent the suppressed position (the closed *I*) from speaking freely.

2. In order to reduce ambiguity about the terms, *dominance* was specified in the instruction as "the influence a particular valuation has on your thinking, feeling, or action, such that it dominates other thoughts, feelings, and actions." The term *meaningfulness* was specified as "the meaning and sense a particular valuation has to your thinking, feeling, or action, such that it contributes to the quality of your life."

3. Holquist (1990) considers the figure–ground relation as central to dialogism: "Dialogism, like relativity, takes it for granted that nothing can be perceived except against the perspective of something else: Dialogism's master assumption is that there is no figure without a ground. The mind is structured so that the world is always perceived according to this contrast" (pp. 21–22).

4. One and the same person may experience a different age in the quality of one character than in the quality of another. As far as people construe themselves as characters, they do not *feel* necessarily in agreement with their actual age, but sometimes considerably younger or older (for the difference between chronological and subjective age see Barnes-Farrell & Piotrowski, 1989, and Montepare & Lachman, 1989).

5. What we mean by the colloquial expression "strong personality" can be described as a Self that is rooted in a center, a core Self, that provides a certainty and conviction of direction that makes one less dependable on the incidental fluctuations in the self–situation interactions. This core Self can only be established after a learning process in which the person is involved in a series of centrifugal and centripetal forces. This view implies that the integrative capacity of the Self shows considerable differences between people and within one and the same person over time. Adolescence, for example, is the typical developmental period in which centrifugal forces clearly dominate, manifesting themselves in a great diversity of positions that, often unrelated and fragmented, create a great deal of discontinuity. In middle age, however, centripetal forces may be strengthened to a considerable degree if the person, in the transition between adulthood and old age, seeks to develop a core Self in which a great variety of contrasting positions become related and become relative autonomous parts of a synthesizing whole. From another angle, this synthesizing whole is emphasized by Jung (1959) with his concept of "individuation."

6. Picasso once described a painting as "a sum of destructions." This statement inspired Spencer (1971) to describe twentieth century poetry in similar terms: "Like a cubist canvas, such poetry breaks down the elements of an experience in order to create a new synthesis and so represent it more truly" (p. 157). In a similar vein, one could say that Schnittke is breaking down the elements of existing music in order to create a new musical synthesis.

CHAPTER 7

Self and Society: A Reexamination of Mead

One of the most cited books in the field of the self is George Herbert Mead's *Mind, Self, and Society* (1934), which over the years has served as a fertile soil for students working in the tradition of symbolic interactionism. The book certainly deserves its status as a classic in social sciences, as it not only addresses some fundamental problems in the relation between self and society, but also functions as an impetus for further theorizing on the junction of psychology and sociology.

In this chapter we will explore the relation between self and society by taking what has been generally considered Mead's most central concept, the "generalized other," as a starting point for further analysis. Our primary question will be: To what extent is Mead's view "dialogical"? More specifically, we will examine Mead's insights on the two features that we have assumed to be the main constituents of the dialogical self: "intersubjective exchange" and "dominance." This then will lead to a conceptualization of the dialogical self in relation to society beyond some of the limits of Meadian thinking. Because our theoretical proposal profits highly from a critical reading of Mead, we will refer frequently to his thoughts.

7.1 The Generalized Other: Internalization versus Exchange

Mead (1934) was very interested in the genesis of the self and considered it as a product of development: ". . . it is not initially there, at birth, but arises in the process of social experience and activity, that is, develops in the given individual as a result of his relations to that process as a whole and to other individuals within that process" (p. 135). Building on James, Mead took the distinction between "self as subject" and "self as object" as a starting point for his analyses. The word *self* is a reflexive, indicating that it can be both subject and object. That is, the self as a subject can take itself as an object. Essential for Mead is that

102

the individual as a subject knows himself or herself as an object, not directly but indirectly: ". . . from the particular standpoints of other individual members of the same social group, or from the generalized standpoint of the social group as a whole to which he belongs" (1934, p. 138). Individuals become objects to themselves only by taking the attitudes of other people toward themselves within a social context. Communication is only possible if individuals are able to become objects to themselves. Mead does not mean communication in the sense of "the cluck of the hen to the chickens" (p. 139), but communication in the sense of significant symbols (gestures and language) directed not only to others but also to the individual himself or herself.

7.1.1 Play and Game

The genesis of the self goes through two stages in childhood development: play and game. In the *play stage,* children learn to take the attitude of particular others toward themselves. Mead emphasizes that children, playing the role of the parent, teacher, or policeman, address themselves as a parent or a teacher and arrest themselves as a policeman. This means that the children have a certain set of stimuli available which call out in the children themselves the responses that these stimuli would call out in others. Play, thus, represents the simplest form of being another to the self: "The child says something in one character and responds in another character, and then his responding in another character is a stimulus to himself in the first character, and so the conversation goes on" (1934, p. 151).

The fact that Mead speaks of "characters" that respond to one another makes him sensitive to imaginal processes in play. Speaking of the "invisible, imaginary companions which a good many children produce in their own experience," he explains:

> They [the children] organize in this way the responses which they call out in other persons and call out also in themselves. Of course, this playing with an imaginary companion is only a peculiarly interesting phase of ordinary play. Play in this sense, especially the stage which precedes the organized games, is a play at something. A child plays at being a mother, at being a teacher, at being a policeman; that is, it is taking different roles . . . " [1934, p. 150]

The play stage represents an important step in the development of children in taking the attitude of significant others toward themselves. They lack, however, in this stage a more generalized and organized sense of themselves. Therefore, the *game stage* is required to develop a self in the full sense of the term. Whereas in the play stage children take the role of discrete others, in the game stage they are required to take the role of *everyone* else involved in the same game. Moreover, game situations typically include different roles that have a definite relationship with one another. Playing a game requires the participants to be able to take all the roles that constitute the game. Even in a simple game such as "hide and seek" a child must be able to alternate the roles of "hunter" and "hider" and to know these roles in their mutual relationship. A more complicated game situation is provided in Mead's famous example of baseball:

> But in a game where a number of individuals are involved, then the child taking one role must be ready to take the role of everyone else. If he gets in a ball nine [baseball] he must have the responses of each position involved in his own position. He must know what everyone else is going to do in order to carry out his own play. He has to take all of these roles. They do not all have to be present in consciousness at the same time, but at some moments he has to have three or four individuals present in his own attitude, such as the one who is going to throw the ball, the one who is going to catch it, and so on. These responses must be, in some degree, present in his own makeup. In the game, then, there is a set of responses of such others so organized that the attitude of one calls out the appropriate attitudes of the other. [1934, p. 151]

The organization of responses is put in the form of the rules of the game, rules that are absent in play. Whereas in the play stage children respond to the immediate stimuli that come to them, in the game stage these responses are organized in such a way that the different roles are parts of a patterned whole. Only in the game stage the child learns to develop a "whole self" and the organized set of roles is, in Mead's (1934) view, essential to "self-consciousness in the full sense of the term" (p. 152).

7.1.2 The Generalized Other: Singular or Multiple?

The game stage yields one of Mead's most widely known concepts, the *generalized other*. With this term he refers to the organized community or social group which gives an individual a "unity of self." The attitude of the generalized other is the attitude of the entire community. In the example of the baseball game, it was the attitude of the entire team. For a proper understanding of Mead, it must be noted that the community or the team becomes represented *in* the self: ". . . in the case of such a social group as a ball team, the team is the generalized other in so far as it enters—as an organized process or social activity—into the experience of any one of the individual members of it" (1934, p. 154). In this way the social process of the community enters the individual's thinking. Abstract thought is only possible by taking the attitude of the generalized other: "Only by taking the attitude of the generalized other toward himself . . . can thinking—or the internalized conversation of gestures which constitutes thinking—occur" (1934, p. 156). Taking the role of the generalized other rather than that of individual others allows for the possibility of abstract thinking and objectivity. In other words, in order to have a fully developed self, one must be a member of a community and be directed by the attitudes *common* to that community. Whereas play requires only pieces of selves, the game requires a coherent self (cf. Ritzer, 1992).

The preceding discussion might lead us to believe that Mead's actors are little more than conformists and that there is little room for individuality, as everyone seems to conform to the expectations of the generalized other. But, as Ritzer (1992) explains, Mead is clear that each self is different from all others. Although the selves of different people share a common structure, each self receives a unique biographical articulation: "There are parts of the self which exist only for the self in relationship to itself. We divide ourselves up in all sorts of different selves with reference to our acquaintances. We discuss politics with one and religion with another" (Mead, 1934, p. 142). Moreover, it is clear that there is not simply one generalized other, but many generalized others, because there are many groups in society. People, therefore, have multiple generalized others and, consequently, multiple selves. The fact that each person has a unique set of selves makes him or her different from anyone else.[1]

7.1.3 Dialogical versus Monological Acts

Recently, Taylor (1991) made a conceptual distinction that may be helpful in exploring to what extent Mead's theory was truly dialogical, that is, the distinction between "dialogical acts" and "monological acts." From the viewpoint of traditional epistomology, Taylor observes that acts are typically monological, in the sense that they are seen as emanating from separate individuals. Although these individuals may coordinate their acts with those of others, this does not deny the fact that, traditionally, acts are perceived as originating from discrete people. However, this notion of coordination fails to capture the way in which many actions require and sustain an agent who is part of an ongoing *inter*action. Taylor gives the examples of two people sawing a log with a two-handed saw or of a couple dancing. An important feature of such actions is a mutually sustained rhythm. Every gesture has a certain flow. When one loses this flow, as occasionally happens, acts become inept and inefficient. In these cases of sawing a log or ballroom dancing, it is crucial for the rhythm that it be shared. This can only happen when we are able to place ourselves in a common rhythm in which our component actions are taken up.[2]

Taylor emphasizes that sawing and dancing are paradigm cases of dialogical actions. There is frequently a dialogical level to actions that otherwise seems to be merely coordinated. A good example is a conversation. Conversations, particularly those with some degree of ease and intimacy, move beyond mere coordination and have a common rhythm. The interlocutor does not only listen but typically participates with head nodding and "unh-hunh." When the interlocutors take turns, roles are reversed and the common movement continues. The atmosphere of conviviality is thinned in the case of the bore or the compulsive, because he or she is impervious to this rhythm.

An action is dialogical, in Taylor's sense, when it is effected by an agent integrated in some social whole. Actions of this kind depend on "the sharing of agency." Taylor (1991) continues to demonstrate that actions of shared understanding are not necessarily restricted to face-to-face encounters. In a different form they can also constitute, for example, a political or religious movement, whose members may be widely scattered but who coordinate their actions by a sense of common purpose. The students in TienAnMen Square, for example, were related in this way with colleagues back on the campus and with people in town. These kinds of actions, that exist in a host of other forms, indicate that we cannot understand human life merely in terms of individual subjects, "because a great deal of human action happens only insofar as the agent understands and constitutes himself or herself as integrally part of a 'we'" (Taylor, 1991, p. 311). Our selves are never simply defined in terms of individual properties. Rather, we define ourselves partly in terms of what we accept as our appropriate place within dialogical actions, not only in face-to-face interactions but also as parts of larger social units.

Taylor (1991) then proceeds by arguing that his notion of dialogue (described above) is quite different from Mead's conceptions. Central in Mead's view is that a self can only be developed when the individual adopts the stance of the other toward himself or herself. In essence, this is a theory of *internalization*. The self is socially constituted through introjecting the attitudes of others. Mead (1934) holds that the self reaches its full development in the game stage, in which the self reflects the attitudes of the social group:

> I have pointed out, then, that there are two general stages in the full development of the self. At the first of these stages [play], the individual's self is constituted simply by an organization of the particular attitudes of other individuals toward himself and toward one another in the specific social acts in which he participates with them. But at the second stage [game] in the full development of the individual's self that self is constituted not only by an organization of these particular individual attitudes, but also by an organization of the social attitudes of the generalized other or the social group as a whole to which he belongs. *These social or group attitudes are brought within the individual's field of direct experience, and are included as elements in the structure or constitution of his self* . . . [p. 158, emphasis added]

Mead's central notion "taking the attitude of the other" is certainly an important theoretical step. Being able to take the attitude of another enables the child to overcome what Piaget calls "egocentricity," but it is only part of a dialogical self. As Taylor (1991) argues, the self neither preexists all conversation, as in traditional (individualistic) monological view, nor does it arise from an internalization of the interlocutor. It arises, rather, within conversation, in which two or more parties take initiatives in giving form to dialogical processes in mutual ways.

Taylor (1991) criticizes Mead for having no place in his scheme for dialogical action and adds that Mead's scheme cannot include this because his "impoverished behavioral ontology allows only for organisms reacting to environments" (p. 313). Taking the stance of another is, in this context, another monological act, "one that is causally influenced by or at best coordinated with the other." In other words, Taylor holds that Mead's sticking to a theory of internalization results in a conception of the self that is not dialogical, but rather a special form of individualism. This is particularly so in the assumption that an organism is reacting to the other as an internalized stimulus. When this is true, we should conclude that Mead is in this respect perfectly in agreement with the behaviorist tradition of his time and that he is doing justice to the subtitle *From the Standpoint of a Social Behaviorist* added to his main title, *Mind, Self, and Society*. However, before we draw such a far-reaching conclusion, it is necessary to go into another central discussion, his distinction between *I* and *Me*, that directly bears on this notion of internalization.

7.1.4 The I–Me Distinction and the Problem of Intentionality

Mead was well aware of the problems that were raised when he would have limited the social process to the internalization of the attitude of the other within the self. Had he done so, the self would simply be a copy of external social roles and not more than a reflection of social institutions. Individuals would be only conforming to social rules and prescriptions and would have no initiatives from themselves. In that case individuals would not be more than "slaves of customs" and there would be no innovations that would bring social changes and renew institutions. Being aware of this problem, Mead (1934) introduced the distinction between *I* and *Me*:

> I have been undertaking to distinguish between the "I" and the "me" as different phases of the self, the "me" answering to the organized attitudes of the others which we definitely assume and which determine consequently our own conduct so far as it is of a self-conscious character. Now the "me" may be regarded as giving the form of the "I." The novelty comes in the action of the "I," but the structure, the form of the self is one which is conventional. [p. 209]

In other words, the social rules and conventions of the generalized other are placed in the *Me*, whereas innovation derives from the *I*. Mead gives the example of artists who are supposed to break away from convention. It is not that such artists are complete "outsiders." They also accept certain rules of expression, as can be seen in the case of the Greek artists who were, at the same time, the supreme artisans in their society. Yet these artists introduced an originality that made their contribution unconventional. They brought something that was "not in the structure of the 'me'" (p. 210).[3]

The *I–Me* distinction gives Mead (1934) the opportunity to emphasize that not only the *Me* but also the *I* functions as a source of values. The values of the *Me* are those that belong to the group: "The 'me' is essentially a member of a social group and represents, therefore, the value of the group, that sort of experience which the group makes possible" (p. 214). The values of the *I* are found "in the immediate attitude of the artist, the inventor, the scientist in his discovery, in general in the action of the 'I' which cannot be calculated and which involves a reconstruction of the society, and so of the 'me' which belongs to that society" (Mead, 1934, p. 214).

At other times the *I* is described as "impulsive." It is here that Mead's *I–Me* distinction comes close to Freudian notions of impulses and their moral control. Mead is very explicit about this:

> This same emphasis also appears in certain types of conduct which are impulsive. Impulsive conduct is uncontrolled conduct. The structure of the "me" does not there determine the expression of the "I." If we use a Freudian expression, the "me" is in a certain sense a censor. It determines the sort of expression which can take place, sets the stage, and gives the cue. In the case of impulsive conduct this structure of the "me" involved in the situation does not furnish to any such degree this control. Take the situation of self-assertion where the self simply asserts itself over against others, and suppose that the emotional stress is such that the forms of polite society in the performance of legitimate conduct are overthrown, so that the person expresses himself violently. There the "me" is determined by the situation. There are certain recognized fields within which an individual can assert himself, certain rights which he has within these limits. But let the stress become too great, these limits are not observed, and an individual asserts himself in perhaps a violent fashion. Then the "I" is the dominant element over against the "me." [1934, p. 210]

In this quotation, it becomes particularly evident that Mead adheres to a theory of internalization in which the *Me* functions on the basis of introjected moral standards, not very different from psychoanalytic thinking. As we have seen in Chapter 3, the psychoanalytic relations theorists also adhere to the notion of internalization. An important feature of these theorists is that significant others (e.g., the father, the mother) are internalized but, once internalized, they become relatively stable objects that structure experience and guide behavior. As Schwartz (1987) has observed, such internalized objects have no voice, that is, once internalized they function more as stabilized internal standards than as "persons" with whom the individual can entertain dialogical relationships on the basis of mutual exchange.

7.1.5 The I as a "Historical Figure"

Taylor (1991), in his criticism of Mead's theory as nondialogical, is aware that the *I* brings innovative impulses into a society that otherwise would be completely stabilized on the basis of rigid conventions. He also points to the impulsive tendencies of the *I*. However, he observes that Mead's *I* does not have an articulated nature of its own that one can grasp *prior* to action. Here we come to another feature of the *I* that perhaps functions as the main stumbling block for a dialogical theory that transcends the limits of internalization. The problem, in fact, is that the *I* appears only in memory, that is, only *after* it has been active in experience:

> The "I" is the response of the individual to the attitude of the community as this appears in his own experience. His response to that organized attitude in turn changes it. As we have pointed out, this is a change which is not present in his own experience until after it takes place. The "I" appears in our experience in memory. It is only after we have acted that we know what we have done; it is only after we have spoken that we know what we have said. [Mead, 1934, p. 196; for a similar text see p. 203]

The fact that Mead conceives the *I* as knowledgeable only in memories of the past and not in the present and future reduces it to a purely "historical figure" with whom no actual dialogue is possible. This conceptual problem becomes evident when one realizes that people involved in dialogical relations are intentional beings with their purposes and plans, who function with their interlocutors as "co-constructors" of reality. It must be admitted that Mead escapes the objection of conformism and convention by assuming an *I* that is purely "reactive" to the generalized other, in that it is impulsive and introduces innovation. However, the constructive potentials of the *I* are seriously limited by the fact that the *I*, as reduced to memory, is incapable of any intentional and purposeful behavior. Perhaps this is not a surprising conclusion, given that Mead as a social philosopher was more interested in the functioning of the self as part of the society than in the creative potentials of the individual. The essence for him was the *Me* as the generalized other, not the *I*: "I have argued that the self appears in experience essentially as a "me" with the organization of the community to which it belongs" (Mead, 1934, p. 200).

Ritzer (1992), in his discussion of Mead's work as a whole, formulates the conceptual problem of the *I–Me* distinction in a delicate way when he says that the introduction of the *I* gives Mead's theoretical system "some much-needed dynamism and creativity. Without it, Mead's actors would be totally dominated by external and internal controls" (p. 345). However, Ritzer (1992) continues to draw a conclusion that seems to be an overstatement in the light of our previous analyses: "With it, Mead is able to deal with the changes brought about not only by the great figures in history (for example, Einstein) but also by individuals on a day-to-day basis. It is the 'I' that makes these changes possible" (p. 345). The critical question that arises here is: How can great figures change society and how can ordinary people give form to their social environment, when they—as *I*'s, including their own thoughts, ideals, and purposes—are knowledgeable only in the past? It is like saying "I know what I have done in the past, but I do not know what I want to do in the future." In other words, Mead's theory runs into conceptual problems when he accounts for innovation by introducing the *I* while impoverishing its intentional capacities at the same time.

So far we have explored Mead's work from the perspective of an "intersubjective exchange of voices" and conclude that Mead's theoretical view is in this sense not dialogical. At least two features prevent his system from being dialogical: (1) The *Me* or generalized other is conceived in terms of internalization and, as a consequence, cannot function as a relatively autonomous position or creative voice in the self; and (2) the functioning of the *I* is seriously reduced because it lacks intentionality and purpose and, therefore, cannot play a role as an original author with an own view of the world. Before we explore the theoretical implications of this conclusion, we will first examine Mead's theory from the second main feature of dialogue, the notion of dominance.

7.2 Mead's Countertheory on Dominance

In his critical discussion of Mead's work, Gregg (1991) convincingly argued that Mead did not present a fully integrated system of thinking but actually outlined two very different models of the self. Moreover, Gregg demonstrated that it is the tension between the two models that proves critical to continued reflection about the relation between self and society. One model emphasized the society as based on unity and rationality, the other referred to the existence of dominance in social relations as an expression of more irrational human forces. In the following section we will, keeping close to Gregg's analysis, elucidate the difference between the two models.

7.2.1 Society as a System of Unity

In order to understand Mead's generalized other more fully, it is important to note that this concept is a cornerstone in Mead's thinking about rationality and objectivity:

> . . . it is necessary to rational conduct that the individual should thus take an objective, impersonal attitude toward himself, that he should become an object to himself . . . and he becomes an object to himself only by taking the attitudes of other individuals toward himself within a social environment . . . [1934, p. 138]

The generalized other, responsible for rational conduct and able to take an objective stance, brings unity in the self.[4] However, how can such unity be achieved in a self that is a multiple self as a consequence of multiple group membership? Mead finds this unity by referring to the unity of the society as a whole: "The unity and structure of the complete self reflects the unity and structure of the social process as a whole . . . " (1934, p. 144). Going through the stages of play and game, children internalize the whole abstract system of social positions and rules. As adults, finally, individuals are capable of taking the attitude of the community as a whole: "The attitude of the generalized other is the attitude of the whole community" (Mead, 1934, p. 154). The integration of an adult's multiple selves can only come from the generalized other:

> A person is a personality because he belongs to a community, because he takes over the institutions of that community into his own conduct . . . The structure, than, on which the self is built is this response which is common to all, for one has to be a member of a community to be a self. Such responses are abstract attitudes . . . [Mead, 1934, p. 162]

In essence, the community membership works as an extension and elaboration of the game process. The map of rules and institutions, coordinating differentiated social subgroups into a cooperating whole, provides, at the same time, the map for the integration of multiple selves. This social structure indicates how similar Mead's generalized other is to Rousseau's "General Will" in reconciling potentially opposed individual interests in a common good: "Unsocialized, the individual would founder in irrational selfishness; partially socialized, he would founder in the multiplicity of fragmentary selves; fully socialized, he becomes rational and moral, and the interests of his multiple selves are consolidated into a superordinate self-interest, which in its turn has been coordinated with the interests of all" (Gregg, 1991, p. 185). (For a discussion of Rousseau's *Social Contract*, see also Mead, 1934, pp. 286–287.)

It is noteworthy that Mead is very interested in a comparison of primitive and civilized societies, given that they differ from the perspective of the generalized other. More specifically, he compares the primitive's conception of the "double" with children's imaginary playmate (1934, p. 140) and considers them *both* as lower forms of self-development in preceding the higher game stage. Civilized societies should not only be formed on the national level, but should even develop into a universal society on the international level: "We are struggling now to get a certain amount of international-mindedness. We are realizing ourselves as members of a larger community. The vivid nationalism of the present period should, in the end, call out an international attitude of the larger community" (Mead, 1934, p. 265). In other words, civilization depends heavily on the organizing influence of the generalized other, and the highest form of the generalized other is the larger (international) community based on gamelike rules that make cooperative relationships possible.

However, Gregg poses some questions of central concern to the notion of dominance: Must not a game have opposing teams? Are games not based on real competition, with winners and losers? Along similar lines, the question may be posed: Is not society, both on a national and an international level, rent by hostile divisions and irreconcilable conflicts? These questions open the door to a countertheory that also can be deduced from Mead's complex text.

7.2.2 Society's Split: In-Group and Out-Group

Mead (1934) was certainly aware that there is in society not only cooperation, but also competition and even animosity. Most clearly this is expressed when he is talking about the notion of "superiority":

> The sense of superiority is magnified when it belongs to a self that identifies itself with the group. It is aggravated in our patriotism, where we legitimize an assertion of superiority . . . It seems to be perfectly legitimate to assert the superiority of the nation to which one belongs over other nations, to brand the conduct of other nationalities in black colors in order that we may bring out values in the conduct of those that make up our own nation. It is just as true in politics and religion in the putting of one sect over against the others. This took the place of the exclusive expressions of nationalism in the early period, the period of religious wars . . . We all believe that the group we are in is superior to other groups. [p. 207]

Mead goes so far as to emphasize, well in the tradition of pragmatism, that superiority, in certain cases, makes people more effective:

> We change things by the capacities which we have that other people do not have. Such capacity is what makes us effective. The immediate attitude is one which carries with it a sense of superiority, of maintaining one's self. The superiority is not the end in view. It is a means for the preservation of the self. We have to distinguish ourselves from other people and this is accomplished by doing something which other people cannot do, or cannot do as well. [1934, p. 208]

The self profits even from the fighting against enemies, and it is in these passages that Mead comes close to an in-group/out-group structuring of society, and a "survival of the fittest" ideology:

> We are normally dependent upon those situations in which the self is able to express itself in a direct fashion, and there is no situation in which the self can express itself so easily as it can over against the common enemy of the groups to which it is united . . . There has to be something to fight against because the self is most easily able to express itself in joining a definite group [1934, pp. 220–221]

The paragraph that immediately follows is most revealing, because it offers a view on the difference between primitive and civilized society that is clearly at odds with his earlier view on the same topic. It is here that Mead's countertheory becomes most evident:

> One difference between primitive human society and civilized human society is that in primitive human society the individual self is much more completely determined, with regard to his thinking and his behavior, by the general pattern of

the organized social activity carried on by the particular social group to which he belongs, than he is in civilized human society. In other words, primitive human society offers much less scope for individuality—for original, unique, or creative thinking and behavior on the part of the individual self within it or belonging to it—than does civilized human society; and indeed the evolution of civilized human society from primitive human society has largely depended upon or resulted from a progressive social liberation of the individual self and his conduct . . . [1934, p. 221]

As Gregg (1991) notes, this paragraph appears "out of the blue" and has no consistent relation to the themes discussed in the preceding pages. Moreover, it blatantly contradicts Mead's preceding thesis, formulated as part of his play–game theory, that it is the generalized other that is responsible for civilization, which primitives just lack. The contradiction between theory and countertheory can also be formulated in terms of the *I–Me* distinction. Mead's main theory considers the *Me* (the generalized other) as characterizing civilization (in which objectivity and rationality are achieved), whereas in the countertheory it is the *I* (personal liberation) that marks civilization.

The conclusion is that Mead has developed two different theories about the relation between self and society: one that centers around the concept of unity, and the other around the concepts of superiority and opposition. As Gregg already emphasized, this conclusion is not drawn in order to reject Mead's theory. On the contrary, the tension between theory and countertheory becomes an especially fertile starting point for further analysis. Before we look for the consequences of the preceding analysis, we summarize, using some of Gregg's terms, the difference between the two theories:

Theory: The differentiation of social groups and roles in society produces multiple selves; these are integrated by internalizing the rules of the macrosocial game, and thus the self is structured as a social *unity.*

Countertheory: Society is defined by an affectively charged *opposition* between a generalized other, with which the self identifies, and a generalized enemy other, with which the self stridently disidentifies.

7.3 The Generalized Other as a Collective Voice

Until now we have critically reviewed Mead's theory, and his conception of the generalized other in particular, from the perspective of "intersubjective exchange" and "dominance." The conclusion is that Mead's self represents a theory of internalization, rather than a theory of dialogue, in which two parties are exchanging knowledge on the basis of mutuality. Moreover, the notion of dominance is neglected in his theory, as far as it is based on the notion of unity, but is recognized in his countertheory, in which "superiority" and "fighting against the enemy" are incorporated.

As already said, it is the tension between theory and countertheory that is fertile enough to continue theoretical reflection about the relation between self and society. The kernel of our proposal is that the generalized other is reformulated as a collective voice. As a collective voice, the individual speaks the words of the group, social class, or society to which the individual belongs and reflects the unity of the group, class, or society. However, collective voices may also conflict, oppose, and disagree with one another, with the result that one voice becomes more dominant than the other. Let us explore the implications of this proposal in more detail.

7.3.1 Conflicting Voices: An Example from James

Mead's generalized other was preceded by James' social self. More specifically, Mead's multiple generalized other was preluded in James' multiplicity of social selves: ". . . a man has as many social selves as there are individuals who recognize him and carry an image of him in their mind" (James, 1890, p. 294). In his elaborations of the concept of social self, James was very sensitive to the conflicts among its constituent components. In one of his examples he says: "As a man I pity you, but as an official I must show you no mercy; as a politician I regard him as an ally, but as a moralist I loathe him" (p. 295). Several features make this example noteworthy from a theoretical point of view.

First, an individual person is speaking. The person has a voice and is expressing an utterance. Second, although the person uses the pronoun *I*, he or she is expressing the viewpoint of a group and, in Mead's terms, takes the attitude of a generalized other (e.g., as a politician, as a moralist). Third, the voices involved are in a relationship of disagreement. Two collective attitudes, coming together in the mind of the individual person, conflict with one another. Fourth, from the present perspective the most significant word in the utterance is the word *but*. This word reveals that the person is *actively relating* the two attitudes to one another. There are not simply two different statements from two unrelated persons (one from a politician, the other from a moralist). On the contrary, the two opinions are concentrated in the mind of a self-reflecting person and brought in a relation of opposition to each other. The term *but* indicates that the two attitudes function as voices that stand in a relationship of "dialogical opposition" toward one another. This dialogical opposition implies that the two voices, in their disagreement, entertain mutual relationships having the quality of an exchange.

Although James does not elaborate on his example, the two voices, once taken up in the process of exchange, create in their disagreement a tension that makes the dialogical relationship dynamic and open. As we have seen in the discussion of Bakhtin's view (Chapter 3), the utterances "life is good" and "life is not good" create a tension that energizes the dialogue and stimulates its continuation. Moreover, this tension is the beginning of a dialogue that is open ended: The two voices are co-constructing a standpoint that is not predictable from the beginning.

7.3.2 Collective Voice: I or Me?

It must be noted that James had good reasons to differentiate between *I* and *Me*. The conception of the *I* enabled him to account for the continuity (sameness through time) of the self. The *Me* accounted for the discontinuities in the self. For example, the *Me* is represented by the "many social selves" that may draw the self in opposing directions (as in the example above). The *I–Me* distinction could thus account for the paradoxical finding that a person, being different in different social contacts, still feels himself or herself as the "same" person. In developing his theory about the generalized other, Mead, in fact, reversed the functions of the *I* and the *Me*. The continuity was guaranteed by the *Me*, because Mead saw in the rules and conventions of the generalized other the sameness of the self. The *I*, on the contrary, became an innovative force, bringing change and discontinuity in the self and in the social process as a whole.

In the view we are proposing in this book, the continuity/discontinuity distinction is incorporated in the term *I position*. The term *I position* is deliberately chosen because it places the continuity in the term *I* and the discontinuity in the term *position*. As far as the individual takes different and contrasting positions (and associated attitudes), there is discontinuity; because it is the same *I* that is involved in these changes, there is continuity. In other words, the composite term *I position* covers both the continuity and the discontinuity of the self.

However, what is the advantage of translating the generalized other as a collective voice and considering it not as a *Me* but as an *I*? The answer to this question can be given by returning to James' example. The person as a politician is, rather than a generalized other (in Mead's terms), a collective voice speaking through the mouth of the *I*. The politician, then, functions not as responding to an internalized and stabilized attitude or set of rules, but as a person-in-a-social-position, who is involved in a process of construction and co-construction with other people. In this constructive activity he or she is shaping the world of politics. When the *I* speaks as a collective voice, the attitude of the collectivity is present in the form of rules, conventions, and established views of the world. At the same time, however, the *I* is able, as an active (co-)constructor, to bring innovations to the same rules and conventions.

The theoretical meaning of the term *I position* would be underestimated if one would stick to only one collective position. In James' example, a similar reasoning could be followed for the person as a moralist. But above all, the *I* has the capacity to shift *between* different or contrasting positions. As we discussed in the preceding chapter, it is possible to conceive, in the case of two contrasting positions, a third position, that we have described as the synthesizing (capital) Self. The central characteristic feature of this Self is that it is capable of an active process of interrelating different, relatively autonomous positions in such a way that they are brought together as components of an organized whole. In the simplified case of two collective positions, for example, that of politician and moralist, the Self has the capacity of making dialogical switches between the two positions such that the two positions are influenced and more or less changed by the process of interrelation. This means that for the person in question, the world of politics and the world of morality do not function as separate domains but rather both become influenced by the synthesizing efforts of the Self.

In Mead's main theory the generalized other is based on unity, and the multiplicity of generalized others are united on the level of the greater society that he had in mind, which is, in fact, a social superstructure based on coopera- tion. In this theory there is no place for conflict and dominance, as we have argued. Mead's countertheory, in contrast, acknowledges the important role of superiority and dominance in the formation of the self. As we have seen, however, it is not clear how this countertheory is related to the main theory of the generalized other. Specifically, Mead does not provide a model that brings together his reasoning about unity as expressed in the generalized other (his main theory) and his reflections about conflict and superiority (his countertheo- ry). It is our proposal that the notion of dialogue is able to bridge the domains of social conflict and unity, because dialogical relationships allow for the existence of both agreement and disagreement and for both intersubjective exchange and dominance.

7.3.3 Collective Stories and Society as a Macrostructure

In his review of symbolic interactionism, Ritzer (1992) concludes that Mead has relatively little to say about society, in spite of its centrality in his theoretical system. At the most general level, Mead uses the term *society* to mean the ongoing social process that precedes both the mind and the self and he considers society as important in shaping the mind and the self. At a lower level of generality, society represents an organized set of responses that are taken over by the individual in the form of the Me. In this sense, individuals carry society around with them, and the internalized set of rules enables them, through self- criticism, to control themselves. Despite these contributions, the emphasis of Mead's work is not on society but on the mind and the self. Even John Baldwin (1986), who is inclined to see a macrosocietal component in Mead's thinking, is forced to admit: "The macro components of Mead's theoretical system are not as well developed as the micro" (Baldwin, 1986, p. 123, cited by Ritzer, 1992).

Mead (1934) deals, however, explicitly with social institutions, that he defines as the "common response on the part of all members of the community to a particular situation" (p. 261) or "the life-habits of the community" (p. 264). In his treatment of institutions, Mead emphasizes the commonality in underlying values, although individual people subscribe these values in different ways:

> This common response is one which, of course, varies with the character of the individual. In the case of theft the response of the sheriff is different from that of the attorney-general, from that of the judge and the jurors . . . and yet they all are responses which maintain property, which involve the recognition of the property right in others. [1934, p. 262]

Although Mead's (1934) emphasis is on the commonality and sharing of values, he recognizes that there are "oppressive, stereotyped, and ultra-conservative social institutions—like the church—which by their more or less rigid and inflexible unprogressiveness crush or blot out individuality . . . " (p. 262). However, he hastens to add that "there is no necessary or inevitable reason why social institutions should be oppressive or rigidly conservative . . . " (p. 262).

What Mead's analyses lack, Ritzer (1992) concludes, is a true macro sense of society in general, and institutions in particular, in the way that theorists like Marx, Weber, and Durkheim dealt with. Interested in the unity of society and the "objective" attitude of the generalized other as he was, he did not elaborate a systematic theory of macrosocial conflicts, social stratification, and ethnic- and gender-based inequality. In fact, Mead's theory represented a "homogeneous society" metaphor, with a heavy emphasis on microsocial gamelike processes.

One of the reasons that we are interested in the notion of a "collective voice" is that a voice can tell narratives and, by implication, a collective voice can tell a collective story. In translating Mead's generalized other as a collective voice, the next step is to pose the question: What stories are told by a collective voice? And more specifically, to what extent do collective stories reflect and even sustain existing power differences in macrosocial structures? These questions may open a fruitful discussion about the nature of collective stories and the characters involved. Indeed, storytelling is pervasive, in the world of both children and adults. Not only is the variation in collective stories astonishing, they also accompany people throughout their lives and penetrate deeply in their ways of thinking about characters and social types. People are influenced by fairy tales, legends, myths, parables, famous books, well-known movies, social talk at parties and on the street, rumors about the economic position of particular companies, jokes about social minorities, gossip about celebrities, stories about the sexual escapades of politicians, homosexuals who adopt a child, people who marry at old age, etc.

The influence of collective stories on daily lives can only be properly understood when one realizes that such stories are not simply a copy of everyday life.

As Carol Christ (1980) has argued, significant experiences result in the creation of stories and, once told and shared, stories organize experiences. An important feature of collective stories is that they are preexistent, that is, many of them exist before the individual becomes a member of the community. As Mead's society precedes the individual self, collective voices precede individual voices and influence them.

As Christ (1980) has convincingly argued, the biblical story about the sinful Eve, and her seductive qualities in particular, had and still have a long-lasting influence in Western civilization, on men and women and their relationships. The contrast between the sinful Eve and the Holy Mary also functions as an example of collective stories that have lasting influence on the way women in our culture have been educated. The story of the "prince on the horse" that may penetrate the daydreams of many girls, expecting a life-long, heavenlike marriage, is certainly not without influence on the self of many individuals.

The contrast between the sensual but sinful Eve (with whom one learns to disidentify) and the insensual but holy Mary (with whom one rather learns to identify) is particularly interesting, because such stories convey particular values but also a splitting of values. It implies the message: "When you are sensual, you cannot be spiritual; when you are a spiritual person, you cannot be sensual." This split may be so deeply rooted in our Western civilization that it is almost impossible to us to understand the meaning of "heavenly prostitutes" in the Hindu tradition. The evaluative splitting between the words *heaven* and *prostitute*, reflecting irreconcilable values, makes it difficult for us to understand that these "prostitutes" had the duty to give the holy person heavenlike experiences that were sensual and spiritual at the same time.

The irreconcilability of spirituality and sensuality has not simply been conveyed via collective stories from generation to generation; it has also deeply affected the self of people in their everyday life. As a consequence of the splitting of values on the cultural level, people experience personal conflicts in their daily lives. A person who is educated in a traditional religious milieu and has a sexual experience with a friend may be confronted with two irreconcilable positions: She feels like a whore and a "decent girl" successively, or even simultaneously. And she will have difficulty achieving a synthesis of these two positions. A difficulty that, to a great extent, is prestructured on the level of culture (in terms of values) and on the macrosocial level (in terms of social classes). The fact that the girl is not an actual prostitute does not prevent her from feeling like she is one. The girls' self is organized on the basis of affectively charged societal positions that become combined as elements of a personal construction.

The above examples indicate that collective stories reflect the "attitude of the other" concerning a great variety of matters in the everyday life of people, including the rules and conventions that guide human interactions. In contrast with Mead's concept of "generalized other," that is based on "rationality" and "objectivity," collective stories, like individual stories, are highly affective and evaluative. Mead has put great emphasis on abstract thinking and rationality and considers the self "essentially a cognitive rather than an emotional phenomenon" (1934, p. 173). He noticed, however, that with this view he departed from James and Cooley, who "endeavor to find the basis of the self in reflexive affective experiences, i.e., experiences involving 'self-feeling'" (p. 173). Because both the telling of and the listening to stories require cognitive organization *and* affective experiencing (Hermans, 1987a; McAdams, 1985b), the concept of collective voice comes, in this respect, closer to James than to Mead.

7.3.4 Splitting versus Synthesis

In the line of his discussion of Mead's countertheory, and influenced by Hegelian thinking, Gregg (1991) argues that the self consists, not of a collection of *Me* attributions, as cognitive personality theories would have it, nor of ego-syntonic identifications, as most psychoanalytic personality theories would have it, but of a system of *Me*/not *Me* oppositions. He holds that every *Me* attribution or identification must have at least two defining relations (implying at least two meanings); a positing, which establishes the self as the presence of something, and a negation, which establishes the self as the absence or opposite of something else. However, the "thing" negated also must be, in some sense, the same sort of entity as the "thing" posited. For example, the self of the person who prefers tofu as a symbol of a pure and spiritual way of life and rejects chemical "junk food" includes not only the meaning of "tofu," but also its negation and opposite (junk food), although the person may qualify the latter kind of food as "not *Me.*" This splitting of subjectivity is not to be regarded as an attributional or inferential error, or as something inherently pathological, but rather as something that is at the basis of the formation of the self. There is no rigid boundary between self and not-self. On the contrary, the self/world boundary is highly permeable. In simple terms, "self/world boundaries are constituted in or as the self, not around it" (Gregg, 1991, p. 120).

The splits between self and not-self (e.g., white/black, normal/gay, beautiful/ugly) are not simple distinctions, but active oppositions or contradictions. To "split" is not just to distinguish, but to value and judge things in their opposition. Splitting is an affectively charged process with moral implications: To split is to establish an opposition between "higher" and "lower." It represents the conflict between good and evil forces, a continuous struggle in which one tries to dominate the other.

Building on his distinction between *Me* and not *Me,* and the corresponding distinction between in-group and out-group, Gregg (1991) holds that the self not only includes the self/in-group identification, but also the anti-self/out-group disidentification. In line with this thinking, we conceive of the self as a multiplicity of *I* positions in which the other, positively or negatively evaluated, cannot be dissolved from the self. This is reflected in personal contact: My friends, my children, my wife, my opponents, my enemies, and the people I despise and may try to avoid are all *I* positions in the self. The people with whom I positively identify and the ones with whom I disidentify are both part of my self. In their opposition and irreconcilability, they call upon a struggle of the Self. The same view applies to myself as part of society. I may identify with particular groups, classes, or categories of people and disidentify with other ones. Both compose the self in rather antagonistic ways. My view and experiences of people who represent these groups are strongly and pervasively influenced by collective stories in which these groups and their representatives function as characters that are depicted in highly colored and affective ways. As a consequence of the intensive transactional relationships between self and society, the self, in the form of a multiplicity of *I* positions, becomes infiltrated by the evaluations of the characters involved in collective stories. This means that the *I* positions also assume the quality of collective positions.

As soon as children are so far that they can address themselves with the pronoun "I," (and even sooner on the basis of nonverbal interactions), they are capable of making evaluative contrasts between positions that result in a complexity of identifications and disidentifications. In the developmental process, particular *I* positions may become dominant in the self. However, both the content and the organization of the *I* positions are highly dependent on the way the child is addressed by others and socially located in society (e.g., as white, boy, but son of delinquent and from a broken family). This means that the child's self is greatly influenced by a process of collective positioning that is often of a highly evaluative nature.

In his reflections about the dialogical nature of the self, Taylor (1991) supposes that Mead, with his theory of internalization, overstates the initial dependence of the child and that he fails to capture what happens after. From the present perspective, one could say that the child is highly dependent on the voices of significant others and the (collective) stories told about him or her. In the course of development, however, the growing child and adult learns not only to incorporate an increasing variety of opposing and conflicting positions in the self, but is also challenged to synthesize them in such a way that he or she learns, more or less, to live with a complex mixture of positive and negative self-valuations. In this development, the developing person finds himself or herself somewhere between splitting and synthesis and, therefore, the struggle of synthesis is always associated with a continuous shifting of the self/non-self boundaries.

Notes

1. Mead (1934) is very aware of the multiplicity of the self: "A multiple personality is in a certain sense normal" (p. 142). He gives the example of a professor of education who disappeared and later turned up in a logging camp. In this way he freed

himself of his occupation and turned to the woods where he felt more at home. The pathological side of it, Mead continues, was the forgetting, the leaving out of the rest of the self. Mead's observation is in agreement with Watkins' (1986) observation that the dysfunction known as "multiple personality" is more a sequential monologue than a simultaneous dialogue.

2. Taylor refers here to actions that, in our terminology, represent forms of exchange with a high degree of symmetry and a low level of dominance. See also Shotter's (1984) concept of "joint action": In many of our ordinary, everyday life activities, we must interlace our actions with those of others in such a way that the final outcomes of such exchanges cannot *exclusively* be traced back to the plans or intentions of any of the individuals concerned. Consequently, in dialogical exchange, there are no completely preformed, orderly, and constant relations between thoughts and words but only ones that we "develop" or "form" as we attempt to express them to

real or imaginal others in some way (Shotter, 1992).

3. In their discussion of Mead's work, Valsiner and Van der Veer (1988) draw similar conclusions: "The 'I' aspect of the self introduces personal innovation into the process of social role-taking ('me'), while the latter curbs the excess of such innovation" (p. 128).

4. There are at least two main differences between Mead's concept of rationality and Descartes' *Cogito*. First, Mead, like James, assumes the other to be not outside, as in Descartes' dualistic view, but represented *in* the self (as a "social self" with James, and as a generalized other, or *Me*, with Mead). Second, Mead's rationality and "objective" thinking goes from the outside inward, whereas *Cogito* represents a purely internal thinking isolated from the environment. Conceived in this way, Mead's self is, well in the tradition of American pragmatism (see Chapter 3) "subjected to" the (internalized) social environment.

CHAPTER 8

Psychology's Three Separations: Division versus Cross-Fertilization

There are three separations that deserve the attention of those interested in psychology as an integrative disciplinary field: between psychologist and subject, between theory and practice, and between different psychological subdisciplines. The first separation, between psychologist and subject, derives from, or is at least facilitated by, the Descartean notion that subject and object are radically disparate. This implies that the object of study has an existence "on its own" and, hence, represents a reality that is "out there," that has only to be "discovered" by the investigator. The second separation, between theory and practice, presupposes the Descartean notion that "doing" requires an activity of the body that is inherently different from thinking as a disembodied *Cogito*. The last separation, between several psychological subdisciplines, can also be considered an expression of the basic Descartean attitude, which is more analytical as it reduces the whole to its parts rather than synthesizing the parts into a working and living whole.

In this chapter we explore the three separations described above from a dialogical perspective and from the concept of the dialogical self in particular. The gist of our proposal is not only that there is a growing need of such a perspective in psychology, but that one can trace developments in the field that are actually moving in that direction. In other words, a dialogical psychology is not a mere utopia, but implicitly or explicitly underlying much of recent thinking and research.

8.1 The Growing Cooperation between Psychologist and Subject[1]

In this section we will first demonstrate that in the work of two classic authors in the field of personality and social psychology, Kelly and Heider, there are important impulses permitting the subject to play a more active and collaborative role in the research situation. This is in marked contrast to the subject as a "naive" object of study. Second, it will be observed that precisely because of the empirical limitations inherent in classical trait psychology, psychologists have, since Mischel's (1968) groundbreaking publication on the consistency problem, *nolens volens* turned to individual subjects as experts of themselves and their own situations. Last, we extend these developments by discussing the position of the subject as co-investigator in psychological research.

8.1.1 Psychologist and Subject as Colleagues

In his discussion of constructive alternativism, which formed the philosophical basis for his personality theory, Kelly (1955) started from the assumption that "each man contemplates in his own personal way the stream of events upon which he finds himself so swiftly born" (p. 3). Kelly chose the metaphor of man-the-scientist in his bold attempt to answer the question of *how* people process this stream of events. In the discussion of this metaphor he indicated that he was speaking "of all mankind and not merely a particular class of men who have publicly attained the stature of 'scientists'" (p. 4). Kelly observed that there is a basic similarity between ordinary people and scientists in the processing of experience. And as far as they both are scientists, they are also colleagues in this processing of experience.

Personal construct psychologists have attempted to elaborate this general approach into an interactional (conversational) strategy. For example, Bonarius (1977) modified Kelly's Rep (Role Construct Repertory) Test into the Repgrid Interaction Technique, assuming a symmetrical relationship between two participants. These partners (for example, two students or a couple) administer the Repgrid to each other and thereby enter into a process of changing roles. Mair (1970) also proposed a conversational model for the Repgrid and later elaborated his conversational model for use in psychotherapy (Mair, 1989).

8.1.2 Intuitive Knowledge and Common-Sense Psychology

Another pioneer, Heider (1958), also provided the building blocks for conceiving the psychological relationship as a dialogue. In the introduction to his book, *The Psychology of Interpersonal Relations* (1958), Heider emphasized the value of intuitive knowledge and the value of common-sense psychology. One cannot explain Heider's view more eloquently than with his own words:

> . . . psychology holds a unique position among the sciences. "Intuitive" knowledge may be remarkably penetrating and can go a long way toward the understanding of human behavior, whereas in the physical sciences such common-sense knowledge is relatively primitive. If we erased all knowledge of scientific physics from our world, not only would we not have cars and television sets and atom bombs, we might even find that the ordinary person was unable to cope with the fundamental mechanical problems of pulleys and levers. On the other hand, if we

removed all knowledge of scientific psychology from our world, problems of inter-personal relations might easily be coped with and solved much as before. Man would still "know" how to avoid doing something asked from him, and how to get someone to agree with him; he would still "know" when someone was angry and when someone was pleased. He could even offer sensible explanations for the "why's" of much of his behavior and feelings. In other words, the ordinary person has a great and profound understanding of himself and of other people which, though unformulated or only vaguely conceived, enables him to interact with others in more or less adaptive ways. [1958, p. 2]

In a similar way Heider (1958) defended the merits of common-sense psychology:

> . . . the study of common-sense psychology may be of value because of the truths it contains, notwithstanding the fact that many psychologists have mis-trusted and even looked down on such unschooled understanding of human behavior. For these psychologists, what one knows intuitively, what one understands through untrained reflection, offers little—at best a superficial and chaotic view of things, at worst a distortion of psychological events. They point, for example, to the many contradictions that are to be found in this body of material, such as antithetical proverbs or contradictions in a person's interpretation of even simple events. But can a scientist accept such contradictions as proof of the worthlessness of common-sense psychology? If we were to do so, then we would also have to reject the scientific approach, for its history is fraught with contradictions among theories, and even among experimental findings. [p. 5]

In essence, Kelly and Heider agree on the similarity between psychologist and subject although they had different starting points and operated in different fields of inquiry. The man-as-scientist notion is present in Heider's observation that ". . . fruitful concepts and hunches for hypotheses lie dormant and unfor-mulated in what we know intuitively" (Heider, 1958, pp. 5–6). The physicist Oppenheimer (1956) also claims with equal firmness that ". . . all sciences arise as refinement, corrections, and adaptations of common sense" (p. 128). It is but a small step to argue that all psychologists must rely on common sense in understanding their subjects and that, despite apparent role differences, they share a common stock of (intuitive) knowledge with their subjects and the language of everyday life needed to enter into a dialogue with their subjects. This common-sense basis also means, of course, that the subject can easily be consulted and that his or her "hunches" about his or her own behavior should be taken seriously.

8.1.3 The Person as Self-Assessor

Of particular historical significance in personality psychology is Mischel's (1968) publication, in which he seriously questioned the consistency of person-ality and the predictive utility of most assessment methods. Particularly, the term *personality coefficient* challenged the predictive pretensions of many personality psychologists. With this term, Mischel described the correlation (between 0.20 and 0.30) that seemed to be ". . . found persistently when virtually any personality dimension inferred from a questionnaire was related to almost any conceivable criterion involving responses sampled in a different medium—that is, not by another questionnaire" (Mischel, 1968, p. 78).

Mischel himself later considered his statement about the personality coefficient ". . . a gross and too casual summary of typical coefficients in the literature reviewed at that time . . . " (Mischel, 1983, p. 78). Nevertheless, the statement and its motivation were persuasive enough for other personality psychologists to confront the thorny problem of consistency and examine alternative solutions. A new surge of interest was instigated by Bem and Allen (1974) who, assuming that not all traits apply equally well to all individuals, divided their subject groups based upon the subjects' self-reported cross-situational consistency on a given trait. It was found that the actual cross-situational consistency was higher for the group high in self-reported consistency than for the group low in self-reported consistency. These findings suggested that the 0.30 ceiling could be broken by taking the subjects' judgment of themselves into account. This judgment functioned as a "moderator variable" because it influenced the height of the correlation among the variables under study.

Other researchers expanded on the moderator variable approach proposed by Bem and Allen (1974), also assuming that the subject is in the best position to reflect on his or her own behavior (Monson & Snyder, 1977). For example, Kenrick and Stringfield (1980) reasoned that it should be possible to use the subject's own phenomenological perspective to determine the public observability of a particular trait at a given moment in time. They asked their subjects to indicate the extent to which their trait behaviors were observable to others and found that by isolating highly observable trait behavior it was possible to increase predictability. Cheek (1982) replicated the basic effects found by Bem and Allen (1974) and Kenrick and Stringfield (1980). In Cheek's study self-ratings were correlated with ratings by peers and again a moderator analysis was performed. The results showed the self–peer correlations to be stronger for subjects who rated themselves as low in variability or highly observable on a given trait. (For a review and discussion on this line of research, see Kenrick & Dantchik, 1983; Zuckerman, Koestner, DeBoy, Garcia, Maresca, & Sartoris, 1988, and Zuckerman, Bernieri, Koestner, & Rosenthal, 1989.)

The moderator analysis can be considered a significant step toward viewing the person as an active participant in personality research. Based on the notion that some traits are consistent in some people and not in others, a shift toward the subject as a knowledgeable individual was made. Moreover, the moderator analysis approaches the person as a self-knower and this self-knowledge bears *directly* on the conceptual system of the psychologist. The person is seen as the owner of knowledge relevant to the researcher's interests. Only by consulting the person as a self-expert can this information be accessed. And by using this "front-door approach" the subject is—in a rudimentary form—considered the psychologist's co-worker.

8.1.4 The Turning to Everyday Life in Trait Psychology

Discussions of the consistency of traits have not only led to elaborate self-assessment procedures, but also to a renewed interest in the workings of the situation at hand. One of the major criticisms of trait psychology was Mischel's (1968) claim that situational determinants account for more of the behavioral variance than individual differences. In the ensuing controversy between situationists and trait advocates, it was concluded that the "amount of variance" questions was a pseudo-issue and reconciliation was found in the interactionist position (e.g., Blass, 1977; Magnusson, 1981). The interactionist view brought increased attention to (1) the assessment of the personal meaning of a trait in close relation to the situation, and (2) the assessment of the personal meaning of the situation in close relation to trait behavior. Both forms of assessment are discussed briefly below. An illustrative example of the former is the act-frequency approach of Buss and Craik (1983a,b) and an example of the latter is the free-response methodology proposed by Pervin (1976, 1984).

In Buss and Craik's (1983a) view, a dispositional—or trait—assertion is seen as a "categorical summary statement," referring to the frequency with which the individual has displayed acts counting as members of a particular category over a specified period of observation. One of the main techniques used in this approach for assessing the trait characteristics of an individual is the prototypicality ratings, in which panels of judges rate the extent to which a number of acts are typical of the dispositional construct in question. The procedure can simply be illustrated by rating the prototypicality of colors. The subject is asked to imagine a true red, then an orange-red, and then a purple-red. Although the orange-red or the purple-red may be named with the term *red*, they are not as good examples of red as the clear "true" red. In short, some reds are redder than others (1983a, p. 395). Similarly, traits can be rated for their prototypicality. For dominance, for example, a more prototypical act would be "I forbade her to leave the room," while a more peripheral act would be "I walked ahead of everybody else" (1983b, p. 110). Note, however, that there is no measure of personal meaning at this point.

In an attempt to elaborate the act-frequency approach in an individualized way, Buss and Craik (1983a) suggest a procedure where the individual is asked to sort the acts observed in his or her own conduct over an observational period and then rate their prototypicality. *Prototypical acts may then be characteristic of a particular individual.* A further step in individualizing the act-frequency approach is to enlist the individual under study in generating the actual trait categories for the acts in question. In this procedure, the individual might be presented with an inventory of his or her monitored acts over an observational period and asked to sort them into meaningful categories. In the end, then, the individual has generated a list of self-formulated personal dispositions.

Pervin (1976), working in the spirit of interactionism, was also interested in the characteristics of traits for individual people, but his methodology was primarily concerned with the situational component. He observed that in studies dealing with person–situation interaction, data are typically analyzed across subjects to determine the proportion of the variance that can be accounted for by person differences, situation differences, and person–situation interactions. Often these studies use questionnaires where the subject is presented with a variety of situations and responses. The situations described and the responses provided for selection may, however, have limited applicability from the standpoint of the individual person. If we are going to consider persons in their situations, Pervin reasoned, then we need to look at situations and responses that are relevant to individual subjects.

The above considerations led Pervin (1976, 1984) to develop a free-response methodology, where each subject is asked to list a number of situations in his or her life (e.g., "Mother blows up at me"; "Have to participate in class"; "Come home from Philadelphia"). Then the subject lists characteristics of these situations, feelings associated with them, and behaviors expressed by the subjects in the situations. The subjects then rate the applicability of each characteristic, feeling, and behavior to each situation. These lists, elicited from each subject and specific to each subject, are then factor analyzed so that individual structures can be detected. The question can now be raised as to what is the position of the subject in the approaches described.

8.1.5 Comparison of the Different Approaches to Personality

The several approaches described above have in common that they all, in one way or another, originate from trait psychology and that they all, more or less, consult the individual as an expert of himself or herself. They do this, however, in quite different ways. Bem and Allen (1974), using moderator analyses, continue to work with trait terms phrased in the traditional way but put subjects in a metaposition concerning their own trait behaviors and then consult them. Although the person is approached as somebody capable of self-reflection and self-knowledge in this approach, the procedure is individualized in a very limited way: Subjects are divided into two groups on the basis of a moderator variable, the one group having higher correlations between predictor and criterion than the other group. Little attempt is made to approach the individual as an organized whole, involving *many* variables or components of the self.

The individualized patterning of variables is given more weight in the approaches of Buss and Craik (1983a) and Pervin (1976), for which the former emphasizes the trait aspect of the person–situation interaction (in terms of acts) and the latter stresses the situational aspect. In addition, the research strategies of Buss and Craik and Pervin refer to naturalistic settings and call for the analysis of behavior in close connection with the everyday life of the individual. In contrast, research along the lines of Bem and Allen lacks this explicit reference to the daily life events of the individual.

The individual's expertise and its relevance for personality research was foreseen by Mischel, who repeatedly pointed to people as "expert assessors and predictors." In his 1968 book, referred to by many as having caused an earthquake in personality psychology, he concludes his discussion of the weak correlation between self-reports and observer ratings as follows: "These associations, however, say nothing about the ability of people to describe and predict behavior under more appropriate conditions. When persons are asked to describe, anticipate, or predict behavior, with minimal interpretation of its meaning, they may be as successful, or even more accurate, than other 'experts' or tests" (pp. 69–70). Similarly, ". . . persons are potentially excellent assessors and predictors of behavior including their own . . . " and "even young children have been found to be remarkably expert in their knowledge of psychological principles and processes . . . " (Mischel, 1983, p. 586).

In sum, the individual has taken on increasing importance over the last decades in personality psychology. This position is characterized by at least two features: (1) The subject is an individual with his or her own perspective and knowledge that cannot be replaced by any alternative body of knowledge; and (2) the individual's knowledge is of direct relevance to the scientific aims of the personality psychologist and, therefore, the individual should be consulted. Such a role on the part of the individual, however, requires a highly open relationship between psychologist and subject. Let us, therefore, continue our exploration by viewing personality as an open system which then will lead us to the notion of a dialogical relationship between psychologist and subject.

8.1.6 The Subject as Co-Investigator: Theoretical and Methodological Prerequisites

On the basis of recent developments in personality and social psychology, Hermans and Bonarius (1991a,b) and Hermans (1992a) envisage the subject as co-investigator in psychological research. That is, the subject is expected to actively enter into a psychological relation that is structured as a dialogue. Such a relationship will thereby take the form of an *intersubjective exchange*, where the two parties both contribute from their own specific perspectives to the scientific process. It must be acknowledged, however, that in this cooperation the two parties have different starting points. The psychologist, as a representative of science, knows of *general* theories, concepts, and methodologies. The subject, as a representative of his or her personal history and life, knows about *specific* behaviors, experiences, and situations. Put differently, the psychologist as a scientist is primarily interested in developing a "global theory" with a high degree of generality, while the subject is most interested in understanding his own particular situation with a "local theory" (Hintikka, 1968; Fischoff, 1976). In order to become dialogical, the different starting points require psychologists to "translate" global theories into the local concerns of the subject in such a way that intersubjective exchange becomes possible.

It should be noted that by a dialogue we do not simply mean a conversation, although this is certainly an important aspect of the interactive approach we propose. The basic relationship between psychologist and subject and, even broader, between psychology and the world of the subject, is of prime concern. From this perspective, three sets of theoretical/methodological criteria seem to be of vital importance for future research.

1. On the level of theory, *order and organization* are of prime concern: What are the constituents of personality and how do they function as parts of an organized whole? Order and organization in personality or self are *not* assumed to be of a fixed nature. Rather, the environment, including the exchange with the psychologist and, more generally, the science of psychology are critical to the understanding of individuality.

On the methodological level, order and coherence require careful attention to the *patterning* of different variables and aspects of personality. The psychologist should select and interrelate the relevant variables in close cooperation with the subject and develop procedures that permit the co-investigator to translate the psychologist's variables into everyday terminology. In such a way, the process of exchange will clearly be facilitated and the resulting patterns can be studied by both parties.

2. *Open* concepts are required, whose formulation is *highly sensitive* to the experiences, behavior, and life situation of the individual. Only in this way can the intuitive knowledge of the individual be translated into the conceptual terms of the psychologist. The notion of open and sensitizing concepts was also stressed in the "grounded theory" of Glaser and Strauss (1967), who formulated their theory in the tradition of symbolic interactionism. An important difference from the approach presented here is that we start with general concepts (i.e., "nomo-concepts") and adapt these to become "idio-concepts" (Hermans, 1988), while grounded theory works the other way around: It starts with a situational analysis (i.e., a "substantive theory" with a low level of generality) which later gets developed into a "formal theory" with a higher level of generality.

An example of adaptation of nomo-concepts into idio-concepts is the case of Alice presented in Chapter 6, where the term *I position* functions as a nomo-concept and the terms *open* and *closed* are, as idio-concepts, chosen by the individual to characterize her own personality.

On the methodological level, open concepts require free-response procedures that are sensitive to everyday life situations and the intuitive insights of the individual. People must be able to give their accounts in terms that are nuanced and detailed enough to permit an adequate representation of their life situation. It is not the intention, however, that the person only react to the questions of the researcher. The subject, interacting with the psychologist, may well arrive at a point where he or she generates questions that may or may not develop into further research questions.

3. On the assumption that a fruitful collaboration can most profitably be realized when personality is viewed as a process evolving over time, *dynamic* concepts are required. Certain knowledge and basic insights may *emerge* from the interaction with the co-investigators. Accordingly, the concepts utilized in the investigation, on the side of both the investigator and the co-investigator, should be subject to modification and specification. In addition, the possibility of inventing new concepts should always be kept open.

From the perspective of methodology, *longitudinal* procedures are optimal. Longitudinal does not simply refer to being "followed" over time here; but rather to an extended cooperation between investigator and co-investigator, which allows for the accumulation of basic insights. In other words, the "experienced subject" is more welcome than the "naive subject" so typically required by the experimental paradigm. Given a theory-based individualized approach to personality with the character of an ongoing dialogue, personality research is expected to be an exciting process where both parties learn from each other on the basis of their mutual exchanges.[2]

8.1.7 Consensus among Colleagues and the Asymmetrical Relation between Psychologist and Subject

What is the reason that psychology often develops concepts and methods that are not sensitive to the everyday world of the individual and that are closed to the personal world of the subject? This question may, of course, give rise to a variety of answers. One factor, however, must certainly be taken into account: the particular nature of scientific communication. In fact, scientific communication in psychology takes place on at least two levels: (1) the subject level, where the psychologist has to communicate with the subject in order to organize the research situation in a meaningful way, and (2) the scientific level, where psychologists present the products of their thoughts and research endeavors to the forum of their colleagues in the form of articles, books, congress papers, proposals for financial support, etc. Because the two levels are interconnected, institutionalized requirements and practices on the one level have far-reaching implications for the other level. The scientific level requires a certain degree of consensus regarding theoretical concepts and methodology in order to enable scientists, working in diverse settings, countries, and even cultures, to exchange information on the basis of mutual understanding. A problem arises when consensus requirements on the scientific level have the intended or unintended implication of constraining the dialogical possibilities on the subject level. An example of such a constraining system is, in our view, the *Diagnostic Statistical Manual* (DSM) (1987) of clinical dysfunctions that, in its successive versions, fulfills the desire of those psychiatrists and clinicians who want to dispose of a system of diagnostic categories that permits a certain degree of conceptual agreement among colleagues. However praiseworthy such an endeavor may be, the produced taxonomy is comprised of a huge number of closed and static concepts that are entirely insensitive to the viewpoint of the subject in question.

The striving of personality psychologists to arrive at an encompassing classification of trait terms in the form of the "big five" (e.g., Costa & McCrae, 1988) is another example of a consensus system that is highly closed on the subject level. Such classifications typically include large numbers of items that force the subject to respond in terms of a limited number of alternatives, which are invariably presented irrespective of the subject's personal history and entirely neglect the subject's personal meanings. Traits, examined in this way, are closed entities, insensitive to the particular world of the individual. Moreover, it is unclear what the *dynamic* interrelation of those factorial traits is in the case of *this* particular individual. (For a criticism of traditional trait psychology and the individual differences paradigm, in general, see Lamiell, 1987; for a criticism of the big five, specifically, see McAdams, 1992.)

The DSM taxonomy of dysfunctions and the "big five" trait classification are examples of a dialogical structure in which the communication on the scientific level is superimposed on the subject level in such a way that the psychologist–scientist communication is dominating the psychologist–subject communication to a large degree. The result has been that the conceptual system of the psychologist as a scientist has become so prevailing over the conceptual system of the subject that there has not been much room left for the expression of the voice of the individual person as a knowledgeable individual.

Closely related to the dominance of the one level of communication over the other is the fact that scientific communication requires the use of well-defined concepts and valid methods. Communication with the subject, however, is simply impossible on the basis of (existing) scientific terminology. Productive communication on this level is only possible if one uses the language of everyday life and the intuitive knowledge that concerned Heider (1958) so much. When it is our serious intention as psychologists–scientists to open the door to the farther reaches and complexities of self and personality, it is a necessary condition that we devise theories, concepts, and methods that enable subjects to contribute to these theories, concepts, and methods from their own position, that is, from the subjects' intuitive knowledge and specific expertise acquired in their own local situations. It is, moreover, necessary that subjects have the opportunity to communicate their stock of knowledge in the language of everyday live, that is more suitable than any scientific language for communicating the subtleties and nuances of the individual's experiences. Only if these requirements are met will the relationship between psychologist and subject develop into a more symmetrical dialogue and enable the subject to become a co-constructor of psychological reality.

8.2 The Problematic Cooperation between Scientist and Practitioner

Recently, Hoshmand and Polkinghorne (1992) presented a review of the literature about the science–practice relation with the purpose of redefining this relation in the direction of a more cooperative enterprise. Their proposal is of direct relevance to what we called, at the beginning of this chapter, the separation between scientist and practitioner and what Mahoney (1989) characterized as "the regrettable schism within modern psychology." We will therefore, keeping close to Hoshmand and Polkinghorne's work, discuss some of the arguments that are in support of a more symmetrical dialogical relationship between psychologist and subject.

8.2.1 Problems with the Traditional Model of Knowledge

Hoshmand and Polkinghorne observe that there is not only a "split" between science and practice, but that, moreover, science is held as "superior" to the knowledge emerging from practice. This combination of split and subordination has its roots in a particular epistemological conception that is usually described as "positivism." An essential characteristic of positivism is that humans, with the aid of the tools of science, can gain "true" knowledge of a reality that exists outside of human thought. It is believed that formal procedures of science (such as experimentation and mathematical models) will produce a progressively accurate picture of reality. Implied in this conception is the belief that everyday language is too imprecise for scientific description and communication among scientists. Moreover, the kinds of problem solving and thinking about problems such as those employed in practice are presumed to be inferior to the more logical modes of thought associated with the scientific reasoning in research. The natural language that practitioners use in their contact with clients is presumed to be less suitable as a means to scientific understanding of reality than are mathematically formulated statements.

The positivistic model has begun to function as the single foundation for "true" knowledge, not only for scientific research but also for professional work. It encourages, moreover, the belief in a one-way relationship between research-tested theory and practice. Under the dominance of the positivistic model, only scientific statements that are justified by the "hard" methods of research are admissible as the knowledge base of the discipline as a whole. The hard scientists are expected to develop theories and methods as the primary means of producing a knowledge base that is than translated into techniques and procedures for use by practitioners. As a consequence, practitioners are assigned a secondary role as appliers rather than contributors of knowledge. In the best case, practice may serve as a source of hypotheses that are later on tested by more scientific procedures. Practice itself, however, is assumed not to be in a position to generate valid knowledge from its own. The secondary role of practice is exposed, for example, in the view of Schein (1972), who proposed a hierarchy of professional knowledge in which basic science is considered highest in rigor and purity, with the implication that researchers involved in basic sciences are ascribed higher status than the practitioners of applied science. A similar view was expressed by Glazer (1974), who distinguished between "major" and "minor" professions, believing that the problem-solving and service-oriented professions, labeled as minor professions, are inferior to the more scientifically oriented major professions. Just because practitioners often seem to act on the basis of practical experience or trial and error and act in ways that seem unsystematic and unpredictable, it is believed that the problem-solving professions cannot establish a rigorous knowledge base. As is well known, the prevailing positivistic view is also reflected in the government's relatively stronger support of the hard sciences and in the pecking order for different disciplines in universities.

In spite of the unifying pretensions of the positivistic value system, psychology as a profession is experiencing, particularly at present, tensions of division. In fact, researchers and practitioners are divided more than ever by a basic conflict of epistemic values and world views. Whereas scientists are striving for generalizing knowledge statements that prove to be true at increasingly higher levels of abstractions, practitioners depend on knowledge derived from experience and direct interaction with clients in their local situations. The latter kind of knowledge, however, is conflicting with the accepted scientific models that require a knowledge base that is not only highly generalizable, but also of an impersonal nature, that is, not dependent on the findings and experiences of a particular psychologist in communication with a particular client.

Differences in orientation and professional education add to the problem of bridging the gap between science and practice. Early in graduate training separate curricula are offered for the teaching of research and practice. Different inclinations of students in the beginning of their study are only strengthened by the organization of curricula that often systematically separate these two orientations. In this way the positivistic value system and the organization of curricula cooperate in the continuation of the division of the two orientations.

In light of the above considerations, Hoshmand and Polkinghorne (1992) conclude that we are in need of a professional inquiry that (1) can bridge the gap between the formal knowledge base of research and the knowledge processes of practice, and (2) allows practitioners to contribute to the knowledge base of the profession. If psychology is expected to be a problem-solving profession, it is crucial not only for practice-oriented individuals but also for academic researchers to respond to the challenges of experiences in practice.

8.2.2 Redefining the Relationship of Theory and Practice

In agreement with the positivistic character of psychology as a science, the main function of scientific activities has become that of theory testing. This has resulted in a knowledge base for psychology as a discipline, that has generally been considered to be the *only* legitimate source of knowledge for the profession. The emphasis on theory testing has, unfortunately, resulted in a relative neglect of discovery research (e.g., Mahrer, 1988; McGuire, 1983; Wachtel, 1980), that is of direct relevance to both theory and practice. Discovery research is oriented to relatively unexplored terrains of practice in which problems are ill defined and, therefore, intensive observation and comprehensive description precede hypothesis testing. Indeed, the advantage of approaches like discovery research is that they do not simply reject hypothesis testing and theory development, but emphasize those research activities that, in the confusional richness of the field, concentrate on findings and phenomena that, in a later stage of research, give a fertile influx of theory testing. Moreover, discovery research allows the practitioner to contribute to the scientific process from an original source of data production rather than as a mere applier of the insights of basic science. Basic scientists, in their turn, are invited to listen to the impulses from practice and allow themselves to become inspired by the resulting observations and insights emerging from the process of discovery.

However, it is perhaps naive to expect that scientists and practitioners will come to a systematic cooperation on a larger scale based on the above considerations alone, regardless of how praiseworthy the purposes and activities of discovery researchers may be. The problem at hand is more basic and touches the basics of our professional education and our epistemological value system. In order to define the problem more precisely, let us first look to the report of a recent conference on scientist–practitioner education (Belar & Perry, 1992).

The National Conference on Scientist–Practitioner Education and Training for the Professional Practice of Psychology was held in Gainesville, Florida, 1990. The purpose of the conference was to define the essential characteristics of the scientist–practitioner model that, since its promulgation at the Boulder Conference in 1949 (Raimy, 1950), has served as the framework for the majority of training programs in clinical psychology and also to a large extent in school, counseling, and industrial psychology. In the 40 years since the model's inception, however, it had never been fully articulated by a national conference of leaders in the field.

As Belar and Perry (1992) note, the delegates of the Florida conference represented a wide diversity in psychology education, training, and work settings, and the final policy document was accepted by acclamation after debate by the entire group. The delegates asserted that the scientist–practitioner model of education and training was essential for the ever-changing discipline of psychology. They emphasized, moreover, that interlocking skills in science and practice were the foundation for generating the knowledge base and applications to practice needed for a developing psychology. The relationship between scientist and practitioner that was most desirable in the eyes of the delegates can best be summarized this way:

> Working groups repeatedly underscored that the scientist–practitioner model is not a summation of its parts, nor is it a point on a continuum between programs emphasizing science and programs emphasizing practice. Education and training in either research or practice alone, or concurrently without integration, were viewed as not fulfilling the requirements for implementation of this model. There was consensus that many programs that currently identify themselves as adherents of a scientist–practitioner model fail to meet this fundamental requirement. To better represent the integrative aspect, many delegates wished to replace the dash in *scientist–practitioner* with a symbol reflecting the integration and interaction of the two aspects (e.g., scientist ~ practitioner, scientist × practitioner). [Belar & Perry, 1992, p. 71][3]

The general support of the Florida conference in favor of a scientist–practitioner interaction is well in agreement with Hoshmand and Polkinghorne's (1992) conclusion, that a revised conception of the relationship of science and practice is needed "in which there is a productive interplay rather than elevation of one form of knowledge above the other" (p. 63). In other words, a dialogical relationship is required among scientists and practitioners, moving from an asymmetrical relation in which one of the parties is intrinsically dominant over the other toward a more symmetrical relation in which both scientists and practitioners function as co-constructors of psychological reality.

As phrased above, the dialogical relationship between science and practice may sound like an ideal that encounters insurmountable obstacles. Indeed, we must not close our eyes to the fact that the Boulder model is often described as a failure. Not without reason, Barlow, Hayes, and Nelson (1984) start their book with the question: "Why is the model of a scientist–practitioner or clinician who will remain in the mainstream of scientific research in our fields still the most popular and highly revered model of training . . . despite the seeming failures of this model over the years?" (p. 4). Moreover, these authors observe that the clinical psychologists who are interested in both research and service appear to be rather small. There are even pessimists who hold that it is simply impossible to provide high-level professional and research training simultaneously (Stricker, 1975).

The above arguments are, however, not decisive objections against the validity of the model. First of all, one has to take into account, as Garfield (1966) does, that there is a lack of adequate role models. Students of psychology are not given an integrated model with which to identify, but are instead confronted by two apparently conflicting models. Second, the participants in the Boulder conference expressed their worst fears that psychotherapists would be "little more than glorified technicians switching from procedure to procedure, depending on what is in vogue or what new charismatic leader in the field of psychotherapy happens to be most visible or is giving the most workshops" (Barlow *et al.*, 1984, p. 35). It would be too simplistic to blame practitioners for proceeding this way, as long as they are educated in a system that has not provided them with an adequate knowledge base for their practice. This leads us to another, deeper reason why the Boulder model has met such obstacles.

8.2.3 The Voice of Decontextualized Rationality

The deeper reason for the scientist–practitioner split is found in the tremendous, often not fully recognized, influence of the Descartean *Cogito* that we have described in Chapter 1. One of the long-lasting implications of Descartes' view is that disembodied thinking has begun to be seen as superior and the embodied doing as inferior, resulting in a unilateral relation between science and practice in which the former has become dominant over the latter. It was Vico, who at an early stage realized that we can think *because* we have a body and that inventions are the product of "corporeal imagination." It is just this imagination that should be used in the process of "activity-oriented thinking," systematically fostered in our curricula.

It is, as Schön (1983, 1987) has proposed, the process of *reflection-in-action* that may play a crucial function for a science of practice. Reflection can bring to the surface the tacit understandings that underlie the repetitive experiences of practice and can make new sense of situations of uncertainty or uniqueness. Systematic reflection in close proximity to action may result in knowledge that is of direct relevance to the local situation in which the practitioner and the client are at work. An important characteristic of reflection-in-action is that practitioners do not postpone thinking when they act and do not simply stop action when they start a thinking process. It is rather the capacity to take, in the midst of an action, a multiplicity of views of the situation (Schön, 1983, p. 281). It is the juxtaposition of different perspectives that, in terms of Vico, draws things into new relationships and may stimulate the development of theoretical views relevant to the practical situation at hand.[4]

But why have reflection and action been separated so long in our curricula? The best answer to this question can be given in terms of what Wertsch (1987, 1991) has called "the voice of decontextualized rationality." Wertsch explains that this voice is usually associated with the Enlightenment, and its use continues to be an issue today. It typically involves that Bakhtin would call a "social speech type" rather than a purely individual voice. The voice of decontextualized rationality represents objects and events in terms of formal, logical, and, if possible, quantifiable categories. These categories are decontextualized in the sense that their meaning can be derived from abstract theories or systems that exist independently of their historical situation. For example, the meaning of "five" or "electron" can be, and often is, established by definitions that are abstract and hence identical across various contexts. An important part of Wertsch's reasoning is that the voice of decontextualized rationality is only one of several possible voices a speaker can appropriate. The fact that rationality is more a product of historical development than it is *the* defining characteristic of the human mind has led several investigators to analyze institutional and cultural factors, and the institution of formal schooling in particular (e.g., Scribner & Cole, 1981). Such research suggests that one of the messages of formal schooling is that one should value decontextualized rational modes of discourse over contextualized ones.

It is Wertsch's contention that the privileging of the rational voice is not limited to formal instructional settings. Instead, it reflects a wider tendency in modern society to allow this voice to occupy a privileged position and hence to dominate and silence other voices. The dominating rational voice has been the topic of a great deal of debate among social theorists. Lukacs (1971) has examined it under the heading of "reification," and Habermas (1970) has analyzed it in terms of "instrumental rationality." It has been observed that decontextualized rationality has traditionally been dominant even though its efficacy has often been called into question (Wertsch, 1987).

Building on Wertsch's voice of decontextualized rationality, we consider present-day psychology as a more or less divided institution in which, in terms of the previous chapter, at least two collective voices can be heard, the voice of scientists and the voice of practitioners. As long as there is a scientist–practitioner "split" or "schism," the active exchange among the two groups is seriously limited. As long as there is a unilateral relationship between science and practice in which science is considered as superior over practice, the scientific voice dominates the practical voice, with the deplorable effect that—from an epistemological perspective—practitioners cannot contribute from their own perspective and expertise to the practical–scientific process as a whole. Moreover, in a situation of asymmetry that is highly biased to "basic science," the possibility that the two parties cooperate in the co-construction of psychological reality is seriously limited. After all, the scientist–practitioner split is rooted in a value system that is hierarchically organized (with rational thinking as higher than embodied doing). It is precisely for this reason that the scientist–practitioner split represents one of the most challenging problems to psychology in the future. It requires a change from a decontextualized, analytical approach of psychological reality to a contextual, synthesizing approach.[5]

At the end of their article, Hoshmand and Polkinghorne draw two conclusions that are well in agreement with the dialogical view and the notion of synthesis proposed earlier in this book. The first is a remark from Schön (1983) that "it is unlikely that the new roles and relationships of practice and research will wholly displace the old . . . It is more likely that the two systems of relationship will coexist" (p. 325). In other words, science and practice should function as "positions" that entertain dialogical relationships and cooperate in the co-construction of psychological reality. The two positions may exist in one and the same individual who is trained in both views and systematically alternates between them. They may also exist in two separate individuals, one a scientist and another a practitioner, who cooperate on the basis of a shared system of understanding. Second, a greater role for the knowledge of practice in the scientific base of the profession is proposed. This, however, will require what Hoshmand and Polkinghorne call a "pluralistic view of knowledge." Only to the degree that there is a productive diversity of science and practice can psychologists be involved in a process of synthesis.

8.3 Centrifugal and Centripetal Forces in Psychology

In her presidential address, Spence (1987) raised a question that touched the heart of the problem of synthesis in psychology by observing that there are two tendencies at work in psychology, one in a centrifugal and another in a centripetal direction. More specifically, the question was whether psychology is a unitary discipline with a strong central core (prevalence of centripetal forces) or a series of relatively independent areas (prevalence of centrifugal forces). It may be evident that this topic concerns not only the American Psychological Association and other psychological institutions, but also, and perhaps primarily, psychology as a discipline. Let us follow Spence's observations in some more detail.

8.3.1 Psychological Science or Sciences?

Spence (1987) noted that the greatest political and organizational conflicts within the American Psychological Association have occurred along the scientist–practitioner fracture line. Psychologists' preoccupation with this split, however, has masked other centrifugal tendencies that have the potential to weaken psychology as a scientific discipline, if not to tear it apart. Without doubt we have witnessed an explosive growth of psychological knowledge in recent decades due to the support of research funding agencies and the increase in the numbers of research scientists in the years following World War II. However, psychology seems not to be any closer to a unified discipline that is founded on a shared set of theoretical principles or methodological assumptions. In this context Spence refers to Koch (1981), who holds that a unified science of psychology is an impossibility. Even when one considers this view as too extreme, it is hard to dispute the observation that contemporary psychology is composed of a collection of more or less independent areas of inquiry.

Rather than advancing toward substantive unity, Spence observes, the tide is currently moving in the centrifugal direction. Cognitive science centers, for example, draw their members from several traditional departments, including psychology. At some universities new academic units are formed that literally pull cognitive psychologists out of the departments of psychology where their initial appointments had been. A similar trend can be observed in neuroscience.

In her worst nightmares, Spence foresees a decimation of institutional psychology as it is familiar to us. Human experimental psychologists desert to the growing discipline of cognitive science; physiological psychologists go to departments of biology and neuroscience; industrial and organizational psychologists are snatched up by business schools; and psychopathologists find their place in medical schools. Clinicians, school psychologists, and other health care practitioners would found their own free-standing professional schools or schools of education. Only personality psychologists, social psychologists, and some developmental psychologists would have no place else to go. As a result of this process, departments of psychology would be "pale shadows of their former selves" (Spence, 1987, p. 1053). Their members would be outnumbered and outclassed by the natural sciences on the one hand and the humanities on the other hand.

Spence is not pessimistic to such a degree that she expects that her doomsday scenario will ever be literally played out. She observes, however, that we are at the present time uncomfortably close to having a psychology with not just two cultures (scientists and practitioners), but three cultures (each with their subcultures) that *at best* get along by ignoring each other. These cultures are hard science, soft science, and professional practice. In other words, psychology is not only split along the scientist–practitioner fracture line, but also within the realm of science, in which hard science is generally considered as "higher" or "more scientific" than soft science.

Although Spence's diagnosis of present-day psychology is certainly emphasizing centrifugal forces, she concludes her contribution in a moderately optimistic way. Although various groups are drawing apart, the growth of knowledge is also leading to developments that bridge areas and result in applications that were simply not visible a few decades ago. As examples, she refers to the emergence of health psychology and the growing collaboration of social and clinical psychologists. She expressed the ambivalence of the situation by saying with the words of Dickens, that we are in the worst of times and in the best of times.

8.3.2 Opposing Forces in Psychology and the Synthesizing Process

Psychology is an institution in which various (collective) voices can be heard. As far as there are divergent cultures (e.g., hard science, soft science, professional practice), different voices tell different stories about what psychology is or should be. Such collective voices determine to a large degree what the main themes are and "pet variables" (Scarr, 1985) of a particular group in a particular period. Such themes and variables are central elements in the communication of psychologists in their specialized journals, congresses, workshops, and meetings. As far as these collective voices ignore one another, there simply can't be any productive exchange. As far as one group sees another as inferior or even develops a unilateral epistemology (e.g., practitioners apply what scientists have invented), dominance relationships may develop resulting in a monocultural view of psychology as a field.

It is worthwhile to consider psychology as if it is a self in which centrifugal and centripetal forces are at work, as we have described in Chapter 6. As Spence (1987) describes, centrifugal tendencies are certainly prevalent at present, although centripetal tendencies are not absent. Rather, both tendencies are at work, the one perhaps counteracting the other, as if evoking a response. Altman (1987) also observed that in every period in the history of psychology, both centrifugal and centripetal forces are simultaneously present. Despite this simultaneity, he argues that there are enough indications that they also are alternatingly dominant in successive periods. In view of this relative dominance, he divided the history of psychology into three periods: (1) The pre-1900 period that was primarily centrifugal; (2) the period from 1900 to 1960 in which centripetal forces were strongest; and (3) the period from 1960 to the present, in which powerful centrifugal forces are at work.

The modern era of psychology may be said to have begun with the founding of Wilhelm Wundt's psychological laboratory in 1879 and the organization of the American Psychological Association in 1892. Prior to 1879, Altman observes strong centrifugal trends in psychological studies. The main reason was that psychology as a "field" did not exist in the decades and centuries prior to the modern era. Early scholars of psychology were often identified with other disciplines such as philosophy, medicine, biology, or with no discipline at all. There was little sense of a defined field of psychology with common values, methods, and approaches. In a time in which there were simply no psychology departments, early scholars explored psychological phenomena in an independent and noninstitutional fashion.

In the beginning of the second period, different philosophical and theoretical views vied to be the dominant paradigm in the field. These included structuralism, functionalism, instinct theory, gestalt approaches, and behaviorism. Eventually, the behaviorist perspective dominated American psychology, although the gestalt orientation continued to play a significant role. Although there were several variants of the behaviorist perspective, they collectively provided a unifying centripetal anchor for American psychology in subsequent years (theories of Watson, Hull, Tolman, Skinner). There were also nonbehaviorist unifying theories that emerged in this period, such as the field theory of Lewin, the personality approaches of Murray and Allport, and stage theories of child development. In this period of "grand theories," psychological theorizing and research were increasingly centripetal. From a methodological perspective, there was a significant degree of unification also. The pervasive influence of the physical and natural sciences contributed to a strong belief in the value of experimental, laboratory-oriented research and a veering away from introspection, self-report, and phenomenology. Emphasis was placed on rigorous quantification and measurement.

The third period, from 1960 onward, was an ideal time, Altman observes, for building departments and colleges and expanding state systems of education. Universities expanded and included many disciplines and subdisciplines. Psychology departments became increasingly focused on their own development without regard to the institution as a whole. Achieving excellence and being in the "top 10 or top 20" were the slogans of many administrators. Excellence was usually measured by research productivity, publications, grant funds, and national visibility. On the contrary, teaching excellence or participation in university affairs counted to a lesser degree. More and more seminars were offered on narrower topics and specialization was emphasized. In the same period there was a shifting allegiance of APA members to other constituencies. Together with the proliferation of specialities and the emergence of interest groups, this shifting allegiance functioned as a strong centrifugal force that led to the loss of a common core of ideas in psychology as a whole.

Although Altman (1987) gives sometimes the impression that he deplores some of the developments in the third period, he explicitly emphasizes that he does not consider one of the two forces as "better" than the other:

> I must reiterate that neither centrifugal nor centripetal trends are intrinsically "good" or "bad." One can praise or decry centripetal trends, for example, as reflecting status quo and stagnation on the negative side, or unity, harmony, and stability on the positive side. Similarly, centrifugal trends can be viewed negatively, for example, as indicating divisiveness and disunity, or positively, for example, as allowing for enrichment and exploration of new directions . . . we should not evaluate either trend as intrinsically good or bad. Rather we should attempt to assess their respective strengths, directions, and characteristics in order to adjust to and capitalize on their qualities. [pp. 1062–1063]

From this perspective, psychology at the institutional level is involved in a synthesizing process that is basically similar to the synthesizing process that is at work at the individual level (see Chapter 6). In this synthesizing process, both centrifugal and centripetal forces are necessary and complement each other. If only centripetal forces are at work, psychology and the self run the risk of becoming highly centralized with only one position as dominant, abandoning creative diversity in the service of the unity of the status quo. Psychology and self would become rigid and closed off from the surrounding world and society and devoid of renewing and innovating impulses. If, however, only centripetal forces are at work, self and psychology would dissolve into fragmentation and disintegration and lose their core. Only if centrifugal and centripetal forces are dialectically related, complementing each other and alternating each other in the course of time, can self and psychology be involved in a process of synthesis.

Both on the individual level and on the institutional level there is a multiplicity of voices that, in the process of interrelationship, may at times sound like a cacaphony. Nevertheless this multiplicity permits a juxtaposition of contrasting views that, if dialogically related, will contribute to the never-ending process of synthesis. Moving on the basic rhythm of centripetal and centrifugal forces, psychology and the self both develop like an unfinished symphony.

8.4 Psychology as a Field of Relative Independent Positions: The Danger of Premature Unification

In this chapter we have dealt with three separations that have played a central role in psychology as a discipline: between psychologist and subject, between science and practice, and between psychological subdisciplines. We have discussed these separations from the standpoint of two defining characteristics of dialogical relationships, exchange and dominance, and analyzed them in terms of collective voices. Moreover, we have brought to attention that psychology is involved in a continuous oscillation of centrifugal and centripetal forces and that the synthesis of psychology can only be captured in terms of this dynamic opposition. As in the case of the individual self, psychology as a "collective self" is dynamized by the interplay of relative autonomous "positions."

In discussing the first separation, we have demonstrated that the person is not merely an "object of study" that can simply be analyzed. We have reacted to such a reification of the person, in fact, and have emphasized the original position of subjects in the research situation, from which they can cooperate with the researcher and contribute to the scientific process from their own specific expertise and irreplaceable knowledge of their local situation. It would be a great misunderstanding if one were to think here that the expert knowledge of the psychologist would be reduced or even replaced by the knowledge system of the subject. On the contrary, as we have demonstrated in actual developments in personality psychology of past decades, the psychologist *as a scientist* apparently profits from the contribution of the knowledgeable subject.

The second separation is also discussed by placing scientist and practitioner in different positions that again are dialogically related. As Hoshmand and Polkinghorne have emphasized, the role of the scientist will not be replaced by the role of the practitioner. Instead, they expect that the two roles will coexist. In other words, a diversity of positions, even if they are contrasting, is expected to be profitable for psychology as a field.

Finally, the third separation also refers to the existence of a multiplicity of positions, that is, those corresponding with diverse psychological subdisciplines. All those differentiations belong to the multicolored field of psychology that acknowledges the complexity of the discipline as it acknowledges the complexity of the individual self. It is our belief that, thanks to diversity and multiplicity, there is the possibility of cross-fertilization, a notion that so much inspired the members of the Boulder conference.

The acknowledgment of the relative autonomy of positions in psychology as a discipline is of particular importance if one is aware of "the danger of premature unification." With this term we refer to the risk that what may appear to be a "unification" at first sight might be unmasked as the ideologically justified dominance of only one position. We already discussed the example of the unilateral relationship between science and practice. Another example is the idea that unification can be achieved by developing broad, generalizing concepts that are based on the consensus of specialists in the field. The subjects and the public have no voice in this case, because their perspective on the topic is considered irrelevant. Further, one might hear some colleagues say: "Only cognitive psychology and the neurosciences have demonstrated real progress in the past decennia, therefore the other subdisciplines better borrow their models from these fields." At the epistemological level we discussed Wertsch's (1987) "voice of decontextualized rationality" that seemed for so long the only true voice of science. In our era, however, more and more psychologists have become convinced that it is, as a historical acquisition, only one of the *possible* voices. All these examples, however divergent they may be, have in common that they adhere to some form of unification with the simultaneous absence or deliberate avoidance of diversity and opposition. It is our strong belief that synthesis in psychology has to confront the challenge of diversity and opposition in order to become a science that will become better equipped to meet the richness and complexity of the human person.

Notes

1. The material in this section has been published in more detail by Hermans and Bonarius (1991a) and Hermans (1991). These articles were critically discussed by Lamiell (1991) and led to a rejoinder by Hermans and Bonarius (1991b).

2. For a discussion of the advantages and disadvantages of such a dialogical model see Hermans and Bonarius (1991a).

3. Recent support of the Boulder model was also provided by O'Sullivan and Que-

villon (1992), who approached the Clinical Psychology program directors at 138 American Psychological Association (APA) approved doctoral programs and 96 terminal master's programs. Directors of 97.8% of the 90 doctoral programs and 74.1% of the 58 master's programs who responded stated that their programs follow the Boulder model.

4. Action research (e.g., Argyris, Putnam, & Smith, 1985) is only one example of this approach. It is our belief that we are only at the beginning of a development that will result in new models for a productive relationship of theory and practice.

5. It must be noted that the dominance under discussion is of an epistemological kind. This does not exclude that practitioners may become dominant over scientists in other respects. For example, Howard, Pion, Gottfredson, Flattau, Oskamp, Pfafflin, Bray, and Burstein (1986) and Spence (1987) pointed to the fact that the number of health care providers has rapidly expanded within the APA to the point of rivaling or outstripping the number of those in academic specialties, resulting in a shift in the balance of power.

CHAPTER 9

The Construction and Co-Construction of Meaning: Explorations into a Psychology of Valuation

In this final chapter we address the issue of meaning, a concept that is at the heart of what may be called "the second cognitive revolution" in psychology (Bruner, 1990; Harré, 1992). More specifically, we will raise the question of what "meaning" is from the perspective of the dialogical self. In addressing this question, we will not limit ourselves to the promises of the dialogical self for future research, leaving it to others as to what to do with the theoretical discussions of the preceding chapters. Rather, we will focus on some methodological work we have done in the recent past, in which we have confronted ourselves with the question: What has the concept of the dialogical self to offer to the empirical study of meaning? The reader should be aware that it is certainly not our position that the work to be presented here is the only or even the best way to empirically investigate meaning from the perspective of the dialogical self. Rather, it is merely *one* method that serves as an *example* for other attempts that may follow in the future. It is a first elaboration that expresses, as Kelly (1955) would say, an "invitational mood" rather than an exclusive methodological program. In brief, it is our main purpose here to make the rather abstract theoretical discussions more concrete so that future researchers and practitioners may learn from them and explore other and better alternatives as a response.

9.1 Manifest and Latent Levels of Meaning: A Structural Approach

One of the most conspicuous features of stories and narratives is their immense diversity among individuals, groups, nations, and cultures. There are not simply many different stories to tell, but even the "same" story is told in a variety of ways. Depending on historical and cultural circumstances and, not in the least, on the imagination of the storyteller, a story such as, let's say, Snow White, Narcissus, or Faust is transmitted in many different versions. The immense diversity of stories was reason for scholars to investigate the basic structure of stories in order to reduce their great phenomenal variety to a more limited number of basic forms or types. As we have discussed already in Chapter 3, Lévi-Strauss was interested in myths of diverse origin and considered them as expressions of a small number of basic structures. Another pioneer, Propp (1968) was also looking for a deep structure underlying the immense diversity of Russian folk tales and took grammar, the "abstract substratum" of living language, as a model for his study. In the area of linguistics, Chomsky (1966) posed the problem of generativity: How can humans generate, from a finite base of experience, an infinite set of realizable surface expressions? In order to tackle this problem, he studied language on two levels, a surface and a deeper level of functioning. In the realm of psychology, Freud's theory is probably the most elaborated example of a generative approach. His conceptualization of dreams, symptom formation, and defense mechanisms explicitly describes the transformation of latent thoughts into manifest ones. More recently Gregg (1991), analyzing open-interview data, proposed a model that concentrates on the continual shifting of identity among contradictory "surface" discourses of the self and showed how each discourse is defined as a reconfiguration of a stable cluster of "deep" structurally ambiguous elements.

Building on the contributions mentioned above, the following question is of central importance to our thinking: Is there a basic structure underlying the immense diversity of self and dialogue? This question is critical as there are as many dialogues and selves as there are people in the world. This point becomes even more compelling when we realize that in the dialogical self one and the same person can tell different stories from a multiplicity of positions.

9.1.1 Basic Similarity of Self and Dialogue

In this book we have made an attempt to combine and integrate two concepts, self and dialogue. Can this integration be further pursued by looking for a basic structure that applies not only to one of the conceptual components, self and dialogue, but to both? Is it possible to find in the realm of the self a basic structure that is similar to the basic structure that can be found for the notion of dialogue? Let us first formulate the answer to this question and then look for the evidence. It is our thesis that both self and dialogue can be characterized by two basic components, one that accounts for the independence and closeness of positions, the other for their interdependence and openness.

A variety of students have argued for the duality of self and mind. A well-known formulation is from Bakan (1966), who distinguished between *agency* (self-maintenance and self-expansion) and *communion*. A comparable view on the duality of the self was presented by Angyal (1965), who discussed *autonomy* (self-determination) and *homonomy* (self-surrender) as two mutually complementing forces. Similarly, Loevinger (1976) described the reconciliation of *autonomy* and *interdependence* at the highest (i.e., autonomous and integrated) stages of ego development. Klages (1948) considered *Bindung* (solidification) and *Lösung* (dissolution) as two complementing components of human character. In a clinical–developmental study, Gutmann (1980) observed a blending of *masculinity* and *femininity* after midlife. In a study of mystic and meditative experiences, Deikman (1971, 1976) distinguished between an *action mode* and a *receptive mode* of consciousness and argued that the mature person is able to alternate between these two modes. Fowler (1981) described the rapprochement of the *rational* and the *ecstatic* at the highest stage of human faith. McAdams (1985a) has identified the distinction between *power* and *intimacy* within an explicitly narrative context. Hermans (1987a) distinguished the striving for *self-enhancement* (self-maintenance and self-expansion), or S motive, and the longing for *contact and union* with the other, or O motive, as mutually complementing orientations in the world. Recently, Markus and Kitayama (1991) emphasized the importance of *independence* and *interdependence* for the self from a cultural point of view. All these characterizations seem to have in common that there are two fundamental, mutually complementing forces in the self: one that attempts to maintain or even increase its separateness and autonomy, and another that aims to open the self to the surrounding world in order to participate in some large whole (see also Kempen, 1990).

The description of the self in terms of two basic motivational characteristics is highly similar to the two defining characteristics of the concept of dialogue that we have extensively discussed: dominance and intersubjective exchange. The basic rhythm of dialogue is turn taking. A person taking his or her turn in a conversation has a dominant position at the moment of speaking ("now it's my turn") and has during this turn the opportunity to express his or her own view from a relatively autonomous position. We have already referred to Linell (1990), who has demonstrated that there are several means for exposing one's individual view and controlling the content and direction of the communication: Interactional dominance, topic dominance, amount of talk, and strategic moves (Chapter 5). On the other hand, intersubjective exchange is only possible if parties open themselves to one another and give the *other* party the opportunity to take his or her turn.[1]

Self and dialogue have on a basic level two characteristics in common: (1) the separateness and autonomy of the self correspond with dominance in turn-taking behavior; and (2) the openness and participation in the self correspond with the intersubjective exchange in dialogue. We have described the dialogical self in terms of a multiplicity of relatively autonomous *I positions*. The adjective "relatively" can be further explained from a structural view. If a position would be entirely autonomous, there would be no dialogue because there would be no openness or exchange with other positions. If, however, the position would have no autonomy at all, or would even be suppressed by other positions, it could not express an own specific view and, again, the possibilities of dialogical exchange would be seriously reduced.

In sum, given the myriads of possible stories, which differ among people and also within the multivoiced mind of an individual person (each position has an own story to tell), it makes sense to distinguish two levels of functioning in the dialogical self: a manifest or surface level, and a latent or deeper level. The phenomenological variety of narratives, both between people and within the same individual, are on the manifest level. On a latent level of functioning, however, a limited number of basic forces or motives is supposed, influencing the content and organization of the stories on the manifest level. Note that the distinction between manifest and latent level applies not only to individual stories but also to collective stories (myths, fables, fairy tales, famous films, rumors in town, stories about economic recession, etc).

9.1.2 Manifest Valuations Structured by Basic Motives

The latent–manifest distinction underlies recent work we have done on the basis of valuation theory (Hermans, 1987a,b, 1988, 1992b,c). In this theory, the concept "valuation" is on the manifest level and the concept "motive" is on the latent level. The theory's central concept, *valuation*, is an active process of meaning construction on the basis of self-reflection. It is an open concept and includes anything people find to be of importance when telling their life story: a precious memory, a disturbing problem, a good talk with a friend, an unreachable ideal, etc. A valuation is any unit of meaning that has a positive (pleasant), negative (unpleasant), or ambivalent (both pleasant and unpleasant) value in the eyes of the individual. Because the person is in different situations across time and space, different valuations emerge and are organized in a valuation system (for examples of specific valuations see Alice's case in Chapter 6).

An essential feature of valuation theory is the assumption that each valuation has an affective connotation, that is, each valuation implies a specific pattern of affect: an affective modality. When we know which types of affect are implied by a particular valuation, we also know something about the valuation itself. Note that affect in this theory is not considered a direct "result" of cognitive processing but an inherent part of valuation.[2]

In order to capture specific differences in the functioning of the affective component of the valuation system, it is assumed that a small set of basic motives is represented latently in the affective component of a valuation. The two motives we have used are the striving for self-enhancement (S motive) and the longing for contact and union with the other (O motive). These basic motives are assumed to be similar across individuals and to be continuously active within each individual moving through time and space. At the manifest level, valuations vary phenomenologically, not only across individuals, but also within a single individual across time and space.

To summarize, when a person values something, he or she always feels something about it and in these feelings the basic motives are reflected. When a valuation represents a gratification of the S motive (e.g., "I won that game by training hard"), then the person experiences a feeling of strength and pride implied in the valuation. In a similar way, a valuation can function as a gratification of the O motive (e.g., "I enjoy my daughter playing her instrument"). Feelings of tenderness and intimacy experienced in connection with the specific valuation are indicators of this particular motive. The affective component of individual valuations can be seen as a representation of the latent motivational base.

The central idea behind the empirical illustrations to be described in the next sections is that *each I position has its own valuation system* and that valuations constructed from the perspective of a particular position can be considered *utterances* that can be exchanged with the valuations of other positions. In this way different positions are able to influence the valuations of the other positions in a dialogical fashion. At the same time we will examine if, at the latent level, more basic motivational structures underlie the great variety of valuations at the manifest level.

9.1.3 The Self-Confrontation Method: Qualitative and Quantitative Analyses

A structural approach, in terms of different levels of functioning of the self, can be methodologically elaborated on in various ways. Gregg (1991) proposed an approach in which he used open-ended interviews, including the TAT and the Sentence Completion test. Gregg's procedures are mainly of a qualitative nature. The self-confrontation method that we have devised is based on a combination of qualitative (valuations) and quantitative data (affective indices). In our description of the self-confrontation method we will limit ourselves to those elements that will be used in the following empirical illustrations.

The self-confrontation method, based on valuation theory, is an idiographic instrument that invites the individual to investigate his or her valuation system in close collaboration with a psychologist. The method is designed for the study of the relation between valuations (formulated by the person) and types of affect (provided by the psychologist). The method enables one to study the way in which these variables get organized into a structured whole and change over time (Hermans, 1987a, 1988, 1989). The procedure involves having the subject rate a list of valuations generated by the subject using a fixed set of affect-denoting terms (described below). The result is a matrix in which the affective pattern characteristic of a specific valuation for a particular individual can be seen (see Appendix). The procedure is usually performed more than once, with several weeks or months intervening, in order to detect the constancies and changes in the valuations and their corresponding affective patterns.

The valuations (rows in the matrix) are elicited by a series of open-ended questions administered by a trained interviewer (for the questions see Chapter 6, Table 1). Next, a standard list of affect terms (columns in the matrix) is presented to the subject. Concentrating on a single valuation, subjects are asked to indicate on a scale of 0–5 to what extent they experience each affect in connection with the particular valuation. All statements are successively evaluated with the same list of affect terms. The list used in the present study is the most recent version in use (i.e., a condensed form of the list used by Hermans, 1987a) and contains 16 affect terms.

On the basis of the information contained in each valuation matrix a number of indices can be calculated which refer to the latent motives associated with a particular valuation. The indices relevant for the present study are the following:

1. Index S is the sum score of four affect terms expressing self-enhancement: self-esteem, strength, self-confidence, and pride.
2. Index O is the sum score of four affect terms expressing contact and union with the other: caring, love, tenderness, and intimacy. For each valuation, the $S - O$ difference can be determined. When the experience of self-enhancement is stronger than the experience of contact, $S > O$. When contact with the other prevails, $O > S$. When self-enhancement and contact coexist, $S = O$.
3. Index P is the sum score for four positive affect terms: joy, happiness, enjoyment, and inner calm.
4. Index N is the sum score for four negative affect terms: worry, unhappiness, despondency, and disappointment. For each valuation, the $P - N$ difference can be studied. This indicates the degree of well-being the person experiences in relation to the specific valuation. Well-being is positive when $P > N$, negative when $N > P$, when ambivalent when $P = N$. (Note that the scores for each of the four indices S, O, P, and N range from 0 to 20.) (For reliability and validity data on the above-mentioned indices, see Hermans, 1987b, pp. 166, 169–171.)

The rationale behind these indices is that they give in their combination information about the expression of the basic motives in the specific valuations and in the valuation system as a whole. If the basic motives are fulfilled, positive affect is expected to prevail over negative affect. When, however, the motives encounter insurmountable obstacles, it is expected that negative affect will prevail.

The results of the investigation are discussed with the person, usually 1 week later. This discussion has the quality of an intensive self-reflection and a profound dialogue with the interviewer. Person and interviewer base their discussion on the overall picture provided by the system of elicited valuations. Hitherto hidden meanings and specific patterns of responding become visible and thereby open for discussion. The discussion is fed by information from the individual affects, affect indices, and comparison of the affect patterns across different valuations. The basic motives that are at work also become obvious. The purpose behind the discussion with the person is to gain a deeper insight into the content and organization of the valuation system, to raise new questions, and to stimulate further exploration of the valuation system or relevant parts of it.

After some weeks or months, usually a second (and sometimes a third and a fourth) self-investigation follows. In this case, however, the subjects do not start "from scratch." Instead, they are confronted with the statements they constructed in the first (or previous) session. The interviewer reads the original questions aloud to the subject and produces the statements that the subject provided in the preceding self-investigation. The subjects are invited to consider, for each statement separately, whether they still go along with it. When this is not the case, the interviewer explains that there are various options available: An old valuation may be reformulated (modification), replaced (substitution), discarded altogether (elimination), or a new response may be added (supplementation). In this way the subjects have considerable freedom to express the constant and changing elements in their own valuation systems. In the case that the interviewer and the subject decide to investigate more than one *I* position, then there are more valuation systems and, by implication, the construction and reconstruction of the valuation system are done for each position separately (e.g., Alice's case in Chapter 6).

In the following three illustrations we will deal with several ways in which *I* positions express themselves in valuations and how they enter into dialogical relations.

9.1.4 Illustration 1: Conflicting Valuations in the Process of Synthesis[3]

Jim, age 45, worked as a politician in the Dutch government. A few weeks before he performed a self-investigation, his superiors had informed him during his yearly evaluation that his job performance was inadequate. As a result, he was considering leaving his job and reorienting himself toward another vocation. Six months after the first self-investigation Jim participated in a second investigation. Several months after the second investigation he decided to leave his job and pursue another vocation. Some of his valuations of the first self-investigation (Time 1) and their development in the second self-investigation (Time 2) are presented in Table 3.

In valuation 1 of Table 3, Jim expresses his extreme disappointment with the

Table 3

Jim's Valuations at Time 1 and Time 2 and Their Scores on the Affective Indices S, O, P, and N[a]

Time 1	S	O	P	N	Time 2	S	O	P	N
1. The evaluation in The Hague was bad and I couldn't get out of it; I had my back against the wall.	0	0	0	20	It all went wrong in The Hague because of fear of success and fear of failure.	0	0	0	19
2. My mother always put me on a huge pedestal and I have always liked that very much; it gave me the feeling of being a chosen one, of being a high-standing person.	13	4	8	3	My striving toward excellence is less of a concern to me now than the new awareness that I have to become whole, that is, accepting my dark side, unifying my strengths and weaknesses.	14	0	13	2
3. I don't want to be a prisoner of myself any longer by all of the "shoulds" and plans that I impose on myself; I want to get to the heart of the matter.	17	4	13	1	My developments of the last year; I have become a more gentle person.	8	12	12	2
4. All of my planning and my "shoulds" cut and still cut me off from being spontaneous.	0	0	0	16	The planning and programming were and still are related to not knowing what I really want; it cut and still cuts me off from being spontaneous.	1	0	1	13
5. I want work that permits me to be more socially involved with other people; I want to find the right job for me.	14	8	12	1	I want work that permits me to be more socially involved with other people; I want to find the right job for me.	13	10	10	3
6. The structure of society as it evolved and could evolve.	10	5	6	9	The relationship from human to human in society; the human rights, the sad awareness that the human is far from perfect; still I want to continue my efforts for improvement.	7	7	5	10

[a]S, affect referring to self-enhancement; O, affect referring to contact; P, positive affect; N, negative affect.

critical judgment he received from his superiors (see also the maximum score for negative affect). This event created an irreconcilable conflict with the feeling he had hitherto of being "on a huge pedestal" and a "high-standing person," a feeling particularly fostered by his mother (valuation 2). At the same time, Jim was aware that his striving toward perfection, his strains in his planning, and his sense of "shoulds" were detrimental to his personality development (valuations 3, 4, and 5). The uncertainty of his position was also reflected in his view of society (valuation 6).

In fact, two positions are involved in the irreconcilable conflict described above, one representing the perspective of his superiors, the other, the perspective of his mother (as constructed by Jim). A most conspicuous change in Jim's valuation system is his attempt to resolve this conflict. The modification of valuation 2 from Time 1 to Time 2 refers to his "new awareness" that he wants to accept his "dark side" and to reconcile his strengths and weaknesses. In this modification, Jim has brought together elements of two different valuations from two positions that were rather separated at Time 1. This reconstruction is only possible if Jim has proceeded to actively interrelate the two valuations.

The modified valuation 2 at Time 2 is a good example of what we have described in Chapter 6 as the process of synthesis. This process requires a metaposition from which the person is able to juxtapose and interrelate other positions. The modified valuation 2 could be described as representing a "third position" from which the two original positions (expressed in valuation 1 and 2 at Time 1) are actively interrelated in such a way that a new construction results. The inclusion of this valuation into the system certainly does not mean that the system as a whole is "synthesized." Rather, part of the system is in the process of synthesis. It remains to be seen if this process is continued. If it is continued, it is possible that other valuations also are taken up in this process.[4]

What conditions must be met for the subject to express his or her knowledge as a "meaning expert" (Chapter 8) in psychological assessment? In order to answer this question, let us look more closely at what happened in Jim's case. We have seen that the reorganization of his valuation system implied that the conflict *between* valuations 1 (referring to failure) and 2 (referring to success) at Time 1 was contracted *within* valuation 2 at Time 2 (referring to a new relation between success and failure). Such a reshuffling can only take place if, at the theoretical level, the existence of open and malleable "units of meaning" is supposed. The concept of valuation is open to the extent that new insights resulting from a vast array of experiences can be expressed. It is malleable in so far as new connections and insights, including those resulting from the investigation itself, can lead to modified or even completely new units of meaning.

Finally, Jim's case also demonstrates the usefulness of the latent–manifest distinction. Although the formulations of Jim's valuations are more or less referring to different aspects of his life situation, they show a clear commonality from the perspective of latent level. Four of the six valuations at Time 1 have higher levels for self-enhancement than for contact and union. On the other hand, no valuation at Time 1 has a prevalence of contact and union over self-enhancement. In view of this rather extreme imbalance, the development of valuation 3 is conspicuous: It develops from a prevalence of self-enhancement at Time 1 to a prevalence of contact and union at Time 2. Although there remains a considerable imbalance between the two basic motives at Time 2, the development of valuation 3 is a remarkable one and deserves special attention in the discussion between psychologist and subject.

It must be noted that the analysis of Jim's case is, from the perspective of the conceptual characteristics of the dialogical self, a limited example. Although it includes several positions and significant interrelationships between the valuations associated with these positions, the investigation of the self proceeds in a rather centralized way. That is, there is only *one* central *I* position, the position of Jim, who has been invited to phrase a number of valuations. The resulting valuations referred to several positions (e.g., mother, superior), but none of *these* positions was given a separate voice. Therefore, we will go one step further in the next illustration.

9.1.5 Illustration 2: Personality Traits as Opposing Characters

The next illustration is based on Bakhtin's (1929/1973) discussion of agreement and disagreement as basic forms of dialogue, which we discussed in Chapter 3. Our subject is Peter, a social worker, 38 years old and a part-time college student. The interviewer invited Peter to describe, in his own terms, two opposite aspects of his personality, which then were examined in terms of two contrasting *I* positions. Peter formulated these aspects as "my active side" and "my passive side." The interviewer then invited him to take the role of his active *I* and, reflecting on himself as an active person, to formulate two valuations referring to his past, two valuations referring to his present, and another two valuations referring to his future. In a second round, Peter was invited to take the role of his passive *I* and to follow the same procedure, now from the perspective of his passive *I*. After the formulation of the valuations, he was invited to rate all valuations from the perspective of *both* positions. This procedure implies that the active *I* characterized not only the affective properties of its own valuations but also gave its affective response to the valuations from the passive *I*. In reverse, the passive *I* responded affectively to its own valuations and to the valuations from the active *I*.

The procedure described above can best be understood by drawing a parallel with two friends in conversation. One says: "I want to visit France, where my parents were born" (valuation) and adds "I like it" (positive affect). The friend answers, "I don't like it" (negative affect), in which case they disagree in their affective response concerning the same valuation. When the friend, however, answers, "I like it," the two parties agree. In our investigation we proceed in a similar way, with the difference that there are not two persons, but two positions. That is, we compare the affective responses of the two positions for each valuation separately.

For demonstration purposes, some conspicuous results of Peter's investigation are presented in Table 4. As this table shows, there are valuations that receive similar affective meanings from both I positions (Nos. 1 and 3), particularly on the indices P and N. On the contrary, there are also valuations (Nos. 2 and 4) where the two positions strongly disagree concerning the affective meaning of the valuation. In the latter case, we observe the existence of contrasting affective patterns with respect to the same valuation. In other words, for some valuations we find clear agreement between the two (opposite) positions and for other valuations we find strong disagreement (a typical finding also for other subjects who have applied the same procedure).

Peter's case exemplifies also the significance of the notion of collective voice (Chapter 8). When Peter mentioned the opposite trait pair active–passive, he explained that it was not really a problem for him to be an active person. Not only did he himself like to see himself as active, but also the people in his surrounding. This was not only true for the people of his work and his fellow students, but also for his wife "who prefers to see me as a person taking initiatives." His passive side, on the contrary, was more problematic as there was simply nobody in his present life who had a rewarding attitude toward his passivity (which meant for him such divergent things as daydreaming, looking at distracting TV programs, or simply "doing nothing"). In other words, the people in his surrounding were mainly representatives of an active, achieving society that had little tolerance for his passive side. Why would Peter not give up his passive side and concentrate on his active side only, rewarding as it is from a societal point of view? This question can be answered by looking to valuation 2 in Table 4, a valuation formulated by the active I. As expected, this valuation is negative for the active I.[5] For the passive I, however, it is clearly positive. Why? Peter explained that—as a passive I— he liked situations of confusion simply because in situations wherein "all goes wrong" activities have to be suspended and there is the chance "to switch" and "to relax," which he enjoyed as a passive and not as an active person. More in general, he fostered his passivity because it gave him something that his activity could not provide: peace of mind.

The fact that Peter's active side is dominating his passive side is also expressed in the valuations. In valuation 4 he says that—as a passive I—he is more and more accepting of himself. This indicates that the passive I, being in an underdog position, has to take care for its own existence given a collective voice that denies or rejects it. The problem of self-acceptance indicates that the collective voice is not simply outside, but also inside the self. It is present *in* the active I that experiences the growing self-acceptance of the passive I as clearly negative

Table 4

Valuations From Peter's Active *I-Position* and Passive *I-Position*

Valuation	Active I				Passive I				Relationship
	S^a	O	P	N	S	O	P	N	
From active I									
1. After the engagement with my girlfriend (my wife later) was broken off I felt a sparkle of activity and became suddenly aware that I had to fight for something.	12	8	12	2	7	14	14	0	Agree
2. In my activities, I am often chaotic, confuse all kinds of things so that I often don't know what is the point.	13	0	0	12	8	9	12	0	Disagree
From passive I									
3. I was bothered by the fact that I always stood alone in my contact with others; people always said about me, "Still waters run deep."	6	2	6	9	4	5	2	8	Agree
4. More and more I am accepting myself as passive.	5	1	4	10	9	15	12	2	Disagree

^{a}S, affect referring to self-enhancement; O, affect referring to contact; P, positive affect; N, negative affect.

(see the indices P and N). It is perhaps significant to observe that *not* the active *I*, but the passive *I* explicitly touches the problem of self-acceptance. The passive *I* can raise this problem because it has received, as part of the self-investigation, a voice to speak from its own specific perspective. If Peter, at some point in his development, had made a split between his "higher" active and his "lower" passive side (which he has apparently *not* done), only the active self would speak, the passive self perhaps being projected on a minority group.

From the perspective of self-organization, it is important to note that in the supposed case, there is only one voice speaking, the voice of the active character. There is not much interest in this character speaking about the self-acceptance of other characters that are split off or suppressed. Speaking about the self-acceptance of the other character would be only to the detriment of the dominating position of the active *I*. Such a centralized self may not even be aware of any problem of self-acceptance since the parts that were seen as "rejectable" have already been deleted from the self. A more complete picture of self-acceptance would only be achieved if the interviewer could consult those *I* positions that are suppressed or split. However, if they are split, they are not available. And if they are suppressed, their voices may be so silenced that they cannot be heard. Special educational or training procedures are needed then to stimulate the imagination and the dialogical contact among positions. In Peter's case, however, we can observe that this contact has not disappeared. He is fostering his passive side *despite* the dominance of the collective voice, and he does so in the conviction that this contributes to the enrichment of his personality.

That the self becomes enriched by the inclusion of the passive position is also evident from a motivational point of view. The affect from the active position shows a consistent tendency to have higher S than O scores, whereas affect from the passive position, on the contrary, tends to have higher O than S scores. This suggests that the passive side of Peter's personality may redress the imbalance resulting from the striving for self-enhancement so typical of his active side.

9.1.6 Illustration 3: Dialogue as a Three-Step Procedure

The preceding illustration included two positions, each with its own set of valuations. Moreover, the two positions responded to each other. This, however, is still a dialogue in a rather restricted sense. As Marková (1987) has argued, a truly dialogical model is not based on two steps (from A to B and from B to A), but on three steps:

step 1: A to B
step 2: B to A
step 3: A to B

In this model, A in step 3 is no longer the same as A in step 1 but changes to some extent by the dialogical process itself. This is what happens in conversations in which people permit themselves to be influenced by the other's point of view. In the first step, A might say: "This is my view." In the second step, B responds: "I have another way of seeing it." In the third step, A changes more or less his or her initial view: "Now I look at it in another way."

The following illustration is based on the three-step model. The material used is inspired by Murray's TAT procedure, one of the first systematic attempts to develop an assessment technique using people's narratives. The TAT pictures show a remarkable feature from a dialogical point of view. *The pictured people make no contact with the subject looking at the picture.* If people are pictured alone (e.g., a boy with a violin), they are seen as separated from the viewer and do not make contact with him or her. When there is more than one person on a picture, they may make contact with one another, but not with the viewer. The guiding idea for our exploration was to provide subjects with a picture in which the portrayed person makes eye contact with the viewer, so that the pictorial constellation facilitates an imaginal dialogue with the viewer.

The picture selected (Fig. 3) is a copy of *Mercedes de Barcelona* (1930), a painting of the Dutch artist Pyke Koch (1901–1992). Although Koch was an autodidact with a unique artistic development, he has been classified as representative of *Magic Realism*. This trend has been described as: "A naturalistic or photographic kind of twentieth-century painting in which the artist is at great pains to reproduce the elements of nature as carefully as possible but in which he also creates an emotional tension and a sense of suspense" (Myers, 1979, p. 314).[6] Koch himself characterized this trend by distinguishing it from surrealism: "Magic realism uses images that are possible but not probable; surrealism, on the contrary, makes use of impossible, not existing situations" (Blotkamp, 1972, p. 37). Typical features of Koch's art are his placing of figures frontal to the viewer and his use of space. By making space shallow and small, the figure is strongly foregrounded and pushed forward so that it is as if she approaches the viewer (Blotkamp, 1972).

The procedure was as follows: Subjects completed a self-investigation in which they constructed an exhaustive amount of valuations (e.g., Hermans, 1987a). Upon completion, they were provided with the picture of the woman. They were invited to concentrate on this picture and imagine that the woman would respond to one of their valuations. They then selected one valuation which they presented to the woman in order to elicit her imaginal response. After the woman had given an imaginal reaction to their valuation, subjects were invited to respond to the woman from the perspective of the original valuation. In fact, this procedure involved three steps:

step 1: subject presents a valuation to the woman
step 2: woman gives an imaginal response
step 3: subject responds to the woman

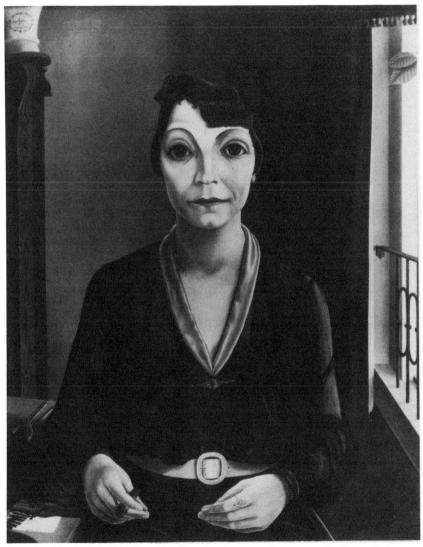

Figure 3 *Mercedes de Barcelona* (1930), reproduction of a painting by Pyke Koch. Reproduced with permission of the Gemeentemuseum Arnhem (Municipal Museum Arnheim), The Netherlands.

We present the results of two subjects, one that showed a minimal change from step 1 to step 3, and another who more drastically modified his original view. Bob, the first subject, is a 50-year-old man who worked as a teacher. He did this investigation after a 4-year period of depression, from which he was cured. His valuations are presented in Table 5. As the affective indices show, Bob selected an extremely negative valuation to present to the woman on the picture. The woman then responded with a statement that was for her negative too. In his response to the woman, Bob again formulated a negative reaction, although less negative than his original valuation. The reason for this decreasing negative affect is probably the experience of sharing with the woman (see the increased O feelings in step 3). It is noteworthy to mention that Bob's response to the woman does not refer in any explicit way to the content of the original valuation. The original valuation seems to be entirely unchanged.

A quite different construction was made by Frank, a 48-year-old man who worked as a manager in a company. He selected a moderately negative valuation for presentation (Table 6), but the imaginal response of the woman was markedly different in comparison with the preceding example. The woman was clearly placed in the position of a wise advisor, who provided him with some guidelines to be used in the situation referred to in the original valuation. In the third step, Frank gave a reaction that differed from his original valuation on all of the affective indices and came close to the affective pattern associated with the woman's advice in step 2. Moreover, the content of his answer in step 3 involved not only a main element of the woman's reaction (reservation), but also a central element of his original valuation at step 1 (negative thinking). In other words, Frank's response to the woman has a synthesizing quality in so far as it combines elements from step 1 and 2. Perhaps it is important to add that an

Table 5

Bob's Valuation (Step 1), the Woman's Comment (Step 2), and Bob's Answer to This Comment (Step 3)

		Valuations	S^a	O	P	N
Step 1	Bob	I always had to manage things on my own; didn't receive any attention, or affection; was superfluous at home; this has made me very uncertain.	0	0	0	20
Step 2	Woman	This sounds very familiar to me; I've had the same experience.	0	1	2	14
Step 3	Bob	I recognize the sadness in your eyes.	4	8	3	14

^{a}S, affect referring to self-enhancement; O, affect referring to contact; P, positive affect; N, negative affect.

Table 6

Frank's Valuation (Step 1), the Woman's Comment (Step 2), and Frank's Answer to This Comment (Step 3)

		Valuation	S^a	O	P	N
Step 1	Frank	I trust people in advance; however, when this trust is violated, I start to think in a negative way; this can have harmful consequences.	6	7	6	12
Step 2	Woman	You should keep your openness; however, your trust should become somewhat more reserved and take into account the topic involved.	16	12	19	5
Step 3	Frank	You are right; I must pay attention to this; reservations in this will also help me to control my negative feelings.	14	11	17	2

^{a}S, affect referring to self-enhancement; O, affect referring to contact; P, positive affect; N, negative affect.

inspection of the content of Frank's valuation system as a whole revealed that the content elements of the woman's advice were *not* included in the original system. This means that the advice by the woman and Frank's reaction were new elements in Frank's valuation system. More generally, in a co-construction in which two positions contribute to the process in a reciprocal way, new elements are introduced into the valuation system.

The exploration described above may function as exemplifying a three-step dialogue, suggesting possible ways to devise assessment procedures that are more dialogical than the projective techniques traditionally used in our field. However, there are also limitations that have to be taken into account. It is, of course, uncertain if a subject will "accept" a particular painting, photograph, or any piece of art as a means for self-exploration. For some people, a specific artistic picture will be inviting and stimulating, for others not. This objection can be met by presenting subjects with a greater number of pictures among which they can choose the ones they prefer to work with. Another limitation is that the picture is provided by someone else, in this case the psychologist. In order to deal with this problem one may invite subjects to introduce a piece of art that they themselves have found of value in their own lives.

Of course, there are other means available for stimulating dialogical processes. In our dream research (Hermans, 1987b) we have, inspired by Foulkes' (1978) work, treated a dream as a story that can be described as a series of valuations, each with their own specific affective connotation. Part of this project was to relate the dream images (as pictorial valuations) to the meaning units of waking life (as conceptual valuations). In agreement with the so-called continuity hypothesis (Webb & Cartwright, 1978) it was found that there was a clear continuity between the valuations of daily waking life and the symbolic expressions in the dream. Moreover, it was found that, when the subjects re-flected on the relationships between their dreams and waking life, they started to incorporate the dream symbols (e.g., being buried under shifting sand) in their valuations referring to their waking life (e.g., "Literally and figuratively I don't have enough space with John"). Such research could be continued in a dialogical direction by applying the three-step procedure to dreams. In step 1 the subject is invited to phrase his or her valuations. In step 2 an important dream character is invited also to formulate valuations from his or her specific position. Finally, in step 3 the subject modifies the original valuations under the influence of the valuations from the dream figure. Such research can function as a promising direction for research on meaning and meaning extension at the interface be-tween theory and practice. At the same time, it can result in methods that may be useful for the cooperation between practitioner and client.

We must certainly take into account that there are large variations among people in the extent to which they are open to dialogical change. With refer-ence to the cases described above, this was exemplified in the difference between Bob and Frank. Although they were confronted with the same picture, Frank showed more change in his valuations than Bob. More generally, the possi-bilities of dialogical change may be highly restricted, for example, in people with traumatic experiences, as psychoanalysts have observed. De Levita (1992) de-scribes the case of parents who have lost a child and oscillate between the fantasy that the child is still alive and the perception that the child is no longer alive. Their fantasy may then be projected on a newborn child that functions as a substitute of the first child. The parents then force the second child to identify with the image that they have about him or her. It is as if the parent says to the child: "I can only see in you what I put there; and so if I don't see that in you, I see nothing" (Ogden, 1979, p. 360). This case can be understood in terms of a position (the lost child) that is rigidly dominating other positions. If another position (the new child) is entering their lives, this position is denied any autonomy, subordinated to the existing position or even identified with it. Examples such as this demonstrate that dialogue, perhaps the highest faculty of human existence, may be highly constrained by past experiences that have overly stabilized the organization of the self.[7]

9.1.7 Not-Conscious and Unconscious Voices

An often-heard objection against the self, as an I–Me relation in the James-ian sense, is that it is heavily biased to conscious processes and, therefore, runs the risk of neglecting unconscious factors. A similar objection could perhaps be raised against the dialogical self as we have described it. In addressing this question, we should first deal with the nature of positions in the self and the way they are organized.

As we have extensively discussed, the different positions in the self are not only relational, in the sense of dialogical exchange, but also organized according to dominance of relationships. On the basis of one's personal history or the values of the community to which one belongs, one position gets a more central place in the self than another. We have even seen that, if a position is rejectable or sharply dichotomized in terms of "higher" versus "lower" or "good" versus "bad," such a position, and its including valuations, may even be split from the self, resulting in a restricted or even impoverished self-narrative.

As the above considerations suggest, dominance relations may become so prevailing in the self that some positions may become suppressed or even excluded from the self. The result may be that the process of exchange is seriously reduced or even made impossible. In the organization of the self, the notion of centralization, as discussed in Chapter 3, plays an important part. As a result of a strong centralization, so typical of our Western collective voice, some positions never receive enough attention to be included as part of the self. In this case, the person is "trained" to define the self in a specific way, with the exclusion of alternative possibilities. One of the implications of the process of centralization is that the Western self is not well equipped to deal with polar opposites. Centralization often implies that one pole of an opposition is used to characterize the self in an exclusive way. A person may then organize his or her self-narrative in such a way that it is, for example, "active" and *not* "passive," "good" and *not* "bad," "hard" and *not* "soft," "winning" and *not* "losing," "sociable" and *not* "aggressive." In fact, centralization runs against the reconciliation of opposites, because it defines the self in terms of only *one* organizing center. If this center is characterized in terms of one pole of a pair of opposites, the opposite pole will often be excluded from the self and prevented from playing a constructive role in self development. The issue of polar opposition is particularly relevant, as narratives and also self-narratives typically imply the interplay of opposite characters. The protagonist meets an antagonist, and it is in their opposition and confrontation that they develop a meaningful story. If one would reduce a story to only one figure, that is, an isolated protagonist, stories and storytelling would miss the dynamic interplay of opposing forces that, in their exchange and clashes, contribute to the co-construction of self and reality.[8] As Watkins (1986) observed, it is strange that we are familiar with many stories in which opposing characters are part of the dynamic interrelationships, whereas we have often great difficulty admitting that similar opposing forces are part of our own selves. Along with Sampson (1985) we hold that the cultural ideal of the centralized self runs against the recognition of the basic multiplicity of the self and the simultaneous existence of opposing forces. The centralization, so typical of Descartes' *Cogito,* is a cultural issue since it shapes, as a collective voice, our selves and daily lives.

As Hart (1981) has argued, it would be a misunderstanding to suppose that James (1890) had no eye for unconscious processes. On the contrary, James was well aware that consciousness has "gaps" that cannot be filled with any definite picture. In his comparison between the Jamesian and Freudian views, Hart described James' unconsciousness as "felt but unnamed" and Freud's unconsciousness as "neither felt nor named but causative." By consequence, the unconscious in Freud's case cannot be felt in any direct way, but must be inferred from a variety of indirect expressions that are often denied from consciousness as a result of defenses. The role of defenses is emphasized in Freud's case because the content of the unconsciousness is typically negative and unacceptable, in contrast to James, who acknowledges the role of positive experiences.

As we have argued in the preceding chapters, the dialogical self can be seen as an elaboration of a Jamesian point of view. A decisive step in our reasoning was the supposition of not one centralized *I* position, but a multiplicity of *I* positions. It is precisely the notion of multiplicity that provides the conceptual road to the investigation of the unconsciousness along the lines of James and Hart. The quintessence of the argument is that *I* positions differ in level of consciousness, with the more dominant positions as more conscious and the suppressed positions as less conscious or even unconscious. This point of view has several implications. First, we prefer to speak about different levels of consciousness in order to avoid the misleading notion of a razor sharp boundary between conscious and unconscious, a point of view that Kelly (1955) already presented some decades ago. Second, our conception implies that the unconscious represents—in the form of one or more *I* positions—an authorial position from which the *I* has an own story to tell, if it gets the chance to do so. In other words, the unconscious positions represent more or less autonomous centers of self-organization. Third, the unconscious can become "dialogicized," that is, the suppressed or even split off positions can be taken up in the process of dialogue by giving them a voice, establishing a more symmetrical relation among conscious and unconscious positions. This can only happen when psychologists have available strategies and techniques that, together with their personal qualities, have enough dialogical power to stimulate the dominated positions to enter into the process of exchange.

Of course, it is too simplifying to speak roughly about "the unconscious." A distinction has been made, for example, between "not conscious" and "unconscious." The first term refers to less conscious layers that are not available to consciousness simply because they are never emphasized in one's personal development or have never received any attention in the process of socialization. In the case of the "unconscious" in the Freudian sense, a psychological conflict is supposed that entails forces that actively prevent the unconscious material from becoming conscious. This distinction can be translated into the language of positions and characters. In the case of experiences that are "not conscious" the characters are "sleeping," but they can be awakened by attention, concentration, and training. This may happen, for example, in the case of a person educated in a nonreligious milieu who has religious or spiritual experiences in a later period of life.

Unconscious experiences are, without doubt, the greatest challenge to the dialogical self. The question can be raised of whether dialogical processes have enough potential to break through the barriers of defenses. For example, when a man has recurrent dreams about a devil who is attempting to murder his wife, under what conditions is this man willing to accept that the murderer is a position *in* his own self? And in what way does this acceptance contribute to his meaning system? These questions can only be answered if this person is willing to investigate his valuations from his usual *I* position (step 1); if he is motivated to investigate the valuations from the perspective of the murderer as he knows them on the basis of his dream (step 2); and, finally, if the man, after he has given the murderer a voice, is willing and able to listen to this voice in such a way that he changes his original valuations (step 3). Only if these requirements are met, is there a deepening of the self as a result of taking up unconscious characters into an intensified dialogical process.

The main point of our reasoning can be summarized by saying that it is the *I* who is able to penetrate lower layers of consciousness if it enters into an active dialogical process. The dominating positions represent the higher levels of consciousness, the suppressed positions the lower levels. By giving the latter positions a voice, the *I* gets the opportunity to jump hence and forth between the several positions so that the suppressed voices are taken up in a more symmetrical process of exchange.

9.2 Meaning as Movement

Building on the material presented in the preceding chapters, we will describe in this final section what meaning is from a dialogical perspective. A most succinct formulation is this: Meaning emerges from dialogical movements between *I* positions. More specifically, the process of meaning construction requires the explanation of four terms: imaginal space, positions, exchange, and dominance. Let us briefly discuss these terms, that have already been treated extensively in the preceding chapters, in their interrelationship.

It would be a misunderstanding to see *imaginal space* as something purely "internal." When we go to a place to visit somebody, we are not simply on our bike or in our car on the road. We imagine how it will be to meet our friends again, and we remember how it was the last time that we saw them. When we are not "on the road," but sitting quietly at home, the house, considered as our perceptible space around us, is full of imaginations: the painting on the wall, the photograph of a deceased family member, the chair that is in need of repair, the table that has to be prepared for a dinner with our family members, the plants that are drying and must be watered. We see a case and seeing it, we know that it contains a precious gift we received from our grandmother, a gift that we assume to be in there. In other words, the perceptible space clearly coexists with the imaginal space. Our imaginations about people, objects, and situations are side by side and interwoven with the perceptible things and situations we find ourselves in.

Our experiences are so formed by (imaginal) space and spatial relations that even time can only be described in spatial terms. We say that the future "will come" and the past "has gone." Somebody has stayed a "long" period or was only here for one "short" hour. Apparently, time-related terms are easily spatialized. However, the reversed transformation is difficult or even impossible. How can we describe in temporal terms typical spatial words such as *long, high, broad,* or *deep.* If we try, then we discover that we cannot avoid using additional spatial terms to explain (e.g., "a long distance takes you many hours to *go*"). The fact that spatializing time is easier than temporalizing space indicates the fundamental character of space and imaginal space for the experiences of our daily lives (cf. Traugott, 1978).

Not only the world, but also the self can be conceived as a mind space. We can be opposed to ourselves, be close to ourselves, take a large distance from ourselves, or be overwhelmed by the emotions in ourselves. If we say that we are involved in a self-confrontation, we see ourselves as having a position somewhere in front of us, two positions being in a state of tension. This takes us to the next term that is central to the concept of meaning.

The imaginal space is populated by *positions.* And as imaginal space is side by side and interwoven with perceptible space, imaginal positions are strongly interconnected with perceptible positions. The fact that my mother has "actually" a perceptible position in space does not say much about the meaning she has in my life. The meaning of my mother is much more determined by the position she has in an imaginal space, in which I see myself related to her as a child, adolescent, and adult. These memories and imaginations are certainly not restricted to the positions of hers and mine. I frequently see her related to my father, brother, and sisters and to other people who played a significant role in our lives. Moreover, the feelings I have about her may be influenced by my imagination that there will come a time where she will be no longer with us. In other words, the meaning my mother, or any significant person, has to me is deeply influenced by a network of positions in which she and I participate. From this perspective, she is not an isolated entity, but a person who is perceived as positioned in an imaginal landscape that is populated by other people who are in one way or another related to her. Moreover, I imaginatively see her as a person who is in different positions from a temporal point of view: as a young, caring mother living together with my father, as a widow standing alone needing the care of her children in turn, and as not being with us anymore. Each of these positions is associated with narratively structured events. Altogether, these positions and associated events are not simply successive moments in a purely chronological sense, but—by the activity of imagination—they are brought together, and in their juxtaposition they form a meaningful pattern.

The term *I position* has functioned as a central concept in our theoretical explorations. There are at least two ways in which we have argued against considering the term *I* as an isolated *Cogito*. First, as we have discussed in Chapter 5, there is developmental evidence that (pseudo)dialogues precede the use of the pronoun I and the emergence of the self as an *I–Me* relationship. This implies that the relation with the other precedes the relation with oneself. In Chapter 7, moreover, we have, building on Mead's fertile insights, argued that the *I*, as a center of self-organization, is preceded by collective meanings implied in the cultural institutions and the community to which we belong. This means that self-organization is not only preceded by cultural traditions and values, but also deeply influenced by them. The experience of my mother was certainly not restricted to my relationship with her, it even by far exceeded the boundaries of our family. The meaning she has for others and myself has been more or less shaped and preshaped by her position as a woman, raised in a middle-class family, in a rural environment, educated in a conservative Catholic school, having a busy life as the partner of a man who owned a small company, and not having had much chance to play an active role in her community after her husband died. All she did and said in her life was more or less influenced by the collective voices of the groups and institutions to which she belonged.

It is certainly not so that the collectivity is simply dictating to a person what to do and say. Rather, a person is able to disagree with society and to develop in a direction that more or less deviates from the direction prescribed by collective voices. We have seen this in the case of Peter, who in his active position was supported by the groups to which he belonged but in his passive position followed largely his own direction.

So far we have dealt with imaginal space and the position that indicates the location in this space, however, this is still a rather static way of dealing with the notion of meaning. The third term, *dialogical movement*, transforms meaning into meaning making, or meaning construction. As Bakhtin (1973) has argued, question and answer and agreement and disagreement are basic dialogical activities. With these dialogical procedures, we are not any more *in* a particular position but, rather, *between* two or more positions (see also Rychlak, 1988, who considers meaning a relational term *par excellence*). Giving a meaningful answer is only possible if one takes the question into account and the nature of the question (or anticipated next question) structures the answer "on the spot." In posing a question, one has to reckon with the intelligibility and knowl-edgeability of the other party at the moment of questioning itself. Also agree-ment and disagreement can only make sense if they are conceived as happening *between* parties, and when a person agrees or disagrees with himself or herself there are two positions within one person. As we have demonstrated in the illustrations at the beginning of this chapter, there is an active process of mean-ing making, when there are at least two positions entering into contact in a way that new meanings emerge that were not present in the same form at the onset of the dialogue. For example, Jim made a synthesizing valuation that resulted from interrelating the incompatible positions of his mother and his superior. Frank also made a new meaning when he combined his original valuation with the imagined utterance of the woman on the picture. The newness of the resulting valuations presupposes a dialogical process that is not within but between the positions in question. Meaning making as a dialogical construction presupposes an *I* that is continuously moving backward and forward between positions.

As Harré & Van Langenhove (1991) have argued, the terms *position* and *positioning* are highly dynamic concepts that are to be preferred above the more static term *role*. One of their arguments was that "it is within conversations that the social world is created . . . " (Harré & Van Langenhove, 1991, p. 394). Indeed, the term *positioning* can be used to suggest that the person is able to construct a position that was not there at the beginning of a process. In order to explain this, let us refer to two examples. The two positions discussed in Jim's case (mother and superior) were *existing* positions that were already there long before the start of the investigation. In Peter's case, however, we proceeded to treat two personality traits ("active" and "passive") *as if* they were characters that could tell a story about their own lives. In this case there is a constructive process of positioning, because Peter put characters in the trait and by the act of imagination personalized them. In other words, the terms *position* and *positioning* may be helpful for imaginatively endowing impersonal phenomena with a voice to speak and create new meanings. This may contribute to the reanimation and "reenchantment" of the self and the world (Berman, 1981).

The last characteristic of meaning follows from the dominance aspect of dialogue. In its most brief formulation, our thesis is that *there are always neglected and suppressed meanings*. Because dominance is an intrinsic feature of dialogue, the prevalence of one meaning implies the necessary neglect or suppression of other ones. We have already discussed the so-called "sleeping" positions and concomitant valuations that have not received much attention in the process of socialization and are in this sense neglected. Discussed also are the positions and valuations that are suppressed or even rejected from dialogue on emotional grounds. We have referred to two reasons why meanings may be neglected or suppressed. One is of a highly general nature and is implicated by the typically Western ideal of the centralized self. The other is rooted in one's personal history: Specific experiences, often negatively tuned, have led to the active suppression or even splitting of unwanted positions or valuations. These are factors that slow down dialogical movements or may even bring them to a standstill, as we see in the case of severe depressions.

Besides the existence of constraining factors in our collective and personal history, there are also purely formal reasons that introduce dominance relationships into dialogue. We have emphasized in Chapter 5 the role of turn taking in explicit dialogical relations. When one party has his or her turn, the voice of the other party is temporarily silenced (suppressed for formal reasons), which is necessary for a meaningful dialogue to develop. Further, according to the figure–ground principle, one of the two is at the center of attention and prevails until figure and ground are reversed.

More generally, the figure–ground relation accounts for the fact that, even when there is a juxtaposition of elements brought in close proximity to one another, as, for example, in a cubist painting (Chapter 4), there is always one part that temporarily dominates the other parts. Even when Flaubert says: "Everything should sound simultaneously" (Chapter 4), there is clearly a figure–ground principle at work as soon as one directs one's attention to one of the instruments. The same is true for positions: Dialogical exchange and dominance do not exclude one another. This, of course, does not deny the desirability of realizing more symmetrical dialogues (Chapter 5), because such dialogues characterize the co-construction of reality, as a never-ending process of meaning enrichment.

Notes

1. Turn taking characterizes *explicit* dialogue. As we have discussed in Chapter 3, dialogue works also in an implicit way. Bakhtin argued that each word is "double voiced." In the conversation with a real or imagined other, the word of the other is present *in* the act of speaking. The "double-voicedness" is even present when the words of the other are omitted. This is what Bakhtin means with the phrase "hidden dialogicality." The interlocutor is invisibly present *in* the words of the speaker. For Bakhtin the notion of dialogue is not identical with explicitly spoken conversation. Rather, it is at the heart of every form of thought. In the context of the present discussion of basic forces in self and dialogue, it must be emphasized that the features dominance and exchange are (implicitly) present in "hidden dialogicality." For example, a person with a self that is excessively dominated by the position of his or her mother may not be able to evaluate things in an independent way. In this case, the voice of the mother, although implicitly present, is highly dominant and reduces the possibilities of symmetrical dialogicality because the communication is largely unilateral.

2. The fact that affect is considered here as a connotative aspect of valuation does, of course, not exclude the possibility of studying affect or passion as an *I* position. For

example, a person can tell his or her self-narrative as an angry person and/or as a peaceful person in terms of different sets of valuations (for a concrete procedure see personality traits studied as *I* positions later in this chapter).

3. The case to be presented in this section is more extensively discussed by Hermans (1992b). The subject, like the subjects of the other illustrations to be presented, participated in a research project at the University of Nijmegen on human valuation. The project typically follows the subjects across time. Many of them perform more than one self-investigation, so that the development of the valuation system can be assessed.

4. A development of a special kind is when a valuation, already synthesized to a certain degree (as valuation 2 at Time 2), is taken up into a next synthesizing move at a later moment in time. In that case we have what one could call a "second-order" synthesis, that is, a valuation that is already synthesized in a first move, is later combined with other portions of the valuation system.

5. The active *I* reacts to this valuation with an affect pattern (high S, low O, low P, and high N) that is at first glance unusual. We have found evidence that this pat-tern expresses some form of anger or opposition (Hermans, 1992c). Most often the text of the valuation explicitly refers to such an attitude (e.g., "I hate . . . " or "I don't like people who . . . "). This attitude may also be implicitly present in the valuation. An element of protest or anger seems to be implicit in the valuation in question.

6. Magic realism is exemplified by the *New Objectivity* painters of Germany, such as George Grosz and Otto Dix, the *Valori Plastici* (literally "plastic values") painters of Italy, and a good many of the modern Dutch painters. The work of some of the social painters of the United States, Peter Blume and Philip Evergood, for example, have some elements in common with magic realism (Myers, 1979).

7. The presented illustrations are of an idiographic nature. For a model that aims at generalizations across the valuations of a larger number of subjects, see Hermans (1988).

8. A systematic attempt to relate self-psychology in terms of "self image" and "other image" to the positions of protagonist and antagonist in psychodrama is provided by Verhofstadt-Denève (1988). For related developments see Rowan (1990).

CODA

The notion of the dialogical self, as exposed in this book, greatly acknowledges the power of imagination. Even Descartes, in the defense of *Cogito*, asked his readers in *First Meditation* to imagine the existence of a *malin génie*, an evil genius, acting as an antagonist:

> I will suppose that . . . some malicious demon of the utmost power and cunning has employed all his energies in order to deceive me. I shall think that the sky, the air, the earth, colours, shapes, sounds and all external things are merely the delusions of dreams which he has devised to ensnare my judgment. I shall consider myself as not having hands or eyes, or flesh, or blood or senses, but as falsely believing that I have all these things. [Descartes, 1641/1984, p. 15]

Despite Descartes' vehement attempts to close himself off from his surrounding world, he could not avoid wandering in an imaginal landscape . . .

APPENDIX
MATRIX OF VALUATION * AFFECT:
RAW RATINGS OF A CLIENT

Valuation number	Affect terms															
	1	2	3	4	5	6	7	8	9	10	11	12	13	14	15	16
1	0	1	0	1	2	1	1	1	2	1	2	1	1	2	2	1
2	1	2	0	5	1	0	5	5	3	3	1	4	2	0	2	0
3	1	3	2	1	3	2	0	1	1	0	2	0	1	2	1	1
4	1	1	1	5	1	1	4	4	2	4	1	3	3	2	1	1
5	0	1	0	4	1	1	4	1	2	1	2	1	2	1	2	1
6	1	2	2	4	2	1	4	2	1	2	3	2	1	1	2	2
7	2	2	2	1	3	1	2	1	1	1	2	0	1	0	2	0
8	3	1	3	4	1	1	4	5	2	4	1	2	4	1	3	1
9	5	3	4	3	2	5	3	5	1	5	2	4	1	2	1	2
10	0	1	1	2	1	0	2	4	1	4	2	4	1	2	1	2
11	3	2	4	1	2	3	4	4	1	4	2	4	1	4	1	3
12	1	1	1	0	1	1	1	1	1	0	1	1	2	0	2	0
13	0	1	0	2	1	0	2	4	0	4	1	4	0	0	1	2
14	0	0	1	1	2	2	1	4	1	4	2	4	1	1	1	2
15	4	2	4	1	2	3	3	4	1	4	3	4	1	2	1	2
16	2	2	3	2	2	3	3	5	1	4	2	4	1	3	1	4
17	0	0	1	5	1	0	3	0	3	0	1	0	4	0	2	1
18	0	1	0	4	0	0	2	3	2	2	1	0	2	0	1	0
19	3	2	3	1	4	4	3	4	0	3	3	3	1	3	1	2
20	4	2	5	1	2	5	4	5	1	4	2	4	1	3	1	3
21	1	2	4	3	1	4	4	5	0	4	2	4	1	4	1	2
22	2	3	2	1	2	2	1	2	0	1	2	1	1	2	1	1
23	3	2	2	1	2	2	1	3	0	2	2	2	0	3	0	3
24	3	2	4	1	2	2	2	4	0	4	2	3	0	3	1	1
25	3	2	4	1	2	4	2	4	1	3	2	3	0	2	1	5

REFERENCES

Ainsworth, M. D. S., Blehar, M., Waters, E., & Well, S. (1978). *Patterns of attachment: Observations in the strange situation and at home.* Hillsdale, NJ: Lawrence Erlbaum.

Altman, I. (1987). Centripetal and centrifugal trends in psychology. *American Psychologist,* **42,** 1058–1069.

American Psychiatric Association. (1987). *Diagnostic and statistic manual of mental disorders-III-R.* Washington, DC.: American Psychiatric Association.

Amsterdam, B. (1972). Mirror self-image reactions before age two. *Developmental Psychobiology,* **5,** 297–305.

Anderson, J. R. (1984). The development of self-recognition: A review. *Developmental Psychobiology,* **17,** 35–49.

Angyal, A. (1965). *Neurosis and treatment: A holistic theory.* New York: Wiley.

Argyris, C., Putnam, R., & Smith, D. M. (1985). *Action science: Concepts, methods, and skills for research and intervention.* San Francisco: Jossey-Bass.

Aronsson, K., & Rundström, B. (1988). Child discourse and parental control in pediatric consultations. *Text,* **8,** 159–189.

Bakan, D. (1966). *The duality of human existence.* Chicago: Rand-McNally.

Bakhtin, M. (1973). *Problems of Dostoevsky's poetics* (2nd ed.) (Translated by R. W. Rotsel.) Ann Arbor, MI: Ardis. (Original work published 1929.)

Baldwin, J. C. (1986). *George Herbert Mead: A unifying theory for sociology.* Newbury Park, CA: Sage.

Barlow, D. H., Hayes, S. C., & Nelson, R. O. (1984). *The scientist practitioner: Research and accountability in clinical and educational settings.* New York: Pergamon Press.

Barnes-Farrell, J. L., & Piotrowski, M. J. (1989). Workers' perceptions of discrepancies between chronological age and personal age: You're only as old as you feel. *Psychology and Aging,* **4,** 376–377.

Beahrs, J. O. (1982). *Unity and multiplicity: Multilevel consciousness of self in hypnosis, psychiatric disorder, and mental health.* New York: Brunner/Mazel.

Belar, C. D., & Perry, N. W. (1992). National conference on scientist–practitioner education and training for the professional practice of psychology. *American Psychologist,* **47,** 71–75.

Bem, D., & Allen, A. (1974). On predicting some of the people some of the time: The search for cross-situational consistencies in behavior. *Psychological Review,* **81,** 506–520.

Bergson, H. (1907). L'évolution créatrice. [The creative evolution.] In *Oeuvres.* Paris: Presses Universitaires de France.

Bergson, H. (1934). La pensée et le mouvant. [The thought and the moving.] In *Oeuvres*. Paris: Presses Universitaires de France.

Berman, M. (1981). *The reenchantment of the world*. Ithaca, NY: Cornell University Press.

Blass, T. (1977). On personality variables, situations, and social behavior. In T. Blass (Ed.), *Personality variables in social behavior*. Hillsdale, NJ: Erlbaum.

Bloom, K., Russell, A., & Davis, S. (1986). Conversational turn taking: Verbal quality of adult affects vocal quality of infant. *Infant Behavior and Development*, **9**. Special issue: Abstracts of papers presented at the Fifth International Conference on Infant Studies, 39.

Blotkamp, C. (1972). *Pyke Koch*. Amsterdam: Arbeiderspers.

Bonarius, H. (1977). The interaction mode of communication: Through experimental research towards existential relevance. In J. K. Cole & A. W. Landfield (Eds.), *Nebraska symposium on motivation: Personal construct psychology* (Vol. 24). Lincoln: University of Nebraska Press.

Brim, O. G., Jr., & Ryff, C. D. (1980). On the properties of life events. In P. B. Baltes & O. G. Brim, Jr. (Eds.), *Life-span development and behavior* (Vol. 3, pp. 367–388). New York: Academic Press.

Bronson, G. W. (1972). *Infants' reactions to unfamiliar persons and novel objects*. Chicago: University of Chicago Press.

Bronson, G. W. (1978). Aversive reactions to strangers: A dual process interpretation. *Child Development*, **49**, 495–499.

Bruner, J. (1985). Vygotsky: A historical and conceptual perspective. In J. V. Wertsch (Ed.), *Culture, communication and cognition: Vygotskian perspectives* (pp. 21–34). Cambridge, MA: Cambridge University Press.

Bruner, J. S. (1986). *Actual minds, possible worlds*. Cambridge, MA: Harvard University Press.

Bruner, J. (1990). Acts of meaning. Cambridge, MA: Harvard University Press.

Bruns, G. L. (1982). *Inventions: Writing, textuality, and understanding in literary history*. New Haven, CT: Yale University Press.

Burgoon, J. K., & Jones, S. B. (1976). Toward a theory of personal space expectations and their violations. *Human Communication Research*, **2**, 131–146.

Burns, R. B. (1979). *The self concept: Theory, measurement, development, and behaviour*. London: Longman.

Buss, D. M., & Craik, K. H. (1983a). The dispositional analysis of everyday conduct. *Journal of Personality*, **51**, 393–412.

Buss, D. M., & Craik, K. H. (1983b). The act frequency approach to personality. *Psychological Review*, **90**, 105–126.

Campbell, J. D. (1956). *The hero with a thousand faces*. New York: Meridian. (Original work published 1949.)

Cassirer, E. (1955). *The philosophy of symbolic forms*. (Vol. 2. Mythical thought). New Haven, CT: Yale University Press.

Caughey, J. L. (1984). *Imaginary social worlds: A cultural approach*. Lincoln: University of Nebraska Press.

Cernoch, J. M., & Porter, R. H. (1985). Recognition of maternal axillary odors by infants. *Child Development*, **56**, 1593–1598.

Cheek, J. M. (1982). Aggregation, moderator variables, and the validity of personality tests: A peer-rating study. *Journal of Personality and Social Psychology,* **43,** 1254–1269.

Chomsky, N. (1966). *Topics in the theory of generative grammar.* The Hague, The Netherlands: Mouton.

Christ, C. P. (1980). *Diving deep and surfacing: Women writers on spiritual quest.* Boston: Beacon Press.

Cicourel, A. V. (1974). *Cognitive sociology.* New York: Free Press.

Clarke-Stewart, A., Perlmutter, M., & Friedman, S. (1988). *Lifelong human development.* New York: Wiley.

Clausen, J. A. (1972). The life course of individuals. In M. Riley, M. Johnson, & A. Foner (Eds.), *Aging and society: A sociology of the age stratification* (Vol. 3, pp. 457–514). New York: Russel Sage.

Cohler, B. J. (1982). Personal narrative and life course. In P. B. Baltes & O. G. Brim (Eds.), *Life-span development and behavior* (pp. 205–241). New York: Academic Press.

Cohler, B. J. (1988). The human studies and the life history: The *Social Service Review* lecture. *Social Service Review,* December, 552–575.

Colapietro, V. M. (1990). The vanishing subject of contemporary discourse: A pragmatic response. *The Journal of Philosophy,* **8711,** 644–655.

Condon, W. S., & Sanders, L. W. (1974). Neonate movement is synchronized with adult speech: Interactional participation and language acquisition. *Science,* **183,** 99–101.

Costa, P. T., & McCrae, R. R. (1988). From catalog to classification: Murray's needs and the five-factor model. *Journal of Personality and Social Psychology,* **55,** 258–265.

Damon, W., & Hart, D. (1982). The development of self-understanding from infancy through adolescence. *Child Development,* **4,** 841–864.

Decary, T. G. (1974). *The infant's reaction to strangers.* New York: International Universities Press.

Deikman, A. J. (1971). Bimodal consciousness. *Archives of General Psychiatry,* **25,** 481–489.

Deikman, A. J. (1976). Bimodal consciousness and the mystic experience. In Ph. Lee et al., (Eds.), *Symposion on consciousness* (pp. 67–88). New York: Viking Press.

De Levita, D. J. (1992). De wolken waarom moeder schreide. [The clouds that made mother cry.] *Inaugural Speech.* University of Nijmegen.

Derrida, J. (1978). *Writing and difference.* Chicago: University of Chicago Press.

Derrida, J. (1981). *Dissemination.* Chicago: University of Chicago Press.

Descartes, R. (1984). Meditations on first philosophy. In J. Cottingham, R. Stoothoff, & D. Murdoch (Eds. and Trans.), *The philosophical writings of Descartes* (Vol. 2, pp. 3–62). Cambridge, MA: Cambridge University Press. (Original work published 1641.)

Diagnostic and Statistic Manual of Mental Disorders (1987). See American Psychiatric Association.

Diehl, G. (1977). *Picasso.* Naefels, Switzerland: Bonfini Press.

Döblin, A. (1961). *Berlin Alexanderplatz:* Die Geschichte vom Franz Biberkopf. [Berlin Alexanderplatz: The story of Franz Biberkopf] Freiburg/Heitersheim, Germany: Walter-Verlag. (Original work published in 1929.)

Dohrenwend, B. P. (1961). The social psychological nature of stress: A framework for causal inquiry. *Journal of Abnormal and Social Psychology,* **62,** 294–302.

Elder, G. (1974). *Children of the great depression.* Chicago: University of Chicago Press.

Elder, G. (1979). Historical change in life patterns and personality. In P. B. Baltes & O. G. Brim, Jr. (Eds.), *Life-span development and behavior* (Vol. 2). New York: Academic Press.

Epstein, R. (1991). Skinner, creativity, and the problem of spontaneous behavior. *Psychological Science,* **2,** 362–370.

Epstein, S. (1973). The self-concept revisited: Or a theory of a theory. *American Psychologist,* **28,** 404–416.

Erikson, E. H. (1950). *Childhood and society.* New York: Norton.

Erikson, E. H. (1963). *Childhood and society* (Revised ed.). New York: Norton.

Evans, G. W., & Howard, R. B. (1973). Personal space. *Psychological Bulletin,* **80,** 334–344.

Fairbairn, W. R. D. (1952). *Psychoanalytic studies of the personality.* London: Routledge & Kegan Paul.

Faulkner, W. (1929). *The sound and the fury.* New York: J. Cape & H. Smith.

Field, T., DeStefano, L., & Koewler, J. H. (1982). Fantasy play of toddlers and preschoolers. *Developmental Psychology,* **18,** 503–508.

Fischoff, B. (1976). Attribution theory and judgment under uncertainty. In J. H. Harvey, W. J. Ickes, & R. F. Kidd (Eds.), *New directions in attribution research* (Vol. 1, pp. 421–452). Hillsdale, NJ: Erlbaum.

Fisher, S., & Cleveland, S. E. (1968). *Body image and personality.* New York: Dover.

Fitzgerald, F. S. (1992). *The great gatsby.* Groningen: Wolters-Noordhoff. (Original work published in 1925.)

Fletcher, A. J. S. (1964). *Allegory: The theory of a symbolic mode.* Ithaca, NY: Cornell University Press.

Florenskaya, T. A. (1989). Psychological problems of dialogue in light of the ideas of M. M. Bakhtin and A. A. Ukhtomskii. *Soviet Psychology,* **27,** 29–40.

Fodor, J. A. (1983). *The modularity of mind: An essay on faculty psychology.* Cambridge, MA: M.I.T. Press.

Foulkes, D. (1978). *A grammar of dreams.* Sussex, England: Harvester Press.

Fowler, J. (1981). *Stages of faith.* New York: Harper & Row.

Fraiberg, S. (1974). Blind infants and their mothers: An examination of the sign system. In M. Lewis & L. S. Rosenblum (Eds.), *The effect of the infant on its caregiver.* New York: Wiley.

Frank, J. (1991). *The idea spatial form.* New Brunswick and London: Rutgers University Press. (Original work published 1945.)

Frye, N. (1957). *Anatomy of criticism.* Princeton, NJ: Princeton University Press.

Gallup, G. G. (1968). Mirror image stimulation. *Psychological Bulletin,* **70,** 782–793.

Garfield, S. L. (1966). Clinical psychology and the search for identity. *American Psychologist,* **21,** 353–362.

Garfinkel, H. (1967). *Studies in ethnomethodology.* Englewood, NJ: Prentice-Hall.

Garvey, C. (1984). *Children's talk.* Cambridge, MA: Harvard University Press.

Gazzaniga, M. (1985). *The social brain.* New York: Basic Books.

Gergen, K. J. (1980). The emerging crisis in theory of life-span development. In P. Baltes & O. Brim, Jr. (Eds.), *Life-span development and behavior* (Vol. 3). New York: Academic Press.

Gergen, K. J., & Gergen, M. M. (1988). Narrative and the self as relationship. *Advances in Experimental Social Psychology, 21,* 17–56.

Glaser, B. G., & Strauss, A. L. (1967). *The discovery of grounded theory: Strategies for qualitative research.* Chicago: Aldine.

Glazer, N. (1974). The schools of the minor professions. *Minerva, 12,* 346–364.

Gregg, G. S. (1991). *Self-representation: Life narrative studies in identity and ideology.* New York: Greenwood Press.

Guardini, R. (1925). *Der Gegensatz.* [The opposition.] Mainz, Germany: Matthias Grünewald.

Guntrip, H. (1971). *Psychoanalytic theory, therapy, and the self.* New York: Basic Books.

Gutmann, D. L. (1980). The post-parental years: Clinical problems and developmental possibilities. In W. H. Norman & T. J. Scaramella (Eds.), *Mid-life: Developmental and clinical issues* (pp. 38–52). New York: Bruner/Mazel.

Habermas, J. (1970). *Toward a rational society: Student protest, science, and politics.* Boston: Beacon Press.

Harré, R. (1992). Introduction: The second cognitive revolution. *American Behaviorial Scientist, 36,* 5–7.

Harré, R., & Van Langenhove, L. (1991). Varieties of positioning. *Journal for the Theory of Social Behaviour, 21,* 393–407.

Hart, J. (1981). The significance of William James' ideas for a modern psychotherapy. *Journal of Contemporary Psychotherapy, 12,* 88–102.

Havighurst, R. J. (1972). *Developmental tasks and education.* New York: McKay.

Hayduck, L. A. (1978). Personal space: An evaluative and orienting review. *Psychological Bulletin, 85,* 117–134.

Heider, F. (1958). *The psychology of interpersonal relations.* New York: Wiley.

Heider, F., & Simmel, M. (1944). A study of apparent behavior. *American Journal of Psychology, 57,* 243–259.

Hermans, H. J. M. (1987a). Self as organized system of valuations: Toward a dialogue with the person. *Journal of Counseling Psychology, 34,* 10–19.

Hermans, H. J. M. (1987b). The dream in the process of valuation: A method of interpretation. *Journal of Personality and Social Psychology, 53,* 163–175.

Hermans, H. J. M. (1988). On the integration of idiographic and nomothetic research method in the study of personal meaning. *Journal of Personality, 56,* 785–812.

Hermans, H. J. M. (1989). The meaning of life as an organized process. *Psychotherapy, 26,* 11–22.

Hermans, H. J. M. (1991). The person as co-investigator in self-research: Valuation theory. *European Journal of Personality, 5,* 217–234.

Hermans, H. J. M. (1992a). The person as an active participant in psychological research. *American Behavioral Scientist, 36,* 102–113.

Hermans, H. J. M. (1992b). Telling and retelling one's self-narrative: A contextual approach to life-span development. *Human Development, 35,* 361–375 (with a commentary by Mark B. Tappan).

Hermans, H. J. M. (1992c). Unhappy self-esteem. *Journal of Psychology, 126,* 555–570.

Hermans, H. J. M. (1993a). Self-narrative in the life-course. In M. Bamberg (Ed.), *New directions for child development,* in press.

Hermans, H. J. M. (1993b). The personal meaning of clinical problems in the context of self-narrative: From assessment to change. In M. J. Mahoney & R. Neimeyer (Eds.), Constructivism in psychotherapy, in press.

Hermans, H. J. M., & Bonarius, H. (1991a). The person as co-investigator in personality research. European Journal of Personality, 5, 199–216.

Hermans, H. J. M., & Bonarius, H. (1991b). Static laws in a dynamic psychology? European Journal of Personality, 5, 245–247.

Hermans, H. J. M., & Van Gilst, W. (1991). Self-narrative and collective myth: An analysis of the Narcissus story. Canadian Journal of Behavioural Science, 23, 423–440.

Hermans, H. J. M., Kempen, H. J. G., & Van Loon, R. J. P. (1992). The dialogical self: Beyond individualism and rationalism. American Psychologist, 47, 23–33.

Higgins, E. T. (1987). Self-discrepance: A theory relating self and affect. Psychological Review, 94, 319–340.

Hilton, D. J. (1990). Conversational processes and causal explanation. Psychological Bulletin, 107, 65–81.

Hintikka, J. (1968). The varieties of information and scientific explanation. In N. van Rootselaar & R. Staal (Eds.), Logic, methodology, and the philosophy of science (pp. 311–331). Amsterdam: North-Holland.

Hofstadter, D. (1986). Metamagical themas. New York: Bantam Books.

Holquist, M. (1990). Dialogism: Bakhtin and his world. London: Routledge.

Hora, E. (1966). Zum Verständnis des Werkes. [For a clear understanding of the work.] In G. Vico, Die neue Wissenschaft: Ueber die gemeinschaftliche Natur der Völker [The new science: Concerning the common nature of the nations] (pp. 229–247). München, Germany: Rowohlt.

Horner, Th. M. (1983). On the formation of personal space and self-boundary structures in early human development: The case of infant stranger reactivity. Developmental Review, 3, 148–177.

Hoshmand, L. T., & Polkinghorne, D. E. (1992). Redefining the science–practice relationship and professional training. American Psychologist, 47, 55–66.

Howard, A., Pion, G. M., Gottfredson, G. D., Flattau, P. E., Oskamp, S., Pfafflin, S. M., Bray, D. W., & Burstein, A. G. (1986). The changing face of American psychology: A report from the Committee on Employment and Human Resources. American Psychologist, 41, 1311–1327.

Hultsch, D. F., & Plemons, J. K. (1979). Life events and life-span development. In P. B. Baltes & O. G. Brim, Jr. (Eds.), Life-span development and behavior (Vol. 2, pp. 1–36).

Jacobson, E. (1964). The self and the object world. New York: International Universities Press.

James, W. (1890). The principles of psychology (Vol. 1). London: Macmillan.

Jantsch, E. (1980). The self-organizing universe. Oxford, England: Pergamon Press.

Jaynes, J. (1976). The origin of consciousness in the breakdown of the bicameral mind. Boston: Houghton Mifflin.

Johnson, F. (1985). The Western concept of self. In A. J. Marsella, G. de Vos, & F. L. K. Hsu (Eds.), Culture and self: Asian and Western perspectives (pp. 91–138). New York: Tavistock Publications.

Johnson, M. (1987). The body in the mind: The bodily basis of meaning, imagination, and reason. Chicago: The University of Chicago Press.

Joyce, J. (1939). *Finnegans wake.* London: Faber & Faber.

Joyce, J. (1986). *Ulysses: The corrected text* (Student's Edition with a preface by Richard Ellmann). London: Penguin Books. (Original publication in 1922.)

Jung, C. G. (1959). Mandalas. In *Collected works* (Vol. 9, Part 1). Princeton: Princeton University Press. (First German edition, 1955.)

Kagan, J. (1980). Perspectives on continuity. In O. G. Brim & J. Kagan (Eds.), *Constancy and change in human development* (pp. 26–74). Cambridge, MA: Harvard University Press.

Katz, J. (1988). *Seductions of crime: Moral and sensual attractions in doing evil.* New York: Basic Books.

Kaye, K. (1977). Toward the origin of dialogue. In H. R. Schaffer (Ed.), *Studies in mother–infant interaction* (pp. 89–117). London: Academic Press.

Kelly, G. A. (1955). *The psychology of personal constructs.* New York: Norton.

Kempen, H. J. G. (1990, August). *Cross-cultural universals of subjectivity.* Paper presented at the William James 1990 Principles Congress, Amsterdam, The Netherlands.

Kenrick, D. T., & Dantchik, A. (1983). Interactionism, idiographics, and the social psychological invasion of personality. *Journal of Personality, 51,* 286–307.

Kenrick, D. T., & Stringfield, D. O. (1980). Personality traits and the eye of the beholder: Crossing some traditional philosophical boundaries in the search for consistency in all of the people. *Psychological Review, 87,* 88–104.

Klages, L. (1948). *Charakterkunde.* [Characterology]. Zürich, Switzerland: Hirzel.

Klaus, M. H., Kennel, J. H., Plumb, N., & Zuelke, S. (1970). Human maternal behavior at first contact with their young. *Pediatrics, 46,* 187–192.

Klein, M. (1948). *Contributions to psychoanalysis 1921–1945.* London: Hogarth.

Koch, S. (1981). The nature and limits of psychological knowledge: Lessons of a century of "qua" science. *American Psychologist, 36,* 257–269.

Lamiell, J. T. (1987). *The psychology of personality: An epistemological inquiry.* New York: Columbia University Press.

Lamiell, J. T. (1991). Valuation theory, the self-confrontation method, and scientific personality psychology. *European Journal of Personality, 5,* 235–244.

Lazarus, R. S. (1984). On the primacy of cognition. *American Psychologist, 39,* 124–129.

Lévi-Strauss, C. (1972). *Structural anthropology.* (Translated by C. Jacobson & B. G. Schoepf.) London: Penguin Books. (Original work published in 1958.)

Levin, H. (1970). The Quixote principle. In M. W. Bloomfield (Ed.), *Harvard English Studies, 1. The interpretation of narrative: Theory and practice* (pp. 45–66). Cambridge, MA: Harvard University Press.

Levin, D. M. (1988). *The opening of vision: Nihilism and the postmodern situation.* New York: Routledge.

Levinson, D. J., Darrow, C. M., Klein, E. B., Levinson, M. H., & McKee, B. (1974). The psychosocial development of men in early adulthood and the mid-life transition. In D. F. Ricks, A. Thomas, & M. Roff (Eds.), *Life history research in psychopathology.* Minneapolis: University of Minnesota Press.

Lewis, M., & Brooks-Gunn, J. (1979). *Social recognition and the acquisition of self.* New York: Plenum.

Lewis, M., & Brooks-Gunn, J. (1984). The development of early visual self-recognition. *Developmental Review, 4,* 215–239.

Linell, P. (1990). The power of dialogue dynamics. In I. Markovà & K. Foppa (Eds.), *The dynamics of dialogue* (pp. 147–177). New York: Harvester Wheatsheaf.

Litz, A. W. (1961). *The art of James Joyce: Method and design in Ulysses and Finnegans Wake.* London: Oxford University Press.

Loevinger, J. (1976). *Ego development.* San Francisco: Jossey-Bass.

Loveland, K. A. (1986). Discovering the affordances of a reflecting surface. *Developmental Review,* **6,** 1–24.

Lukacs, G. (1971). *History and class consciousness: Studies in Marxist dialectics.* Cambridge, MA: M.I.T. Press.

Magnusson, D. (Ed.) (1981). *Toward a psychology of situations: An interactional perspective.* Hillsdale, NJ: Erlbaum.

Mahler, M., Pine, F., & Bergman, A. (1975). *The psychological birth of the human infant.* New York: Basic Books.

Mahoney, M. J. (1988). Constructive metatheory: 1. Basic features and historical foundations. *International Journal of Personal Construct Psychology,* **1,** 1–35.

Mahoney, M. J. (1989). *The future of scientific psychology.* Paper presented to the American Association for the Advancement of Science. January 15. San Francisco, CA.

Mahrer, A. R. (1988). Discovery-oriented psychotherapy research. *American Psychologist,* **43,** 694–702.

Mair, J. M. M. (1970). Psychologists are human too. In D. Bannister (Ed.), *Perspectives in personal construct theory* (pp. 157–184). London: Academic Press.

Mair, J. M. M. (1989). *Between psychology and psychotherapy: A poetics of experience.* London: Routledge.

Mancuso, J. C., & Sarbin, T. R. (1983). The self-narrative in the enactment of roles. In T. R. Sarbin & K. Scheibe (Eds.), *Studies in social identity* (pp. 254–273). New York: Praeger.

Markovà, I. (1987). On the interaction of opposites in psychological processes. *Journal for the Theory of Social Behavior,* **17,** 279–299.

Markus, H. R., & Kitayama, S. (1991). Culture and the self: Implications for cognition, emotion, and motivation. *Psychological Review,* **98,** 224–253.

Markus, H. R., & Nurius, P. (1986). Possible selves. *American Psychologist,* **41,** 954–969.

Markus, H. R., & Sentis, K. (1982). The self in social information processing. In J. Suls (Ed.), *Psychological perspectives on the self* (Vol. 1). Hillsdale, NJ: Erlbaum.

Markus H. R., & Wurf, E. (1987). The dynamic self-concept: A social psychological perspective. *Annual Review of Psychology,* **38,** 299–337.

McAdams, D. P. (1985a). *Power, intimacy, and the life story: Personological inquiries into identity.* Chicago: Dorsey Press. (Reprinted by Guilford Press.)

McAdams, D. P. (1985b). The "imago": A key narrative component of identity. In P. Shaver (Ed.), *Self, situations, and social behavior. Review of personality and social psychology* (Vol. 6, pp. 115–141). Beverly Hills: Sage.

McAdams, D. P. (1992). The five-factor model in personality: A critical appraisal. *Journal of Personality,* **60,** 329–361.

McClelland, D. C., Atkinson, J. W., Clark, R. A., & Lowell, E. L. (1953). *The achievement motive.* New York: Appleton-Century-Crofts.

McCrae, R. R., & Costa, P. T., Jr. (1982). Aging, the life course, and models of personality. In T. M. Field, A. Huston, H. C. Quay, L. Troll, & G. E. Finley (Eds.), *Review of Human Development* (pp. 602–613). New York: Wiley-Interscience.

McGuire, W. J. (1983). A contextualist theory of knowledge: Its implications for innovation and reform in psychological research. In L. Berkowitz (Ed.), *Advances in experimental and social psychology* (Vol. 16, pp. 1–47). San Diego, CA: Academic Press.

Mead, G. H. (1934). *Mind, self, and society.* Chicago: University of Chicago Press.

Michotte, A. (1963). *The perception of causality* (Translated by T. R. Miles & E. Miles). London: Methuen. (Original work published 1946.)

Mischel, W. (1968). *Personality and assessment.* New York: Wiley.

Mischel, W. (1983). Alternatives in the pursuit of the predictability and consistency of persons: Stable data that yield unstable interpretations. *Journal of Personality,* **51,** 578–604.

Monson, T. C., & Snyder, M. (1977). Actors, observers, and the attribution process: Toward a reconceptualization. *Journal of Experimental Social Psychology,* **13,** 89–111.

Montaigne, M. de (1603). *The essayes: Or morall, politike and millitarie discourses* (Translated by J. Florio). London: Blount. (Original work published 1580.)

Montepare, J. M., & Lachman, M. E. (1989). "You're only as old as you feel": Self-perceptions of age, fears of aging, and life satisfaction from adolescence to old age. *Psychology and Aging,* **4,** 73–78.

Murray, H. A. (1938). *Explorations in personality.* New York: Oxford University Press.

Myers, B. S. S. (1979). *Encyclopedia of painting* (4th ed.). New York: Crown.

Newson, J. (1977). An intersubjective approach to the systematic description of mother–infant interaction. In H. R. Schaffer (Ed.), *Studies in mother–infant interaction.* London: Academic Press.

Ogden, T. H. (1979). On projective identification. *The International Journal of Psycho-Analysis,* **60,** 357–373.

Oppenheimer, R. (1956). Analogy in science. *American Psychologist,* **11,** 127–136.

Ornstein, R. (1986). *Multiminds: A new way to look at human behavior.* Boston: Houghton Mifflin.

O'Sullivan, J. J., & Quevillon, R. P. (1992). 40 years later: Is the Boulder model still alive? *American Psychologist,* **47,** 67–70.

Pascal, B. (1963). Pensées et opuscules [Thoughts and opuscules]. (L. Brunschvicg, Ed.). Paris: Hachette. (Original work published 1667.)

Pepper, S. (1942). *World hypotheses.* Berkeley: University of California Press.

Pervin, L. A. (1976). A free-response description approach to the analysis of person–situation interaction. *Journal of Personality and Social Psychology,* **34,** 465–474.

Pervin, L. A. (1984). Idiographic approaches to personality. In N. S. Endler & McV. Hunt (Eds.), *Personality and the behavioral disorders* (2nd ed). New York: Wiley.

Piaget, J., & Inhelder, B. (1969). *The psychology of the child.* London: Routledge & Kegan Paul.

Polkinghorne, D. E. (1988). *Narrative knowing and the human sciences.* Albany, NY: State University of New York Press.

Polti, G. (1977). *The thirty-six dramatic situations* (Translated by L. Ray). Boston: The Writer. (Original work published 1921.)

Prigogine, I., & Stengers, I. (1984). *Order out of chaos: Man's new dialogue with nature.* New York: Bantam.

Prince, G. (1982). *Narratology: The form and functioning of narrative.* Amsterdam: Mouton.

Propp, V. (1968). *The morphology of the folk tale.* (Translated by L. Scott & revised by L. Wagner.) Austin: University of Texas Press. (Original work published 1928.)

Raimy, V. C. (1950). *Training in clinical psychology.* New York: Prentice-Hall.

Ricoeur, P. (1970). *Freud and philosophy.* New Haven, CT: Yale University Press.

Ricoeur, P. (1986). *Time and narrative* (Vol. 2). (Translated by K. McLaughlin & D. Pellauer.) Chicago: University of Chicago Press.

Riegel, K. (1975). Adult life-crises: A dialectical interpretation of development. In N. Datan & L. Ginsberg (Eds.), *Life-span developmental psychology: Normative life-crises* (pp. 99–128). New York: Academic Press.

Ritzer, G. (1992). *Sociological Theory* (3rd ed.). New York: McGraw-Hill.

Rosenberg, M. (1979). *Conceiving the self.* New York: Basic Books.

Rosenberg, M. (1983). A metaphor for the identity of tragic heroes. In Th. R. Sarbin & K. E. Scheibe (Eds.), *Studies in social identity* (pp. 274–284). New York: Praeger.

Rosenberg, S., & Gara, M. A. (1985). The multiplicity of personal identity. In P. Shaver (Ed.), *Self, situations, and social behavior: Review of personality and social psychology* (Vol. 6, pp. 87–113). Beverly Hills, CA: Sage.

Rothenberg, A. (1971). The process of Janusian thinking in creativity. *Archives of General Psychiatry, 24,* 195–205.

Rowan, J. (1990). *Subpersonalities: The people inside us.* London: Routledge.

Rychlak, J. F. (1988). *The psychology of rigorous humanism* (2nd ed.). New York: New York University Press.

Ryle, G. (1949). *The concept of mind.* London: Hutchinson.

Sampson, E. E. (1985). The decentralization of identity: Toward a revised concept of personal and social order. *American Psychologist, 11,* 1203–1211.

Sarbin, Th. R. (1986). The narrative as a root metaphor for psychology. In Th. R. Sarbin (Ed.), *Narrative psychology: The storied nature of human conduct* (pp. 3–21). New York: Praeger.

Sarbin, Th. R. (1989). Emotions as narrative emplotments. In M. J. Packer & R. B. Addison (Eds.), *Entering the circle: Hermeneutic investigation in psychology* (pp. 185–201). Albany, NY: SUNY Press.

Sarbin, Th. R. (1990). The narrative quality of action. *Theoretical and Philosophical Psychology, 10,* 49–65.

Scarr, S. (1985). Constructing psychology: Making facts and fables for our times. *American Psychologist, 40,* 499–512.

Schegloff, E. (1982). Discourse as an interactional achievement. In D. Tannen (Ed.), *Analyzing discourse: Text and talk* (pp. 71–93). Georgetown University Round Table on Language and Linguistics, 1981. Washington, D.C.: Georgetown University Press.

Schein, E. (1972). *Professional education.* New York: McGraw Hill.

Schlenker, B. R. (Ed.) (1985). *The self and social life.* New York: McGraw-Hill.

Schön, D. (1983). *The reflective practitioner: How professionals think in action.* New York: Basic Books.

Schön, D. (1987). *Educating the reflective practitioner.* San Francisco: Jossey-Bass.

Schwalbe, M. L. (1991). The autogenesis of the self. *Journal for the Theory of Social Behaviour, 21,* 269–295.

Schwartz, R. (1987). Our multiple selves: Applying systems thinking to the inner family. *The Family Therapy Networker,* March/April, 25–83.

Scribner, S., & Cole, M. (1981). *The psychological consequences of literacy.* Cambridge, MA: Harvard University Press.

Seneca, L. A. (1965). L. Annaei Senecae ad Lucilium epistolae morales (Tomus II). [L. Annaeus Seneca's moral letters to Lucilius (Vol. 2).] (L. Reynolds, Ed.) Oxford: Oxford University Press. (Original work published circa 65.)

Shotter, J. (1984). *Social accountability and selfhood.* Oxford: Blackwell.

Shotter, J. (1992). Bakhtin and Billig: Monological versus dialogical practices. *American Behavioral Scientist, 36,* 8–21.

Smith, M. B. (1985). The metaphorical basis of selfhood. In A. J. Marsella, G. de Vos, & F. L. K. Hsu (Eds.), *Culture and self: Asian and Western perspectives* (pp. 56–88). New York: Tavistock Publications.

Smith, M. B. (1991). *Values, self, and society: Toward a humanist social psychology.* New Brunswick: Transaction Publishers.

Sommer, R. (1959). Studies in personal space. *Sociometry, 22,* 287–360.

Spence, J. (1985). Achievement American style: The rewards and costs of individualism. *American Psychologist, 40,* 1285–1295.

Spence, J. T. (1987). Centrifugal versus centripetal tendencies in psychology. *American Psychologist, 42,* 1052–1054.

Spencer, S. (1971). *Space, time, and structure in the modern novel.* New York: New York University Press.

Stein, G. (1933). *The autobiography of Alice Toklas.* New York: Random House.

Stern, D. N. (1977). *The first relationship: Infant and mother.* Cambridge, MA: Harvard University Press.

Stern, D. (1983). The early development of schemas of self, other and "self" with other. In J. D. Lichtenberg & S. Kaplan (Eds.), *Reflections on self psychology* (pp. 49–84). Hillsdale, NJ: The Analytic Press.

Stone, H., & Winkelman, S. (1985). *Embracing our selves.* Marina del Rey, CA: Devorss.

Straus, E. W. (1958). Aesthesiology and hallucinations. In R. May, E. Angel, & H. F. Ellenberger (Eds.), *Existence.* New York: Basic Books.

Stricker, G. (1975). On professional schools and professional degrees. *American Psychologist, 30,* 1062–1066.

Sullivan, H. S. (1953). *The interpersonal theory of psychiatry.* New York: Norton.

Sundstrom, E., & Altman, I. (1976). Interpersonal relationships and personal space. *Human Ecology, 4,* 47–67.

Taylor, C. (1991). The dialogical self. In D. R. Hiley, J. F. Bohman, & R. Shusterman (Eds.), *The interpretative turn* (pp. 304–314). Ithaca, NY: Cornell University Press.

Teleac Coursebook (1991). *Britse en Amerikaanse literatuur van deze eeuw.* [British and American literature of this century.] Utrecht, The Netherlands: Teleac Foundation.

Traugott, E. C. (1978). On the expression of spatio-temporal relations in language. In J. Greenberg (Ed.), *Universals of Human Language* (Vol. 3, pp. 369–400). Stanford, CA: Stanford University Press.

Valsiner, J., & Van der Veer, R. (1988). On the nature of human cognition: An analysis of the shared intellectual roots of George Herbert Mead and Lev Vygotsky. *Journal for the Theory of Social Behaviour, 18,* 117–136.

Van Rossum, F. (1992). Alfred Schnittke en de zwanezang van de revolutie: Leven met een idioot. [Alfred Schnittke and the swan-song of the revolution: Living with an idiot.] *Muziekjournaal Entr'acte, 3/4,* 32–39.

Vargiu, J. G. (1974). Psychosynthesis workbook: Subpersonalities. *Synthesis 1.*

Vasil'eva, I. I. (1988). The importance of M. M. Bakhtin's idea of dialogue and dialogic relations for the psychology of communication. *Soviet Psychology,* **26,** 17–31.

Verhofstadt–Denève, L. (1988). *Persoon, ontwikkeling en psychodrama: Een existentiëel-dialectische visie.* [Person, development, and psychodrama: An existential-dialectial view.] Louvain: Acco.

Vico, G. (1968). *The new science of Giambattista Vico.* (Translated by T. G. Bergin & M. H. Fisch.) Ithaca, NY: Cornell University Press. (Original work published 1744.)

Vico, G. (1988). *On the most ancient wisdom of the Italians unearthed from the origins of the Latin language.* (Translated by L. M. Palmer.) Ithaca, NY: Cornell University Press. (Original work published 1710.)

Vico, G. (1990). *On the study methods of our time.* (Translated by E. Gianturco & edited and translated by D. P. Verene.) Ithaca, NY: Cornell University Press. (Original work published 1709.)

Vitz, P. C. (1990). The use of stories in moral development: New psychological reasons for an old educational method. *American Psychologist,* **45,** 709–720.

Voloshinov, V. N. (1976). *Freudianism: A Marxist critique* (Translated by I. R. Titunik.) New York: Academic Press.

Wachtel, P. L. (1980). Investigation and its discontents: Some constraints on progress in psychological research. *American Psychologist,* **35,** 399–408.

Warneck, M. (1909). *Die Religion der Batak.* [The religion of the Batak.] Leipzig: T. Weicher.

Watkins, M. (1986). *Invisible guests: The development of imaginal dialogues.* Hillsdale, NJ: Erlbaum.

Webb, W. B., & Cartwright, R. D. (1978). Sleep and dreams. *Annual Review of Psychology,* **29,** 223–252.

Wertsch, J. V. (1987). *Voices of the mind.* Inaugural lecture on the occasion of taking up the Belle van Zuylen professorship at the University of Utrecht, on October 27, 1987. Utrecht, The Netherlands: University of Utrecht.

Wertsch, J. V. (1990). Dialogue and dialogism in a socio-cultural approach to mind. In I. Markovà & K. Foppa (Eds.), *The dynamics of dialogue* (pp. 62–82). New York: Harvester Wheatsheaf.

Wertsch, J. V. (1991). Voices of the mind: A socialcultural approach to mediated action. London: Harvester Wheatsheaf.

White, H. V. (1968). Vico, Giovanni Battista. In D. Sills (Ed.), *International Encyclopedia of the Social Sciences* (Vol. 16, pp. 313–316). New York: MacMillan.

White, H. (1973). Metahistory: The historical imagination in nineteenth-century Europe. Baltimore, MD: John Hopkins University Press.

Winter, D. G. (1973). *The power motive.* New York: The Free Press.

Woolf, V. (1990). *To the lighthouse.* London: Hogarth. (Original work published in 1927.)

Wrong, D. (1968). Some problems in defining social power. *The American Journal of Sociology,* **73,** 673–681.

Zajonc, R. B. (1984). On the primacy of affect. *American Psychologist,* **39,** 117–123.

Zaner, R. M. (1981). *The context of self: A phenomenological inquiry using medicine as a clue.* Athens, OH: Ohio University Press.

Zazzo, R. (1979). Des enfants, des singes, et des chiens devant le miroir. [Children, monkeys, and dogs in front of the mirror.] *Revue de Psychologie Appliquée,* **29,** 235–246.

Zuckerman, M., Koestner, R., DeBoy, T., Garcia, T., Maresca, B. C., & Sartoris, J. M. (1988). To predict some of the people some of the time: A reexamination of the moderator variable approach in personality theory. *Journal of Personality and Social Psychology,* **54,** 1006–1019.

Zuckerman, M., Bernieri, F., Koestner, R., & Rosenthal, R. (1989). To predict some of the people some of the time: In search of moderators. *Journal of Personality and Social Psychology,* **57,** 279–293.

INDEX